In memory

of

Michael Lewis Hyde

Born 14 May 1938
Graduated USAF Academy 8 June 1960
Killed in action 8 December 1966

A Patriot, A Classmate, A Friend

Archie to SAM

A Short Operational History of Ground-Based Air Defense

Second Edition

KENNETH P. WERRELL

Air University Press
Maxwell Air Force Base, Alabama

August 2005

Air University Library Cataloging Data

Werrell, Kenneth P.
    Archie to SAM : a short operational history of ground-based air defense / Kenneth P. Werrell.—2nd ed.
        p. ; cm.
    Rev. ed. of: Archie, flak, AAA, and SAM : a short operational history of ground-based air defense, 1988.
    With a new preface.
    Includes bibliographical references and index.
    ISBN 1-58566-136-8
    1. Air defenses—History. 2. Anti-aircraft guns—History. 3. Anti-aircraft missiles—History. I. Title.

358.4/145—dc22

Disclaimer

Air University Press
131 West Shumacher Avenue
Maxwell AFB AL 36112-6615
http://aupress.maxwell.af.mil

Contents

Illustrations

CONTENTS

CONTENTS

CONTENTS

Foreword

Dr. Kenneth Werrell's history of ground-based air defense performs an important service both to scholarship and, more importantly, to the defense of our nation's freedom. It is perhaps human nature that we tend over time to lose sight of the lessons of the past, especially when they do not conform to certain cherished preconceptions of ours. That such myopia can be dangerous, if not downright disastrous, Dr. Werrell's study richly illustrates. Without sentimentalism, he chronicles a pattern of lessons learned and too quickly forgotten as the marvel of air power was reminded again and again of its limitations and vulnerability. In Korea and in Vietnam, the American people were stripped of their illusions of national and technical omnipotence. The unhappy outcome of those two conflicts was doubly lamentable because the lessons of World War II were—or should have been—fresh in our minds. In that world war, as Dr. Werrell shows, relatively cheap ground-based air defense did make a difference: at Ploesti, at Antwerp, and at the Rhine bridges.

And it will make a difference tomorrow. The greatest value of Dr. Werrell's work is that it provides guideposts and guidance for us as professional soldiers and aviators charged with upholding American security. We have taken history's lessons to heart as we plan and program our ground-based air defenses into the next decade and beyond. In both the forward and the rear areas, we have emphasized the time-honored principles of mass, mix, and mobility. No one weapon, not even today's modern aircraft, can do the job alone. The truism applies with particular force to antiaircraft defense. And at least one other truism emerges from Dr. Werrell's and our own studies: effective air defense requires a joint and combined effort. Our planning has been predicated on the assumption that counterair will play a central role in safeguarding our ground forces from air attack. On the ground, the air defense artillery will count on the cooperation and assistance of our colleagues in the infantry, armor, and field artillery. On our success or failure in working together to meet the challenges of tomorrow will rest our nation's future.

DONALD R. INFANTE
Major General, US Army
Chief of Air Defense Artillery

About the Author

Dr. Kenneth P. Werrell conducted the original study while serving as a visiting professor at the Air University Center for Aerospace Doctrine, Research and Education, Maxwell Air Force Base, Alabama, from 1981 to 1983. He revised the study while working at the Airpower Research Institute in 1999–2001.

Dr. Werrell graduated from the United States Air Force Academy in 1960 and earned his pilot wings the next year. He served with the 56th Weather Reconnaissance Squadron at Yokota Air Base, Japan, from 1962 until 1965, completing the tour as an aircraft commander of the WB-50. He resigned his commission in 1965 and went on to earn his master's and doctorate degrees from Duke University.

Dr. Werrell taught at Radford University, Virginia, beginning in 1970 and retired as a professor in 1996. He also served as a contract historian at the Army War College and taught one year at the Command and General Staff College.

Dr. Werrell has authored numerous articles and books about military history, including *Eighth Air Force Bibliography* (Manhattan, Kans.: *Aerospace Historian*, Kansas State University, 1981); *The Evolution of the Cruise Missile* (Maxwell AFB, Ala.: Air University Press, September 1985); *Who Fears?: The 301st in War and Peace, 1942–1979* (Dallas, Tex.: Taylor Publishing, 1991); *Blankets of Fire: U.S. Bombers over Japan during World War II* (Washington, D.C.: Smithsonian Institution, 1998); and *Chasing the Silver Bullet: US Air Force Weapons Development from Vietnam to Desert Storm* (Washington, D.C.: Smithsonian Institution, 2003). His most recent book is *Sabres over MiG Alley: The F-86 and the Battle for Air Superiority in Korea* (Annapolis, Md.: US Naval Institute Press, 2005).

Preface to the Second Edition

Archie to SAM is a revised and updated edition of *Archie, Flak, AAA, and SAM*. For many years, the Air University Press, most especially Tom Lobenstein, has suggested I revise this work. I finally got the opportunity when I served three years in the Airpower Research Institute (ARI) where Col Al Howey and Dr. Jim Titus helped clear the way. My "boss," Dr. Dan Mortensen, and two other colleagues, Dr. Lee Dowdy and Tom Searle, helped in many more ways than they realized. My coworkers in ARI, especially such computer people as Guy Frankland and La Don Herring, made things much easier. As with the original study, the extremely capable staff at the Air University Library (particularly Steve Chun, Diana Simpson, and Edith Williams) and the Historical Research Agency (with special thanks to Joe Caver and Archie DiFante) were extremely helpful. Bud Bennett at Radford University was very important to this work. I also want to thank the talented staff at Air University Press who made this project possible. Especially important were Dr. Richard Bailey, who demonstrated great competence and patience, and Carolyn J. McCormack, who saved me from numerous embarrassing mistakes. In addition, as always my faithful wife Jeanne helped both directly with typing and editing—and understanding.

A Note for Those Who Read or Used the Original Edition

This brief note shows readers what is different between the original edition and this version. Unlike most reprints where the author updates the text by adding additional chapters, I have in fact refashioned the entire study. Not only have I tinkered with the prose, I have added some materials from sources that have appeared (or that I have uncovered) since the original was printed. This will be most noticeable in the greater attention devoted to the Soviet and US Army surface-to-air missiles (SAM). I have also added events that have occurred since 1986 or so when I cut off research for the original, most prominently the Gulf War experience. In addition, two chapters cover the story of ballistic missile defense, a subject I had excluded from the original for practical purposes. About one-half of the original illustrations were replaced, and the captions were reworked.

Reflecting on the subject of ground-based air defenses, I am struck by a number of observations. First, little attention continues to be given to this subject, despite its impact on air operations. Writers and readers concentrate on the offensive side of the story, most of all on the pilots and aircraft. Second, the emergence of stealth technology has changed the balance between air offense and defense—for the moment. That actually overstates the point, as the potency of SAMs was already in decline (as demonstrated by the Israelis in the 1982 Bekaa Valley operation) before stealth appeared in combat. Nevertheless, air dominance has shifted more toward the offense as this new technology—coupled with the rise of the United States as the sole world superpower—has ushered in a new era in air warfare. Clearly, the United States has massive technological superiority. A third factor is a cautionary one. The cost of modern technology is immense and continues to grow, which translates in practical terms to far fewer airframes available for action. Therefore, the loss (or threat of loss) of only a few machines could affect how an air campaign is waged.

KENNETH P. WERRELL

Preface to the First Edition

Archie, Flak, AAA, and SAM is an operational history of ground-based air defense systems from the beginning of air warfare up through 1988. The title refers to the several names Airmen use, and have used, to describe ground fire: *Archie* in World War I (from the British), *flak* in World War II and Korea (from the Germans), *AAA* throughout, but especially in Vietnam (from the American abbreviation for antiaircraft artillery), and most recently SAM (from the US abbreviation for surface-to-air missiles). This study concentrates on how these weapons developed and how they affected both US and non-US air operations.

The subject of ground-based air defense systems is neglected for a number of reasons. First, research is difficult because source material is fragmented. Even more significant is the fact that the topic does not have "sex appeal." Readers are more interested in the aircraft than the weapons that bring them down. Whereas the airplane appears as a dynamic, advanced, exciting, and offensive weapon, ground-based air defense systems are seen in the opposite light. Further, US experience has been almost exclusively with the offensive use of aircraft, not with the defensive use of flak and SAMs; Americans have seldom fought without air superiority. Too, there is the World War II example that many, if not most, people hold as the archetypical war—during which aircraft defeated all comers on all fronts. Another factor is that the air defense community has been overwhelmed by the air offense community. Not that the former is any less able or less professional than the latter, only that the air offense community has the attention and support of both industry and Congress. Little wonder then that the subject of flak and SAMs has been neglected.

Despite this neglect and the aforementioned reasons, ground-based air defense systems are important. They have been involved, have impacted on most air conflicts, and have achieved notable successes. These weapons have downed and damaged large numbers of aircraft and consequently have forced aviators to make changes and pay higher costs for operations. Clearly, ground-based air defenses have been ever present and have always been a factor in air wars. There is no indication that this influence will diminish in the future.

The neglect of the subject of ground-based air defense systems on the one hand, contrasted with its importance on the other, prompted this study. In it, I have traced the historical record from World War I up through a number of smaller conflicts in the 1980s. Although primarily a narrative, I have tried to analyze the story and draw from it some generalizations, however tentative they may be. I prefer "generalizations" to the often-misused term "lessons."

The acknowledgments indicate where I conducted my research, and the endnotes document the material upon which I based this study. Research was overwhelmingly confined to English language sources, the basis of which was US Air Force, Army, and Navy documents and studies. In addition, I found primary materials dealing with both the Royal Air Force and Luftwaffe. I made considerable use of secondary sources, and I employed a few interviews. Admittedly, the major difficulty with this study is that, while I found materials from both sides covering the World Wars, my coverage of the Korean, Vietnam, and the Middle East Wars is drawn primarily from one side. Finally, I did not use the rich, although spotty, classified materials for obvious reasons.

Without preempting the conclusions, a number of themes are present. A study of the evolution of ground-based air defense weapons provides a classic view of the perennial contest between offense and defense, as well as of the impact of technology on warfare. More than just technology is involved, however; coverage includes such topics as tactics, leadership, change, and innovation. Perhaps most important, this subject cannot be even casually studied without the distinct impression that many of the main features of aircraft versus ground-based air defense battles are repeated over and over again. Clearly, lessons and generalizations abound in this story. I trust my treatment will do justice to the topic; that is, I hope the result makes up for some of the previous neglect of this subject and is commensurate with its past and continuing importance.

Acknowledgments

Many individuals and organizations helped make this book possible. First, I wish to thank those at my home institution, Radford University, who encouraged and made possible my work with the Air University: the Board of Visitors; Dr. Donald Dedmon, president; Dr. David Moore, vice president for Academic Affairs; Dr. W. D. Stump, dean of the School of Arts and Sciences; and Dr. W. K. Roberts, chairman of the Department of History. Lt Gen Charles Cleveland, former commander of the Air University; Maj Gen David Gray, USAF, retired; and Maj Gen Paul Hodges, former commandant of the Air War College, were unsparing in their support throughout this project. Col Thomas Fabyanic, USAF, retired, the founder and first director of the ARI, and Col Kenneth Alnwick, USAF, retired, his successor, deserve much of the credit for helping conceive the concept, encourage the project, and remove many of the barriers encountered. Also, special thanks to Col Neil Jones, USAF, retired; Brig Gen John C. Fryer Jr.; and Col Sidney J. Wise, who provided vital publication assistance. Others at the Air University helped in many important ways, especially Col Dennis Drew, Preston Bryant, Dianne Parrish, John Westcott, and Dorothy McCluskie. Many individuals helped in document processing: Lula Barnes, Sue Carr, Carolyn Ward, Marcia Williams, and Cynthia Hall. For logistical support I am thankful to Capt Harbert Jones, Betty Brown, and Marilyn Tyus. The US Air Force History Program helped in a number of ways. Individuals include Dr. Richard Morse, Lynn Gamma, Judy Endicott, Pressley Bickerstaff, and Margaret Claiborn of the US Air Force Historical Research Center. The Air University Library played a key role in making this book possible, with special thanks due Tomma Pastorett, Ruth Griffin, and Kathleen Golson. The US Army also lent considerable support to this project. Especially helpful were several agencies at Fort Bliss: Air Defense School, Air Defense Museum, and Directorate of Combat Development. Special thanks are due Jesse Stiller, the Air Defense Artillery Command Historian. Overseas, Air Commodore H. A. Probert, Humphrey Wynn, and J. P. McDonald, at the Air Historical Branch, London; the staff at the Royal

Artillery Institute, Woolwick, United Kingdom; and E. Hines and Paul J. Kemp of the Imperial War Museum, London, made research of the British and German side of the story possible.

Finally, I must thank my entire family, especially my wife, Jeanne, who endured much to make this project possible.

Chapter 1

Antiaircraft Defense through World War II

The genesis of antiaircraft defense appeared soon after man took to the air. There are reports of antiballoon artillery in the American Civil War and the Franco-Prussian War. During the latter, 66 balloons are known to have left the besieged city of Paris, with one destroyed by Prussian guns.[1] The first aircraft downed in combat fell to ground fire in the Italo-Turkish War of 1912.

So, when World War I began, there were clear precedents for ground-based air defense systems. However, the ground problem clearly was much more important than dealing with the few insignificant aircraft. Although the Germans had built a few guns designed for antiaircraft duty in the decade before World War I, little attention was given to this issue. Germany began the war with 18 antiaircraft guns: six of them motorized and 12 of them horse drawn. The other European powers gave the matter even less attention.[2] Most of the first antiaircraft guns were artillery pieces modified to elevate higher and traverse through a wider arc than standard artillery pieces (fig. 1). The task of the antiaircraft gunner proved much more demanding than that of the traditional artilleryman. But the target problem was much more difficult. In contrast to the standard artillery problem of hitting a target located in two dimensions, the antiaircraft gunner was working in three dimensions, having to adjust not only for range and deflection but also for elevation. In addition, the aerial target was moving, possibly in all three dimensions, and possibly varying in speed, altitude, and direction. Finally, the projectile was unguided once it left the tube, following a ballistic course over a number of seconds while en route to the target. The technology of the day was inadequate for the tasks of detection, tracking, and fire control.

During World War I, both sides bombed their opponents' cities. German attacks on London and Paris tied down considerable

Figure 1. Improvised antiaircraft artillery (AAA). Early in World War I, the need for antiaircraft protection outstripped the available equipment. This forced the combatants to improvise using standard artillery pieces and makeshift arrangements. (Reprinted from Imperial War Museum.)

Allied resources, estimated in the British case to be eight times the resources expended by the German airmen. However, British defenses became increasingly effective. The Germans launched 43 aircraft on London during their last major raid (19 May 1918) against the British defenders that employed 84 fighter sorties and 126 guns that fired 30,000 rounds. Although the defenders claimed but three bombers destroyed, only 13 reached and bombed London's center. In the war, home defenses claimed 21 airships (of 201 airship sorties) and 27 aircraft (of 424 aircraft sorties), of which ground fire accounted for three zeppelins and

11 to 13 aircraft. In November 1918, the British used 480 anti-aircraft guns and 376 aircraft in the defense of Great Britain.[3]

The bulk of air operations during World War I was not strategic but was in support of ground forces. On the western front, German antiaircraft gunners claimed 1,588 Allied aircraft (19 percent of their total kills), while French gunners claimed 500 German aircraft; Italian gunners claimed 129; British Expeditionary Force gunners, 341; and US gunners, 58. The guns grew increasingly effective as hastily improvised equipment gave way to specially designed equipment, while, relatively speaking, aircraft showed only modest improvements in performance. Among the technologies harnessed by the defenders were sound-detection systems, searchlights, optical range-finders, and mechanically timed fuzes.[4] As a consequence, the number of German antiaircraft rounds for each claim fell from 11,600 in 1915 to 5,000 in 1918; French rounds per claim decreased from 11,000 (1916) to 7,000 (1918); Russian from 11,000 (1916) to 3,000 (1917); and British from 8,000 (1917) to 4,550 (1918). American antiaircraft artillery (AAA) downed 17 German aircraft in three months, averaging 605 rounds per kill.[5]

In contrast to the advances made during World War I, air defenders made little progress between the wars. The three-inch gun of World War I dominated what little AAA there was, and acoustical devices provided the best location equipment (fig. 2). In 1928, the United States adopted as standard equipment the three-inch M3 gun that had an effective ceiling of 21,000 feet, just exceeding the aircraft ceiling of the day. Meanwhile, new technology such as removable barrel liners, automatic breech mechanisms, and continuous fuze setters, improved the antiaircraft guns. However, the revolution in aviation technology of the 1930s, permitting much greater aircraft speeds and altitudes, rendered three-inch guns and acoustical-location gear obsolete.[6] In brief, from the mid to late 1930s, aircraft (offense) had the edge over the AAA (defense).

In the latter half of the 1930s, new equipment began to appear in antiaircraft units around the world. The major powers adopted slightly larger but much more powerful guns, deciding on a caliber of about a 90-millimeter (mm) gun with a muzzle

Figure 2. Standard US heavy AAA gun during the interwar years. The standard US heavy AAA piece during the interwar years was this three-inch gun. Members of the 62d Coast Artillery engage in a practice exercise in August 1941. (Reprinted from USAF.)

velocity of 2,800 to 3,000 feet per second (fps) and a rate of fire of 30 shots per minute (spm). The Germans chose the 88 mm gun (fig. 3), the British built a prototype 3.7-inch (94 mm) gun in 1936, and the Americans began to replace their three-inch gun with a 90 mm gun in 1940. All major powers experimented with new detection devices, but it was the British who forged a lead in the field of radar.[7] Radar was a giant advantage for the defender, at first giving early warning, later control of aircraft interception (initially with ground and then airborne radar), and finally aiming antiaircraft guns.

British Antiaircraft Artillery

Of all the European powers, the British had the most acute air defense problem; for compared to the other European capitals,

Figure 3. German 88 mm gun. The standard German heavy artillery piece during World War II was the German 88 mm gun. (Reprinted from Imperial War Museum.)

London was the easiest to find and closest to the border. In Winston Churchill's colorful and frightening words, the British capital was "a tremendous fat cow . . . tied up to attract the beasts of prey."[8] The British convinced themselves of the decisiveness of air power, fearing what they called the "knockout blow." They accepted the dismal prophecies of such theorists as the Italian Giulio Douhet, the Briton Sir Hugh Trenchard, and the American William "Billy" Mitchell, who predicted that the employment of air power would result in devastated cities, pulverized industries, panic-stricken civilians, and thus surrender. These airmen believed there was no direct defense against the bombers and as Prime Minister Stanley Baldwin succinctly put it, "The bomber will always get through." Without early warning, the air defense problem seemed impossible, as the only potential solution to intercepting high-speed, high-flying bombers through the vast skies was airborne patrols that were impractical. Another factor that led top decision makers to despair was the belief that only a few bombers could deliver adequate firepower (high explosives, incendiaries, and poison gas) that would have decisive results. Therefore, the British put their faith and effort into a strategic bomber force, depending on the fear of retribution to deter enemy air attack. Thus, they neglected most defensive air efforts. Not until 1937 did the Royal Air Force (RAF) shift its emphasis from bombers to fighters. By then, British radar, integrated into a nationwide command and control system, promised a solution and led to a new look at the air defense problem. All the same, British air defenses were inconsequential in the late 1930s (fig. 4). On 1 January 1938, the British had only 180 antiaircraft guns larger than 50 mm. This number increased to 341 by September 1938 (Munich), to 540 in September 1939 (declaration of war), and to 1,140 during the Battle of Britain.[9]

During the decisive Battle of Britain, AAA played a secondary role to RAF fighters, as the gunners claimed only 357 of the 1,733 German aircraft the British believed they destroyed. (A more recent source puts the gunners' scores at fewer than 300.) But an adequate measure of efficiency must include more than simply claims. By the end of September 1940, the British estimated that 48 percent of the German bombers turned back from the defended areas. Even if that is an overestimation, flak unquestionably forced the bombers higher, unnerved the crews, and resulted in reduced bombing accuracy.[10] In addition, antiaircraft guns were the principal de-

Figure 4. 3.7-inch gun on a Pile mattress. Here it is mounted on a "Pile mattress" used during the V-1 campaign and named for antiaircraft artillery commander Gen Frederick Pile. (Reprinted from Imperial War Museum.)

fense against night attacks, as night fighters were in their infancy. By the end of 1940, AAA defenses claimed 85 percent of the British night kills.

British AAA defenses had a number of problems. One continual air defense difficulty that is seldom discussed is "friendly fire." In fact, the first British kill, three days after the declaration of war, was unfortunately a friendly aircraft that had even given the correct recognition signal. The British gunners claimed the first German aircraft over a month later on 19 October 1939. Retention of the older three-inch guns until 1943 was another factor that inhibited the British air defenders. Perhaps most significant was the reliance on visual aiming. It was not until October 1940 that the British began to equip their forces with gun-laying radar. Radar made a big difference—the number of rounds fired per destroyed claim at night fell from 30,000 in September (when German night bombing began) to 11,000 in October and to 4,087 in January 1941.[11]

Personnel problems hampered British antiaircraft defenses throughout the war. The British sent their regular antiaircraft units overseas and relied on territorial forces similar to the

7

American National Guard for home defense. At the beginning of the war, the territorial forces were of top quality. But as the war continued, experienced men were reassigned to other duties, and the overall quality of the forces declined. The first group of 25 militiamen to arrive at one battery, after passing through a medical examination at a recruiting center, included two individuals with advanced cases of venereal disease, one person with a withered right arm, one mentally deficient, one with no thumbs, and a sixth whose glass eye fell out when he ran.[12]

The drain on antiaircraft personnel forced the British to take innovative measures. One was to incorporate women into what they called mixed batteries—the first of which became operational in August 1941 (fig. 5). These units were restricted to deployment in Great Britain until November 1944, when the first one moved to the continent. Women filled all positions except those involving heavy loading and firing.

The women served well—the principal problems resulted not from them but from their parents, friends, and British culture. One historian notes that "women brought an instinctive skill to the handling of AAA instruments and radar; they were less disturbed than men by intervals of inactivity and yet stood up

Figure 5. British women in training. British women training on a AAA gun director. Personnel shortages encouraged the British to employ women in antiaircraft units. (Reprinted from Imperial War Museum.)

well to enemy bombing."[13] In all, about 68,000 women served in British antiaircraft units during the war.

Another approach to the manpower shortage was to use the Home Guard. These men were, for the most part, willing enough but were over age or physically restricted. In addition, they could only serve 48 hours every 28 days. The peak strength of the Home Guard serving guns exceeded 145,000 in January 1944. Beginning in October 1941, one weapon employed by the Home Guard was the unguided rocket (fig. 6).

These proved to be visually impressive, but militarily ineffective.[14] Despite these measures to compensate for shortages in manpower, the number of personnel assigned to antiaircraft duties declined from 330,000 in 1941 to 264,000 in mid-1942. Britain just did not have sufficient personnel for all its needs, and the number of personnel available for antiaircraft duties determined how many guns the British could deploy.[15]

Figure 6. Rocket firings. In addition to guns, the British also employed unguided rockets as antiaircraft weapons. The British deployed thousands of rocket barrels at home; but while impressive when fired, they registered few hits. (Reprinted from Imperial War Museum.)

Initially, Allied AAA in the field proved inadequate as demonstrated in the campaigns in Norway and France. While British guns did better at Dunkirk, nevertheless, this too was a losing proposition. The failures of British arms and AAA were also evident in the 1941 Greek campaign. But even in losing operations, the power of antiaircraft was evident. In Crete, the British were only able to field a scratch force of hodgepodge units, including 16 3.7-inch, 16 3-inch, 37 40 mm, and three two-pound guns against a Luftwaffe force of 280 bombers, 150 dive bombers, and 180 fighters. Nevertheless, the defenders inflicted heavy losses on the Germans and came close to defeating them. In all, the Germans lost 147 aircraft to flak and 73 to other causes. Sixty-three were badly damaged.[16] The Allied antiaircraft gunners continued to improve to the detriment of the German air force (GAF).

At the siege of Tobruk, for example, the Luftwaffe made a determined effort to silence British antiaircraft guns and shut down the harbor. From April 1941 (when the garrison was cut off) until November 1941 (when it was relieved), British flak units engaged 4,105 aircraft with 28 heavy guns, 18 40 mm Bofors, and 42 captured Italian 20 mm Bredas and claimed 374 aircraft destroyed, probably destroyed, and damaged.[17] More to the point, the Germans sank only seven ships during the siege and failed to close the harbor.

In 1941, the Axis airmen attacked Malta, which was only 60 miles from Sicily and was critical in the battle for the Mediterranean and North Africa. The island endured a naval blockade and aerial siege for well over a year, oftentimes defended only by antiaircraft guns. In January 1941, there were 70 heavy guns and 34 light flak pieces on the island, a number that increased to 112 and 118, respectively, by July. One German tactic was to attack the gun positions directly, which the GAF did on 115 occasions in a five-month period, destroying five heavy and three light guns, killing 149 gunners, and wounding 290. In early 1942, the GAF won air superiority over Malta and pounded it ferociously. For two months, only the British antiaircraft gunners defended Malta. The critical month was April when Axis airmen flew 10,323 sorties and dropped about 7,000 tons of bombs, about half the total tonnage unloaded on the island. The British claimed 102 aircraft destroyed that month; however, the correct figure is probably closer to 37. During the entire campaign, the defenders (airmen and gunners) claimed between 860 and 1,000 aircraft destroyed on 1,199 air raids, while the Axis admitted to the loss of 567. Whatever the actual number, the stout and successful defense of Malta contributed immensely to the Axis defeat in North Africa.[18] This action was probably the most important contribution that Allied ground-based antiaircraft made to the war effort.

Developments in technology aided the defenders. By 1943, the British converted from powder to mechanical fuzes. Flashless propellants also increased the efficiency of their guns, as did automatic fuze setters that improved accuracy and increased the firing rate by a factor of two and one-half to three. By this time, electric predictors were also used.[19]

Luftwaffe bombing attacks on Britain trailed off in 1941, as the Soviet campaign began to dominate German attention. On 27 March 1942, the Germans opened a new phase to the air war against Britain with attacks on southern coastal towns by small numbers of low-flying fighter-bombers. A lack of early warning devices to detect low-flying attackers, a wide range of targets, and an inadequate number of light antiaircraft guns created considerable problems for the defenders. The British could do nothing about the first two factors, but they did increase the number of 40 mm guns dramatically from 41 in May 1942 to 267 by the end of September (fig. 7). By April 1943, the British had deployed 917 40 mm guns, 424 20 mm guns, and 506 two-pounders (one-third of their available 40 mm guns and two-fifths of their light flak units) along the southern coast. The increased alertness of the gunners and increased number of guns brought about impressive results. The gunners downed four aircraft of 42 sorties on 23 May, four of 24 sorties on 25 May, and 10 of 35 sorties on 30 May. In this phase of the air war—hit-and-run attacks on fringe targets—the British claimed 56 aircraft destroyed of 1,250 sorties, an attrition rate of 4.5 percent (fig. 8).[20]

11

Figure 7. British 40 mm light antiaircraft gun and crew. Swedish Bofors 40 mm guns saw extensive action throughout the war serving both sides. (Reprinted from Imperial War Museum.)

Figure 8. Diving V-1 bomb prior to impact in London. Although the defenders destroyed almost 4,000 buzz bombs, about 2,400 bombs hit London and killed over 6,100 civilians. (Adapted from USAF.)

The V-1 Campaign

The last major opponents of British home-based AAA were the German V weapons, the V-1, a winged and pilotless bomb, and the V-2 ballistic missile. The flying bomb, also known as the buzz bomb, carried a two-ton warhead about 160 miles at approximately 400 miles per hour (mph). Allied defenses consisted of offensive bombing raids against V-1 targets (launching sites, fabrication plants, and supply depots), fighter patrols, balloon barrages, and AAA. Initially, the defenders assumed that the pilotless bomb would fly at about 400 mph and at 7,500 feet. Later, they revised their assumptions to 350 mph at 7,000 feet and, finally, to 330 mph at 6,000 feet. The British completed a detailed plan on the defense of their homeland in January 1944 (fig. 9). It established fighter patrol lines and an artillery line of 400 heavy pieces and 346 light pieces immediately south of London. But the demands of supporting the D-day invasion and optimism resulting from the bombing of the German launch sites led the British to revise the plan in March. It called for a reduction in the number of guns defending London to 192 heavy pieces and 246 light pieces, a total reduction from 528 to 288 heavy pieces, and from 804 to 282 light pieces. Air Chief Marshal Roderic Hill, the defense commander, pointed out that AAA would have difficulties if the V-1s operated at 2,000 to 3,000 feet and not at the predicted 6,000 feet.[21] Events validated Hill's warning.

After the Allied invasion of Europe on 6 June 1944, Adolph Hitler pushed for the V-1 campaign as a means of relief for his troops. The Germans began the bombardment on 12 June but could fire only two small salvos; however, by 18 June, the Germans launched the 500th V-1; by 21 June, the 1,000th; by 29 June, the 2,000th; and by 22 July, the 5,000th. These V-1 attacks continued until September, when the Germans withdrew from their French bases before the Allied ground advance.[22]

The V-1s traveled fast for the day, crossing the English coast at an average speed of 340 mph and accelerating to about 400 mph as they burned off fuel. Thus, the fighter pilots had but six minutes to sight and down the buzz bombs before they reached their targets. The V-1s were difficult to spot because of

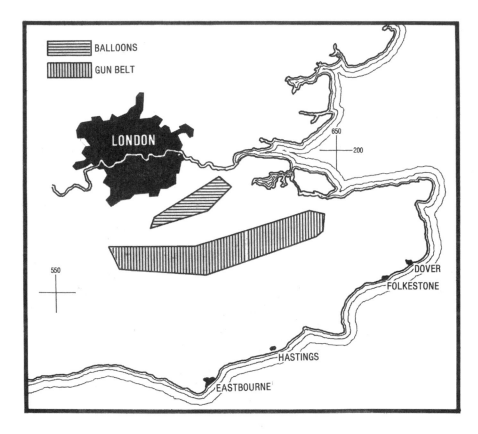

Figure 9. Diagram of initial defensive deployment. Initial defensive deployment of London during the V-1 campaign. (Adapted from USAF.)

their small size, about half that of the FW 190. This problem was exacerbated by the low-altitude approach averaging between 2,100 and 2,500 feet. Not only was the V-1 tough to spot and intercept, it was also tough to down. One source estimated that the missile was eight times as difficult to down as a manned aircraft, even though it flew straight and level. Although that estimate was probably an exaggeration, the V-1 was not an easy target to destroy.[23]

The Allies steadily increased their fighter units to 15 day and eight night fighter squadrons (two were part-time). Rules of engagement gave the fighters full rein in good weather and AAA gunners complete freedom in bad weather. During in-between weather, the most frequent situation, AAA gunners had complete freedom up to 8,000 feet. On 10 July, the British modified a 26 June order allowing fighters to enter the gun belt in hot pursuit of V-1s. Consequently, fighter pilots entered active antiaircraft gun areas at their own risk.[24]

England's third line of defense, after the offensive bombing and the fighter patrols, was its AAA. When the campaign began, the defenders rapidly got 192 heavy guns into position with the support of 200 light guns; and by the end of June 1944, they increased this number to 376 heavy guns, 594 light guns, and 362 rocket launchers.[25] Despite these numbers, V-1s were getting through, as British defenses were not working at optimum efficiency. The V-1's operating altitude of 2,000 to 3,000 feet was the worst possible for the defense: too high for the light guns and too low for the heavy guns. Heavy mobile pieces proved unsatisfactory because they could not traverse smoothly and rapidly. Radar, positioned in hollows and folds in the terrain for protection against German countermeasures that did not materialize, operated at a disadvantage. The proximity of the gun belt to London created another problem. The British hit a number of V-1s that later crashed into London, even though the defenders had done their job.[26] Finally, there was considerable interference between the gunners and the fighters, as pilots chasing the missiles sometimes strayed into the gun belt, inhibiting the gunners who on occasion fired on the fighters as well as the missiles. The defenders made a fast, effective, and flexible adjustment to the situation, which was much to their credit and to a large degree responsible for their ultimate success.[27]

The defenders easily came to grips with some of the problems. On 18 June 1944, the British ordered guns within London silenced and, by the end of June, resited their radar onto higher ground. The defenders built permanent structures for their portable guns (fig. 10). Constructed of 28 railway sleepers and 12 ties, these structures were first called Pile portable platforms; but, they quickly became known as Pile mattresses, named for AAA commander Gen Frederick Pile. In late June, the British began to replace their static guns with mobile guns; and, in early July, they put better gun predictors into action.

Figure 10: Pile mattress. The British emplaced their heavy (3.7 inch) guns on a solid base that became known as a "Pile mattress." (Reprinted from Imperial War Museum.)

The two most difficult problems remaining involved damaged V-1s falling on London (causing damage if they hit something, whether or not the warhead detonated) and interference between fighter pilots and gunners.[28]

Hill and Pile concluded that they should designate an all-gun belt from which all aircraft would be excluded. As this idea emerged, a staff officer suggested moving the guns and radar to the coast. Such a relocation would eliminate the problem of damaged missiles falling on London and would provide radar operators and gunners optimum visibility. This scheme would also give the fighter pilots a clear boundary (the coastline) between the gun and aircraft zones. Almost simultaneously, Robert

Watson-Watt, the eminent scientist and developer of radar, independently came up with the same concept, giving it even more weight.[29]

The plan had a number of dangers. First, there was the question of effectiveness. Would the new concept actually improve the defenses? A split zone would inhibit the fighter pilots, who claimed 883 of the 1,192 V-1 kills as of 13 July. Second, how long would such a redeployment, entailing hundreds of heavy guns, thousands of personnel, and tens of thousands of tons of supplies and equipment, take? What would happen to the defenses in the meantime? Finally, how long would it take to get a clear decision on this proposal? With each passing day, redeployment became increasingly difficult as more of the mobile guns were fitted with Pile mattresses and more guns were added to the gun belt.[30]

On 13 July, Hill made the decision to create an all-gun belt on the coast. This bold, quick exercise of authority was remarkable, as was the speed with which the decision was implemented. By 17 July, the heavy guns, radar, and supporting equipment and supplies were in place, followed in two days by the light guns. This action, which involved the movement of 23,000 people and about 60,000 tons of supplies, was no small feat (fig. 11). The British deployed the guns on the coast between Dover and Beachy Head, creating a zone extending 10,000 yards over the water and 5,000 yards inland. Aircraft were restricted to altitudes above 8,000 feet in this area, but the fighter pilots were free to roam over the English Channel and over England between the gun belt and the balloon line.[31]

Although the redeployment and separation of the aircraft and guns was a major factor in the increased effectiveness of the defenses, there were other factors as well. The number of heavy guns in the coastal belt increased from 376 on 1 July to 416 on 23 July; to 512 on 30 July; and to 592 on 7 August. In addition, there were 892 40 mm guns and 504 20 mm guns plus 254 rocket tubes. The addition of new American radar (SCR-584) and predictors for the British 3.7-inch guns and the American 90 mm guns also improved the defenses.[32] Another major technical improvement was the use of proximity fuzes that detonated at a preset distance from the target. The new

17

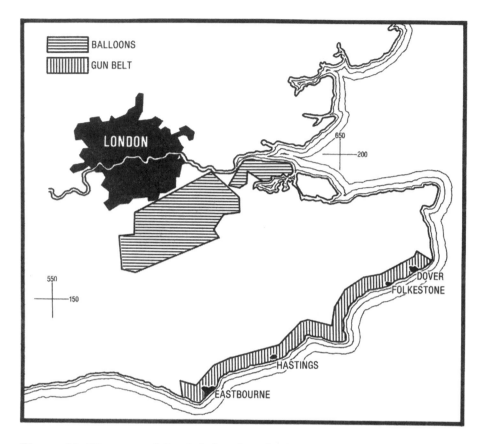

Figure 11. Diagram of final defensive deployment. Final defensive deployment of London during the V-1. (Adapted from USAF.)

fuze proved to be about five times more effective than either time or contact fuzes.[33] Finally, the gunners improved their accuracy as they got more practice.

These defensive improvements, coupled with the known direction, altitude, and speed of the V-1s, enabled the defenders to dramatically improve their effectiveness. Before the redeployment, the defenses downed 42 percent of the V-ls observed; after the redeployment, that figure rose to 59 percent. Another set of data, similar but not exactly coinciding, indicated that the defenses downed 48 percent of those missiles spotted over land before the redeployment and 84 percent of those spotted

18

after the redeployment. The high point occurred on the night of 27 August and early morning hours of 28 August when the defenders destroyed 90 of 97 missiles reported, allowing only four V-1s to get through to London.[34]

The increased power of the defenses resulted largely from the tremendous improvement in the effectiveness of AAA. The gunners got 22 percent of the destroyed credits before the redeployment and 54 percent afterwards. They downed 17 percent of their targets in the first week after redeployment and 74 percent in the last four days of action (29 August through 1 September 1944).[35]

During the summer campaign, the Germans began to launch V-1s from bombers. The first test air launch known to the British occurred on 6 April 1944 at Peenemünde, with the first recognizable use of an air-launched weapon against England occurring on 9 July 1944. Between then and 5 September, the GAF air launched about 400 V-1s. With the withdrawal of German forces from the French launching sites, these air-launched weapons became the chief air threat to Britain in the closing months of the war. Between 5 September and the last air launching on 14 January 1945, the Germans hurled about 1,200 of these V-1s against Britain, but only 66 reached London.[36] Clearly, their accuracy was very poor.

The final act in the V-1 campaign against Britain came in March 1945 when the Germans introduced a long-range version of the V-1. Fitting the V-1 with a lighter wing and warhead (36 percent less) permitted it to carry 50 percent more fuel and enabled it to fly 220 miles compared to the standard missile's range of about 150 to 160 miles. The Germans launched the first modified V-1 from ramps in Holland on 3 March. From then through 29 March, the Germans fired 275 V-1s against Britain, 13 of which reached London. Tipped off by photo-reconnaissance and intelligence reports about this new weapon, the Allies ordered the northern defenses bolstered on 27 February with seven squadrons of day fighters and three squadrons of night fighters. But the AAA gunners performed so well that the British relieved all but one of the day squadrons. The defenders downed 73 percent of the 125 missiles observed.[37]

The Germans fired 10,500 V-1s against Britain, of which about 2,000 crashed shortly after takeoff. The defenders observed 7,500 missiles and downed 4,000 (53 percent); they credited fighter pilots with 1,847 kills, the gunners with 1,878, and the balloons with 232 (fig. 12).[38] Efficiency improved from downing 42 percent of the V-1s observed before the redeployment to the coast (during the period 12 June to 15 July) to 59 percent after the redeployment (16 July to 5 September). The guns downed 63 percent of the air-launched missiles after this period (16 September 1944 to 14 January 1945) and 33 percent of the ground-launched V-1s from Holland. Put another way, the percentage of V-1s that reached London, relative to those launched, declined in these same periods (29, 23, 6, and 5) for an overall figure of 23 percent. About 2,419 V-1s reached the London Civil Defence Region, killing 6,184 civilians and seriously injuring 17,981. About 5 percent of the total casualties consisted of service personnel, and approximately 92 percent of the casualties occurred in the London area.[39]

To put the V-1s into perspective, they must be compared with other German weapons that killed and maimed British civilians during World War II. German bombings killed 51,509, V-2s killed 2,754, and long-range guns, 148. Of the 146,777 British civilian casualties (killed or injured) in World War II, bombings caused 112,932; V-1s, 24,165; V-2s, 9,277; and, long-range guns, 403.[40] The buzz bombs, along with the V-2 ballistic missiles, did more than just kill and maim Britons. They undermined the morale of a nation war weary after almost five years of conflict. The V-weapons assault encouraged almost one and one-half million Londoners to leave the city, more than the number that evacuated during the blitz. During this period, the authorities estimated that production fell by one-quarter.[41] The defensive effort involved squadrons of fighters, about 250,000 personnel, and 2,500 guns.

Another aspect of the V-1 operational story is frequently overlooked. The Germans also launched about 7,400 to 9,000 V-1s against targets on the continent, mostly (4,900) against the port of Antwerp, Belgium. In the city's defense, the Allies deployed 18,000 troops manning 208 90 mm guns, 128 3.7-inch guns, and 188 40 mm guns. In addition, they used

Figure 12. Barrage balloons. Barrage balloons were a relatively cheap device that inhibited many more low-flying aircraft than they destroyed. These devices were also useful against the V-1s. (Reprinted from http://www.raf.mod.uk/bob1940/images.)

280 balloons that later were augmented to 1,400. No fighters were employed in the defense of Antwerp, mainly because of the short distance between the V-1 launcher and its target.[42]

In the attack on Antwerp, the Germans fired their first missiles from the southeast in October. In mid-December, they shifted to the northeast and finally, by the end of January, to the north. The last direction of attack created a particular problem for the defense because a large airfield in that sector was not closed until 21 February 1945. Nevertheless, the defenders downed 2,183 (91 percent) of the 2,394 missiles plotted. More to the point, only 211 V-1s reached a 7,000-yard radius around the docks that the defenders designated as the vital area, of which 150 hit the dock area.[43] The Germans also attacked Liège, Belgium, with about 3,000 V-1s. V-1s killed 947 military and 3,736 civilians and wounded 1,909 military and 8,166 civilians on the continent. Antwerp suffered 1,812 military and 8,333 civilian casualties, or 10,145 of the 14,758 V-1 casualties on the continent.[44]

American Antiaircraft Artillery

American flak made an impressive showing in combat (fig. 13). During the first month of the Normandy campaign (7–30 June 1944), First Army antiaircraft gunners claimed 96 aircraft destroyed of 682 enemy sorties. Following the breakout from the invasion beachhead, between 31 July and 6 August, the Luftwaffe hurled 1,312 aircraft at American forces passing through difficult terrain at the Avranches bottleneck. Although US gunners downed only 58 aircraft, the Germans did not hit a single bridge, dam, or vital target.[45] Another major GAF effort took place on 3 December 1944 when the Luftwaffe launched 80 to 100 aircraft against the First Army and lost 30 to 41 in a 45-minute engagement. During the Battle of the Bulge (16 December 1944–1 January 1945), the First Army antiaircraft units claimed 366 German aircraft destroyed or probably destroyed of 1,178 sorties.[46]

The most spectacular one-day Allied air defense effort occurred on New Year's Day 1945. The GAF plan called for about 900 German fighters, led by Ju 88 night fighters, to attack 16 Anglo-American airfields. Coordination broke down badly as German flak downed about 100 of their own aircraft before they reached Allied lines. (This fratricide is interesting in view of the fact that German AAA was organized within the Luftwaffe.) Poor weather, lack of training, confusion, Allied flak, and Allied fighters further diluted the impact of the raid. Allied losses were much lower than might have been expected, and German losses were much higher. The GAF claimed to have destroyed

Figure 13. US 90 mm M-1 gun. The standard US heavy antiaircraft gun during World War II was the 90 mm M-1. (Reprinted from US Army Air Defense Artillery Museum.)

402 Allied aircraft on the ground and 65 in the air, but the Allies stated their losses as 236 destroyed and badly damaged on the ground and 23 in air-to-air combat. On their part, the Germans put their losses at 304 aircraft destroyed and 232 pilots lost. Anglo-American pilots claimed 102 aerial victories, and Allied gunners claimed 185 to 394 (the former figure, confirmed kills; the latter, confirmed kills plus those awaiting confirmation). The Allies recovered 137 German aircraft wrecks in their area of control and, from their remains, credited the fighters with 57 kills and flak with 80.[47]

A clearer view of the confused battle is perhaps possible by focusing on the attack of one airfield. The German fighter unit JG 11 launched about 65 fighters against the Anglo-American airfield (Y-29) at Asch, Belgium, where four RAF Spitfire squadrons and two US fighter groups were stationed. When the Germans struck Asch, one Spitfire squadron and one Thunderbolt squadron were airborne, and a dozen P-51s of the 352d Fighter Group were taking off. The latter's commander, Col John Meyer, claimed one FW 190 before he raised his landing gear. In the ensuing melee, American pilots claimed 32 kills; British pilots, one. In all, the Allied pilots and gunners at Asch claimed 35 to 41 German aircraft out of 50 attackers. The Allies lost no P-51s and only one P-47 in the air; they lost seven Spitfires and several C-47s on the ground. The Germans admitted losing 27 aircraft in the attack.[48]

A few months later, US flak gunners scored another impressive victory. After American forces unexpectedly captured the railway bridge across the Rhine River at Remagen, Germany, on 7 March 1945, German forces made considerable and desperate efforts to destroy it. By 14 March, the American antiaircraft gunners massed 64 90 mm, 216 40 mm, and 24 37 mm guns as well as 228 quad and 140 single .50-caliber machine guns in their defensive effort (fig. 14). They claimed 142 German aircraft destroyed of 442 attacking. More important, German aircraft did not damage the bridge.[49]

The impact of AAA can be seen in two statistical snapshots. During the European campaign, American forces of the 12th Army Group (First, Third, and Ninth US Armies) recorded 14,776 sorties by the German air force. US gunners claimed the destruction of 2,070 Luftwaffe aircraft. The GAF recorded 29,953 aircraft lost to enemy action or missing in the entire war. Of the 14,938 downed over Germany, the Germans credited AAA with the destruction of 2,598 aircraft.[50]

German Flak

Of all combatants in World War II, the Germans had the most experience with antiaircraft defense. They had come a long way from the Versailles peace treaty that essentially banned German antiaircraft weapons. Although the Germans evaded the provisions of the treaty to a degree, that agreement clearly inhibited them from building any real military force until Hitler came to power in 1933. In April 1934, the Germans assigned the antiaircraft arm to the Luftwaffe. At first, they considered AAA as

Figure 14. US quad .50 gun. The American quad .50 was an effective weapon against both air and ground targets. (Adapted from http://www. strand.com/quad50/halftrk.jpg.)

the primary defense of the homeland from enemy aircraft. The Germans expanded the role of flak as they assessed the lessons of the Spanish Civil War, where AAA also served most notably as an infantry support weapon. Based on that war, the Germans doubled the number of their flak units. When World War II began, the Germans had 2,600 heavy and 6,700 light flak guns, the largest air defense system in the world (fig. 15).[51]

Figure 15: German 40 mm Bofors. The Germans used a wide variety of light flak guns including this truck-mounted 40 mm Bofors. (Adapted from Air Force Historical Research Agency.)

Germany's best-known artillery piece was its 88 mm gun. Although a gun of that caliber was used in World War I, Krupp designers at Bofors in Sweden worked out the details of a new 88 mm gun in the interwar years and returned to Germany with the new model in 1931 (fig. 16). The resulting 8.8-centimeter (cm) Flak 18/36/37 made up about 60 percent of Germany's heavy flak guns during World War II. The gun fired a 20.3-pound shell at a muzzle velocity of 2,600 fps to an effective ceiling of 26,000 feet. This compares to the standard British heavy anti-aircraft gun, the 3.7-inch Mark 3 that fired a 28-pound projectile at a muzzle velocity of 2,600 fps to an effective ceiling of 32,000 feet, and the American 90 mm Mark 1 that hurled a 23-pound shell at 2,700 fps to an effective ceiling of 32,000 feet. These two Allied guns weighed more than the German gun and had a higher rate of fire, 20 spm compared with the German 15-spm gun.[52] The fame of the 8.8 stems mainly from its versatility as a triple-purpose weapon (antiaircraft, antitank, and standard artillery piece) and its ubiquity.

Figure 16. German 88 mm gun. Probably the best-known artillery piece of World War II was this German 88 mm gun. It was the most versatile heavy artillery weapon used in the war, serving very well as a conventional artillery piece, as well as against tanks and aircraft. (Reprinted from Imperial War Museum.)

The Germans began to work on a more advanced model, the 8.8-cm Flak 41 in 1939 but did not get this gun into service until 1943. Although it suffered early mechanical problems, this flak gun had greater performance. It fired a 20.7-pound shell at a muzzle velocity of 3,280 fps to an effective ceiling of 37,000 feet. It also featured a lower silhouette on its turntable mounting than did the 8.8-cm Flak 18/36/37 on its pedestal mounting. Because of the high cost and complexity of this flak gun, the Germans manufactured relatively few of them (556 in all) and, in February 1944, fielded only 279.[53]

The Germans supplemented the 88s with two larger guns. In 1933, the Germans established the specifications for a 105 mm antiaircraft gun and three years later selected Rheinmetall's proposal over Krupp's. The 10.5-cm Flak 38/39 fired a 33.2-pound shell at a muzzle velocity of 2,885 fps to an effective ceiling of 31,000 feet. In 1936, Rheinmetall also won a contract for a 12.8-cm gun designated as the 12.8-cm Flak 40 (fig. 17). It fired a 57.2-pound shell at 2,890 fps to a maximum ceiling of 35,000 feet. Compared with the 88 mm gun, the 128 mm gun used a powder charge four times as great and which resulted in a shell flight time only one-third as long. In late 1944, there were 116 105 mm flak guns mounted on railroad mounts, 827 on fixed mounts, and 1,025 on mobile mounts. For increased mobility, the Germans mounted about 5 percent of their 105 mm and 128 mm flak guns on railroad cars. Germany's best flak gunners, who were correctly considered the cream of the flak arm, manned these potent guns (fig. 18).[54]

In the early years of the war (1939–41), flak protected German troops from the few Allied aircraft that the Luftwaffe had not destroyed and supported the advancing armies as an antitank and direct support weapon. In the Western European campaign of 1940, flak units claimed 854 of 2,379 aircraft destroyed and over 300 armored vehicles. By October 1941, the German flak units credited their gunners with destroying 5,381 aircraft and 1,930 armored vehicles.

One important German flak victory occurred during the evacuation of Axis forces from Sicily over the Strait of Messina in August 1943. Despite Allied air and sea superiority, almost 40,000 German and 62,000 Italian troops—and even their rear guard—got to the mainland with much of their equipment, including nearly 10,000 vehicles. Allied preoccupation with the upcoming Italian invasion and completion of the conquest of Sicily as well as the Axis employment of 500 heavy and light flak pieces helped to account for this Axis success.[55] The Messina evacuation was as much an Axis accomplishment as it was an Allied failure.

During the early years, German home defenses faced light opposition as the British night raiders were few in number, ill equipped, and poorly trained (a bomber could rarely find its target, much less destroy it). But British airmen began to strike telling blows as dramatically seen in the first RAF raid of 1,000 bombers on Cologne in May 1942. Shortly afterwards,

Figure 17. German 128 mm AAA gun. The 128 mm gun was the most powerful antiaircraft gun the Germans put into service during the war. By the end of 1944, they had deployed about 2,000. (Reprinted from Imperial War Museum.)

Figure 18. German railroad-mounted 128 mm guns. The best German gunners manned the railroad-mounted 128 mm guns. Two dozen of the powerful guns defended the Ploesti oil fields. (Adapted from USAF.)

American heavy bombers joined the fray with daylight attacks, but they did not launch large raids into Germany until the spring of 1943.

Oil was critical to war fighting, and Germany was short of oil before the conflict. One key target was the oil complex at Ploesti, Romania, that produced 35 percent of Germany's crude oil. After an ineffective attack by 13 American B-24s on 12 June 1942, the Army Air Forces (AAF) dispatched 178 heavy bombers on a low-level attack on 1 August 1943. American intelligence estimated Axis flak defenses at about 100 heavy guns and several hundred light guns but encountered twice that number (fig. 19). These guns, combined with the vulnerability of the Liberators at low altitude, confusion of the battle, and the mission's long distance (over 2,300 miles round-trip) caused heavy bomber losses. Fifty-four B-24s failed to return; the airmen attributed the bulk of these losses to flak.

Figure 19. B-24 at Ploesti. The AAF lost 54 B-24s at the 1 August 1943 raid on the oil refineries at Ploesti. This battle was but one World War II example of high aircraft losses on low-level missions. (Adapted from USAF.)

The Allies continued to attack Ploesti, conducting 19 high-level raids on Ploesti between 5 April and 19 August 1944 (fig. 20). On 5,479 effective sorties, American bombers dropped 13,469 tons of bombs and lost 223 bombers. Flak downed 131 bombers and 56 fighters.[56]

Besides the 21 heavy bomber raids by the AAF, there were four other bombing attacks on Ploesti. The RAF flew three night missions, dropped 313 tons of bombs on 186 effective sorties, and lost 15 bombers to unknown causes. In contrast, on 10 June 1944, the Americans dispatched 46 P-38s, each carrying a 1,000-pound bomb and a 300-gallon fuel tank, escorted by 48 Lightnings, against the oil target. The Airmen credited 38 P-38s with effective bombing sorties and with get-

Figure 20. Ploesti smoke screen. The Germans used various defensive measures, including smoke screens, to defend the critical Ploesti refineries. The Romana American oil refinery is at the center right of this 17 August 1944 photo. The white dots are bomb craters. (Reprinted from USAF.)

ting 19 bombs on target with good results. But, the Americans met stiff resistance, including 100 enemy aircraft; as a result, they lost nine dive bombers (seven to flak) and 14 of the escorting P-38s. American fighters claimed 28 enemy aircraft destroyed in the air.[57]

In early April 1944, 178 heavy and 203 light guns protected Ploesti. The Germans bolstered this number to 278 heavy guns and 280 light guns by the time of the final attack on 19 August. The heavy guns consisted of 128 mm guns (10 percent), 105 mm mobile guns (15 percent), 88 mm mobile guns (60 percent), and Romanian 75 mm guns. They also captured Soviet 76.5 mm guns (15 percent). Flak took an increasing toll on American bombers, doubling from 1.2 percent of sorties in April to 2.4 percent in August, as losses to enemy aircraft declined from 2 percent of sorties to zero.[58]

The Germans fiercely defended other oil facilities as well. At Politz, they deployed 600 heavy AAA weapons, and at Leuna, 700. At the latter, about 40 percent of the heavy weapons were larger than 88 mm guns. Between 12 May 1944 and 4 April 1945, the Allied airmen waged a bombing campaign against Leuna, Germany's second largest synthetic oil and chemical plant. It clearly illustrated the power of massive antiaircraft protection during World War II. The AAF sent 5,236 bomber sorties, and the RAF sent 1,394 sorties that dropped 18,092 tons of bombs on the target. However, primarily because of weather and enemy opposition, only 10 percent of these bombs fell on the plant complex. Bombs on-target declined from 35 percent in May 1944 to 5 percent in July and finally to 1.5 percent in September. On three missions in October, the Germans reported that no bombs fell on the plant. The Americans lost 119 bombers (2.3 percent of sorties), while the British lost eight (.57 percent), mostly to German flak.[59]

German cities were also heavily defended by flak. Hamburg's defenses included 400 heavy guns, while almost 300 defended Munich, and 327 protected Vienna. The Allies hit the Austrian capital on 47 raids and lost 361 heavy bombers, 229 (63 percent) to flak. On 7 February 1945, the Fifteenth Air Force lost 25 of the 689 aircraft sent against Vienna (19 to flak). The Fifteenth Air Force hit the city again the next day; but this time, it lost none of its 470 bombers. The losses on the first raid were due to the clear weather that helped the gunners and to the Americans' lack of airborne coordination and electronic countermeasures (ECM). The AAF attributed success on the following day to poorer weather (7/10 to 10/10 overcast) and better American coordination and ECM.[60]

The Germans introduced technological improvements to increase flak efficiency. In 1941, flak units began to get gun-laying radar. Radar was a major advance over sound detectors, the existing system used to detect and track aircraft. The older device suffered from short range and erratic performance. However, the German introduction of radar was slow, for as late as August 1944, the GAF was still using over 5,500 sound detectors.[61] Another improvement was the introduction of grooved projectiles. These shells fragmented into 80- to 100-gram pieces instead of the usual 1 to 7 grams, therefore causing much greater damage.[62] Incendiary shells also increased flak efficiency by three times, according to German estimates.

Fuzes were another important advance. The Germans requested double fuzes (contact and timed) in 1943 and introduced them into combat in late 1944. These fuzes increased the effectiveness of 88 mm guns five times; 105 mm guns, three times; and 128 mm guns, twice. But the Germans did not make the big change in fuzes; instead, the Allies introduced proximity fuzes. After the war, an American study calculated that had the Germans used proximity fuzes, they could have increased their flak efficiency by a factor of 3.4, making B-17 operations very hazardous and B-24 operations impractical.[63]

The Germans also experimented with a number of novel approaches to ground-based antiaircraft systems. They tested squeeze-bore and sabot devices, systems that fired a shell of smaller size; for example, an 88 mm shell from a 105 mm gun. Such shells achieved greater velocities than they would have otherwise, as more powder pushed a smaller projectile. Neither system got into service.

The Germans examined yet another concept—flak rockets (later known as surface-to-air missiles or SAM). Although the Germans realized few positive results with the program in the 1930s, they still gave the new technology consideration for the task of combating Allied air attacks. In early 1941, Gen Walter Dornberger, one of the key German decision makers in rocket and missile development, ordered a study of an antiaircraft missile with an altitude capability of up to 60,000 feet. Werner von Braun, chief of missile research at the Peenemünde test site, instead proposed using a rocket-powered interceptor.

This was the initial route the Germans took that yielded the spectacularly performing, yet tactically lame, Me 163. In any case, in September Hitler halted all long-range development projects. The Germans later lifted the stop order on the program, and, in April 1942, drew up the specifications for a variety of flak rockets, both guided and unguided. The Germans made rockets the "centerpiece" of their development program. The Luftwaffe's leader, Hermann Goering, had high expectations. In September 1942, he authorized work on AAA rockets. In response, von Braun forwarded a study in November 1942 that mentioned three types of guided flak rockets: a 28-foot, single-stage solid-fuel missile; a 33-foot, two-stage solid-fuel missile; and a 20-foot, single-stage liquid-fuel missile. Pushed by the German antiaircraft chief, Gen Walter von Axthelm, flak rockets became the core of the 1942 German antiaircraft development program.[64]

Subsequently, the Germans developed a number of guided flak missiles and two small, unguided ground-launched rockets, the Foehn and Taifun. The Foehn was designed to combat low-flying aircraft. It measured less than three inches in diameter and about two feet in length and weighed 3.3 pounds. First fired in 1943, the rocket had a 3,600-foot range and was intended to be fired in ripples from a 35-barrel launcher. The Germans put three batteries into service and credited them with downing three Allied aircraft. The rocket's primary impact was, however, psychological.[65]

The other unguided flak rocket, the Taifun, measured less than four inches in diameter and 76 inches in length, weighed 65 pounds, and carried a 1.4-pound warhead (fig. 21). The Germans fired the liquid-fuel rockets in ripples from either a 30-barrel launcher or a 50-barrel launcher mounted on an 88 mm gun carriage. The Taifun had an altitude capability of 46,000 to 52,000 feet.[66]

In addition, the Germans developed four guided rockets: Enzian, Rheintochter, Schmetterling, and Wasserfall. The Enzian could have passed for an aircraft, albeit a small, radio-controlled one lacking a horizontal tail (fig. 22). Almost 12 feet in length, the missile's sweptback wing spanned 13.5 feet. It weighed 4,350 pounds and was assisted in its launch from an 88 mm gun

35

Figure 21. Taifun. The Germans were developing a family of antiaircraft missiles. Two unguided efforts were the 3.3-pound Foehn and this 65-pound Taifun. (Adapted from Smithsonian Institution.)

carriage by four solid-fuel boosters. The Enzian carried a 1,050-pound warhead to an altitude of 48,000 feet and a slant range of 16 miles at 560 mph. The Germans test-fired possibly 24 Enzians, nine of which they considered successes. In January 1945, the Germans canceled the project, although work continued until March.[67]

Rheintochter I was a subsonic, solid-fuel, two-stage rocket that measured 20.5 feet and weighed 3,850 pounds. The second stage had four canard fins and six wings (which spanned 9.8 feet) and carried a 330-pound warhead to a slant range of 18,000 yards and an altitude of 29,000 feet. The Germans first tested the radio-controlled device in August 1943 and fired 82 flak rockets by early January 1945 (fig. 23). The Germans cancelled the program the next month. Rheintochter II employed

Figure 22. Enzian. The Germans also worked on four guided antiaircraft missile projects. This 4,400-pound Enzian was one of the less successful of these. (Reprinted from Imperial War Museum.)

two booster rockets, as did Rheintochter III. The third version used the same first stage, but its second stage was about 3.3 feet longer. It was powered by a liquid-fuel engine and had slightly better performance than its predecessor, having the ability to reach an altitude of almost 50,000 feet at a range of over 20,000 yards. The Germans tested about six of these (none with radio control) between July 1944 and January 1945 before canceling Rheintochter in favor of the Schmetterling.[68]

The Schmetterling looked like a swept-wing aircraft that measured 12.5 feet in length and 6.5 feet in span (fig. 24). The Germans worked on two versions of the missiles that had an all-up weight of 980 pounds. The Hs 117H was air-launched, while the Hs 117 was ground-launched from a 37 mm gun carriage aided by two solid-fuel boosters. The designers originally intended to use wire guidance but later employed radio controls. The missile carried a 55-pound warhead to a maximum effective slant-range of 17,500 yards and to an altitude

Figure 23. Rheintochter. The Germans test-fired 88 of the solid-fuel Rheintochter I's, shown here, before the project was cancelled in favor of the liquid-fueled Rheintochter II and III. (Adapted from Imperial War Museum.)

of 35,000 feet at a maximum speed of 537 mph. Ordered in August 1943, the Germans first fired it in January 1944 and achieved success on 25 of 59 launches, despite engine (fuel regulation) problems.[69]

Wasserfall, the largest German flak rocket, was a scaled down V-2, from which it was derived. Unlike the V-2, however, Wasserfall had a set of four fins mounted about one-third down its 25.6-foot length and larger tail fins.[70] Wasserfall had a lift-off weight of 7,800 pounds and carried a 200-pound warhead at supersonic speeds. The Germans desired a missile that could down an aircraft flying 560 mph at an altitude of 65,000 feet and at a distance of 31 miles (fig. 25). The Wasserfall fell short of these requirements, but it had the largest engagement envelope of the German antiaircraft missiles: an altitude of 6 miles at a distance of 30 miles, an altitude of 9 miles at 25 miles, and an altitude of 11.4 miles at 16.5 miles. (American bomber formations in 1945 were flying less than 200 mph and seldom flew above 30,000 feet.) The Germans intended to use beam-

Figure 24. Schmetterling. The Schmetterling was about one-quarter the weight of both Enzian and Rheintochter and looked like a swept-winged aircraft. The Germans test-fired about 80 of these missiles. (Reprinted from Air Force Historical Research Agency.)

rider guidance, in which the missile rides along an electronic beam to its target. But telemetry difficulties created problems. The Germans had two schemes for detonating the warhead: ground-activated signals and a proximity fuze. The developers completed design work for the Wasserfall in early 1943 and first flew the missile in February 1944. The Germans tested at least 25 times before canceling the project in February 1945.[71]

Some authors speculate on what might have been if the Wasserfall, the most promising flak rocket, had been built in quantity, rather than the V-2. As it required only one-eighth the man-hours to build as a V-2, clearly a large number could have been built. They overlook some basic factors. The anti-aircraft problem is much more difficult than that of ground bombardment, for the target is small, possibly maneuvering, and fast moving. The Germans lacked an operational proximity

Figure 25. Wasserfall. Wasserfall at Peenemünde in the fall of 1944. It was a smaller version of the V-2 and the largest of the German flak rockets. (Adapted from Air Force Historical Research Agency.)

fuze, and the Allies had a lead in electronics that probably could have nullified, certainly degraded, the German's radio-controlled guidance system.

A number of problems inhibited German flak. Flak personnel declined in quality, especially after 1943, as Germany combed out its forces to make good the war's heavy attrition. The Germans employed women, old men, young boys, factory workers, foreigners, and even prisoners of war in flak units. In November 1944, 29 percent of flak personnel were civilians and auxiliaries; in April 1945, 44 percent. German flak strength peaked in February 1945, when it fielded over 13,500 heavy and 21,000 light pieces. The increasing number of guns deployed by the Germans consumed tremendous amounts of materials, revealing another difficulty—a shortage of ammunition—that in early 1944 forced the Germans to restrict their firing. Another ammunition shortage occurred in November 1944 and was attributed to the bombing of German chemical plants and transportation. One consequence of this shortage was that some German shells were filled with inert materials. By the end of the war, flak units could deliver only one-half of their firepower potential because of these shortages. Another indication of the decline of efficiency of German flak was the increasing number of shells required to down an Allied aircraft. In the first 20 months of the war, it took 2,800 heavy flak rounds per kill, whereas in 1944, 16,000 flak rounds of 88 mm/model 36-37 or 3,000 rounds of 128 mm caliber rounds were required.[72]

Nevertheless, German flak was effective in World War II and grew increasingly potent as the war continued (fig. 26). Through 1944 German gunners inflicted about one-third of Allied aircraft losses and two-thirds of the damage; and after that, they inflicted about two-thirds of the losses and almost all of the damage. To be precise, not only did German flak become more effective through the course of the war but proportionally more important as German aircraft were swept from the skies. In June 1944, for example, the Germans deployed 10,900 heavy and 22,200 light guns in the west. The AAF lost 18,418 aircraft in combat against Germany in World War II (fig. 27). The American Airmen credited AAA with downing 7,821 of these and enemy aircraft with 6,800.[73]

In addition to downing and damaging Allied aircraft, flak also degraded bombing accuracy. A 1941 British report estimated that one-third of bombing accuracy degradation was attributed to flak. A postwar study of Eighth Air Force bombing errors between May 1944 and February 1945 credits almost 40 percent of these errors to enemy guns. An additional 22 percent of the error was attributed to the increased altitude required to counter flak. The Mediterranean air forces put the same message across in another way: with little or no flak opposition, fighters required 30 bombs to hit a bridge, but against intense flak, it took 150 bombs per hit. Medium bombers not encountering flak destroyed 21 percent of the bridges attacked and completely

Figure 26. Falling B-24. During World War II, ground fire downed more American aircraft than did enemy fighters. In the European theater of operations, AAA downed 5,400 American aircraft, while enemy aircraft destroyed 4,300. (Reprinted from USAF.)

missed only 3 percent; but against flak, the bombers destroyed only 2 percent and completely missed 28 percent.[74]

Allied Countermeasures

Allied Airmen used a number of measures to reduce the effectiveness of enemy flak. Planners picked routes around known flak positions, used higher bombing altitudes, employed saturation tactics, and devised tighter formations.[75] Two other measures deserve detailed treatment.

Figure 27. Damaged B-17. This B-17 survived a flak hit over Cologne, Germany. During World War II, the Eighth Air Force suffered 20 percent damage per sortie and wrote off 1,600 bombers as "damaged beyond economic repair." (Reprinted from USAF.)

The importance of radar to the defender as both an early-warning and gun-laying device grew as Allied bombers increasingly operated at night and in poor weather. Fortunately for the Allies, the British held a marked advantage over the Germans in electronic warfare; some say a two-year lead. One countermeasure used against German radar was called window (by the British) and chaff (by the Americans). Aircraft dropped strips of aluminum foil, similar to Christmas tree tinsel, which created false signals on German radarscopes (fig. 28). The RAF first used this electronic countermeasure in the July 1943 Hamburg raids, following a command decision that cleared its use after being withheld for almost 18 months. The second major ECM device, called carpet, electronically jammed German radar. In October 1943, the Allies first employed the device in bomber formations as both a broadband and spot jammer. Estimates vary on the impact of ECM; and ECM impact changed as specific conditions changed, especially weather. Although the ECM device may have decreased the effectiveness of flak

Figure 28. Chaff. Chaff was an effective counter used against radar beginning in World War II. (Adapted from US Army Air Defense Museum.)

by as much as two-thirds, an overall estimate of one-fourth is probably closer to the truth.[76]

The AAF used more direct tactics as well. On the first day of the Market-Garden operation, 17 September 1944, the AAF attacked 112 flak positions. In addition to over 3,000 tons of bombs dropped by B-17s, P-47s dropped 36 tons of fragmentation bombs and expended almost 123,000 rounds of .50-caliber machine-gun ammunition. The relatively light losses suffered by the attackers, the troop carriers, and gliders indicate that the effort worked.[77] The element of surprise, however, may account for Allied success, as the next day proved far different. On 18 September 1944, 38 P-47s of the crack 56th Fighter Group attacked German flak positions in the Turnhout area with .50s and parachute fragmentation bombs. Disaster ensued. Low overcast, haze, and orders requiring pilots to hold their fire until fired upon inhibited the American pilots and put them at a disadvantage. The unit lost 15 aircraft to German flak and one aircraft to Allied antiaircraft fire; in addition, 13 of the 22 aircraft that returned home were damaged by flak. Eleven pilots, three of them injured, returned to Allied lines, while three others were killed and two captured. That day, the AAF flew 104 sorties against antiaircraft guns and lost 21 aircraft with another 17 damaged. These missions claimed 18 flak guns destroyed.[78] In the entire Market-Garden operation, Allied airmen claimed destruction of 118 flak positions and damage to 127 others. But the Anglo-Americans lost 104 aircraft on 4,320 sorties (excluding troop carriers and gliders), of which 37 were lost on 646 sorties to suppress flak. Analysis of the entire operation indicated that flak suppression succeeded only during the first day of the operations.[79] Not surprisingly then, the next month, US Strategic Air Forces in Europe recommended against attacking heavy flak positions with low-flying aircraft as ineffective and costly. The report concluded that alternative measures (ECM, formations, evasive maneuvers, and fragmentation bombing) were more practical.[80]

The Fifteenth Air Force conducted an experiment that bombed flak positions from high altitude. On two missions in April 1945, B-24s dropped 260-pound fragmentation bombs fitted with proximity fuzes on German flak northeast of Venice from about 25,000 feet. The Airmen considered the operations successful.[81]

The Americans also employed artillery to blanket known flak positions as the fighters approached. The American gunners attempted to pin down the flak gunners so the fighters could launch their initial attack against minimal resistance. The Americans employed these tactics with mixed results during the June 1944 siege of Cherbourg, France.[82]

Another Allied effort at flak suppression occurred during the Anglo-American airborne assault across the Rhine River at Wesel on 24 March 1945 in Operation Varsity. Allied aircraft and artillery attempted to silence or neutralize the 922 German flak barrels in the area. Allied bombers dropped over 8,100 tons of bombs on flak positions on 3,741 sorties during the three days before the airdrop. RAF Typhoons used bullets, bombs, and rockets; and Allied artillery fired 24,000 rounds (440 tons) at 95 German positions. Despite this awesome firepower, the Allies accomplished little. Allied Airmen and artillery-men scored few hits and, at best, temporarily lowered the morale of the German gunners. Nevertheless, German flak inflicted considerable casualties on Allied forces. In addition to destroying 53 tow and 16 supply aircraft, the Germans damaged 381 of 853 American gliders and 160 of 272 British gliders, of which 142 had major damage (fig. 29).[83] American Airmen found little profit in attacking flak positions in World War II. Of 338 Eighth Air Force fighters lost to flak during the war, 77 percent were lost while strafing. As Maj Gen Elwood "Pete" Quesada, commander of the 9th Tactical Air Command (TAC), put it: "It was like a man biting a dog."[84]

Fratricide

One problem that antiaircraft gunners would rather not talk about is firing on and hitting friendly aircraft. Fratricide in the speed and confusion of battle is as understandable as it is re-grettable. Ground troops and antiaircraft gunners had fired on friendly aircraft in World War I and formed the attitude: "There

Figure 29. German 20 mm gun. German light flak was very potent. This single 20 mm gun is assisted by the German soldier in the background operating a range finder. (Reprinted from Imperial War Museum.)

ain't no such thing as a 'friendly airplane.'"[85] That attitude and that problem continued.

The most costly Allied fratricide incident in World War II occurred during the invasion of Sicily. On the night of 11 July and the early morning hours of 12 July 1943, the Allies attempted to reinforce the invasion with elements of the 82d Airborne Division. Gen Matthew Ridgway, the division's commander, anticipating difficulties, attempted to get a protected aerial corridor for his forces and got assurances from both the US Navy and the US Army antiaircraft gunners. Unfortunately, Ridgway's worst fears were realized. The troop-filled C-47s and the gliders arrived over the invasion fleet shortly after an Axis bombing raid. The first flight passed without incident, but then one gun opened fire and acted as a signal for Allied gunners both ashore and afloat to cut loose at the rest of the aerial armada. Antiaircraft fire destroyed 23 of the 144 aircraft that departed Africa that night and badly damaged 37 others. Losses in personnel amounted to 97 paratroopers killed or missing and 132 wounded. Sixty Airmen were killed or missing, and 30 were wounded.[86]

Two nights later, a similar incident occurred with similar results. American and British troop carriers attempted to drop British paratroopers to seize a bridge and establish a bridgehead on the east coast of Sicily. Friendly naval and ground fire engaged the transports, destroyed 11, damaged 50, and forced 27 others to abort the mission. Of the 87 aircraft that pressed on, only 39 got their troops within a mile of the designated drop zone. Thus, only 300 of the 1,900-man force reached their objectives; nevertheless, they carried it.[87]

Fratricidal problems continued throughout the war. Fortunately for the Allies, they proved less costly than the Sicilian debacles. On D-day, for example, despite special invasion markings (white stripes), "friendly fire" hit a number of Allied aircraft. At 2025, guns aboard a landing craft downed two P-51s flying at 500 to 1,000 feet. Ten minutes later, Allied flak destroyed two more Allied aircraft. At 2050, gunners fired on four Spitfires but apparently did not score any decisive hits. At 2130, however, Allied flak holed one Spitfire that was last seen smoking and losing altitude. At 2200, gunners engaged two Typhoons and appeared to hit both. These are the recorded cases; we can only speculate on how many other incidents escaped reporting.

Although the Allies instituted several measures to prevent fratricide, including electronic identification devices (identification, friend or foe—[IFF]), recognition signals, and restricted areas, the problem continued (fig. 30). Between 22 June and 25 July, Allied gunners engaged 25 friendly aircraft and destroyed eight. Five of these aircraft, two Spitfires on 22 June and three P-51s on 26 June, were destroyed after they attacked friendly forces. (There were at least 13 incidents of Allied aircraft attacking Allied forces between 20 June and 17 July 1944, killing at least two soldiers and wounding three others.) Fragmentary records indicate that Anglo-American flak crews downed six Allied aircraft in August, two in October, and at least three in November. Even the brass could not avoid the problem. On 1 January 1945, US AAA units fired on an aircraft carrying AAF

Figure 30. George Preddy. George Preddy was killed by friendly fire as he chased a German aircraft in December 1944. He was one of the AAF's leading aces with 26.8 credits. (Reprinted from http://www.wpafb.af.mil/museum/history/wwII/ce32.htm.)

Generals Carl A. Spaatz and James H. Doolittle. Spaatz informed Gen George S. Patton Jr. of his gunners' poor aircraft recognition and shooting skills. The 8th Fighter Command lost seven fighters to Allied flak. US gunners admitted engaging 15 friendly aircraft and destroying 12, all of which the gunners asserted were either committing a hostile act or flying in a restricted zone. On the other hand, US gunners complained that lack of identification restricted them from engaging one-third of 6,000 targets.[88]

Following the 26 June incident with the three US P-51s, the 9th Tactical Air Command restricted free-lance strafing within 10 miles of the bomb line; only prearranged missions were to be flown in that area. The armies established restricted areas that by 7 September 1944 constituted an almost continuous belt from Antwerp, Belgium, to Nancy, France. British Bomber Command protested that this restriction inhibited their operations, and so the Allies limited the zones without satisfying either party.[89]

The problem of fratricide was, of course, not limited to the Allies or to the European theater. All warring powers had the problem—for example, the German fighter attack on Allied airfields on 1 January 1945. The Germans admitted to losing 229 fighters in 1943 and 55 in the first half of 1944 over Germany to their own flak. In the Pacific between December 1943 and June 1944, the US Navy downed at least six of its own aircraft and two or three AAF B-25s.[90] The worst case was probably at the Cape Gloucester, Bismarck Archipelago, assault that began on 26 December 1943. American naval antiaircraft fire downed two B-25s and one P-47 and damaged two other B-25s. US ground gunners also destroyed an American night fighter. Apparently, naval gunners fired on "anything that was not a P-38," the readily identifiable twin-boom American fighter. The Marines credit friendly antiaircraft fire with downing three of their aircraft during the war.[91]

The US Navy in the Pacific

The US Navy made strenuous efforts to defend its ships against enemy aircraft. During World War II, it spent over $4 billion on this problem, almost one-half of this amount on ammunition. The Navy estimated that its antiaircraft guns increased their effectiveness 100 times from the start to the finish of the war. Mid- and short-range light antiaircraft guns presented the major problem as the pre–World War II armament (.50-caliber machine guns and 1.1-inch guns) proved inadequate. The US Navy turned to foreign guns, the 20 mm Swiss Oerlikon and the 40 mm Swedish Bofors.

The Navy estimated that the 20 mm cannon was eight to 10 times as effective as a .50-caliber machine gun and in 1935 bought some of the Swiss Oerlikons, even though Army and Navy aircraft used the French Hispano Suiza 20 mm guns. By war's end, the Navy had 12,561 of the 20 mm guns shipboard and had spent $787 million for one billion rounds of 20 mm ammunition. The investment paid off. Between Pearl Harbor and September 1944, the 20 mm guns downed 32 percent of all Japanese aircraft claimed by Navy guns and 25 percent after that date. Although the 20 mm guns did have certain advantages over heavier guns, the 40 mm began to replace them toward the end of the war (fig. 31).[92]

The Bofors 40 mm gun was the most widely used antiaircraft piece of World War II. The Swedes began the gun's development in 1928 and fielded the first units in the early 1930s. It could fire a two-pound shell to an effective range of 1,500 yards at a rate of 120 shots per minute. The world took notice when the British ordered the weapon in 1937, and, by 1939 the Swedes delivered the Bofors to 18 countries and concluded production licenses with 11 others. Both sides manufactured and used Bofors during the war.

The Navy's interest in the Bofors 40 mm gun began in the fall of 1939; and, in late August 1940, guns and equipment arrived in the United States (fig. 32). Tested in September, the Bofors guns proved superior to both the US 37 mm and the British two pound (pom pom). The US government signed a contract in June 1941 and installed the first 40 mm Bofors aboard ship early the next year. But, there were problems in manufacturing the Bofors. First, the original metric drawings had to be converted to English measurements; second, it was found that the two American manufacturers used different sys-

Figure 31. USN 20 mm gun. The Navy's 20 mm guns accounted for one-third of the Japanese aircraft claimed by ship guns prior to September 1944, and one-quarter of the claims after that date. (Reprinted from http://www.bcoy1cph.pacdat.net/20mm_Oerlikion_AA_USN..jpg.)

tems—York decimals and Chrysler fractions. As a result, parts for the American-made guns were not completely interchangeable. At first 200 parts differed, but this number was eventually reduced to 10. By June 1945, the US Navy had 5,140 40 mm guns in dual and quad mounts. These guns claimed about 18 percent of the Japanese aircraft destroyed by antiaircraft guns through June 1944 and about 50 percent between October 1944 and March 1945.[93]

The United States experimented with dual-purpose (antiship and antiaircraft) guns in the 1920s. It produced the 5-inch/38-caliber gun in the early 1930s that was installed on a destroyer in 1934. The gun had a horizontal range of 10 miles, a vertical range of 6 miles, and a firing rate of 12 to 15 shots per

Figure 32. USN 40 mm gun. The Navy's 40 mm guns, again the ever-present Bofors, accounted for one-half of the Japanese aircraft destroyed by ship guns after October 1944. (Reprinted from http://www. grunts.net/album/navy/guncres.htm.)

minute. The Navy increased the number of these guns from 611 in July 1940 to 2,868 in June 1945.

A major factor in the increased effectiveness of the heavy-caliber gun was the introduction of proximity fuzes. The Navy first fired the proximity fuze in January 1942, and, in its first simulated combat test that August, downed three drones with four shells. In the proximity fuze's first combat engagement a year later, the USS *Helena* downed a Japanese bomber with its second salvo. The Navy estimated that the proximity fuzes increased AAA effectiveness three to four times. The fuze helped account for the high percentage of Japanese aircraft claimed by the 5-inch/38-caliber guns, numbering 31 percent through the first half of 1944.[94]

Japanese Antiaircraft Artillery

Japanese AAA lagged behind the other major powers throughout the war. The Japanese lacked the technological and manufacturing base to deal with their air defense problems and to make good their deficiencies. In addition, the Japanese received only limited assistance from the Germans and failed to fully mobilize their civilian scientists.[95]

The most widely used Japanese heavy flak piece was the 75 mm type 88 that entered service in 1928. It fired a 14.5-pound shell at a muzzle velocity of 2,360 fps to 23,550 feet but was inaccurate above 16,000 feet. The Japanese stuck with this gun throughout the war, while the Americans, British, and Germans went to larger and better performing weapons. Not that the Japanese did not try to upgrade their weapons—they produced an improved 75 mm gun (75 mm type 4) in 1944 but built only 65 and got few into action. Likewise, the Japanese put a 120 mm gun into production in 1943 but built only 154. Only two 150 mm guns saw service. The Japanese also used a few 88 mm naval guns.[96]

In 1941, the Japanese deployed 300 antiaircraft guns in defense of the home islands. By March 1945, they deployed 1,250, and, by the end of the war, over 2,000. As might be expected, the Japanese concentrated the largest number of their heavy guns (in all 509 to 551) around Tokyo: in August 1945, 150 naval 88 mm guns; 72 120 mm guns; and two 150 mm guns. Thus, compared with the Germans, the Japanese deployed fewer and less-capable guns. In addition, Japanese radar was far behind German radar. The Japanese did not capitalize on German technology but primarily relied on technology from captured American and British equipment.

Little wonder that Japanese flak proved less effective than the firepower of the other combatants. Based on overall losses and losses per sortie, the air war against Germany was much more costly to the AAF (18,418 aircraft and 1.26 percent of sorties) than the air war against Japan (4,530 aircraft and .77 percent of sorties).[97] In the entire war, the AAF credited Japanese flak with destroying 1,524 AAF aircraft and Japanese fighters with destroying 1,037 (fig. 33). Japanese AAA did better proportionally against the US Navy than against the US Marine Corps, claiming 1,545 of 2,166 Navy aircraft lost in combat as compared with 437 of 723 Marine aircraft.

Figure 33. A-20 aircraft sequence. This Douglas A-20 was downed by Japanese guns over Karos, Dutch New Guinea. (Reprinted from USAF.)

Figure 33. A-20 aircraft sequence (continued). (Reprinted from USAF.)

In the strategic bombing campaign against Japan, the AAF used its best bomber, the Boeing B-29, which was faster, higher flying, and more heavily armed than either the B-17 or B-24 that bombed Germany.[98] The AAF lost 414 B-29s in combat against Japan. They estimated that 74 fell to enemy aircraft, 54 to flak, and 19 to both flak and fighters (fig. 34). The ineffectiveness of Japanese flak and electronics is highlighted by the American decision to change from their prewar bombing doctrine and European strategic bombing practice of high-altitude day attacks to night attacks below 10,000 feet.

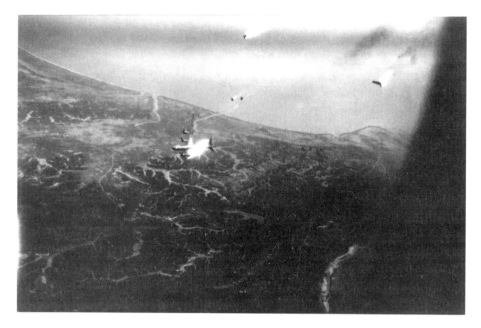

Figure 34. Falling B-29. Japanese air defenses downed about 227 B-29s over Japan, about equally divided between flak and fighters. This Superfortress was shot down on 26 June 1945. (Reprinted from USAF.)

Unlike the campaign against Germany that was dominated by the battle against GAF fighters, this decision resulted from poor bombing results, not aircraft losses. Consequently, the B-29s attacked Tokyo at low altitudes at night and suffered slightly fewer casualties: 39 aircraft on 1,199 sorties (3.2 percent) at night compared with 35 bombers lost on 814 sorties (4.3 percent) on daylight high-altitude missions. At the same time, bombing effectiveness greatly increased. The limited number of Japanese guns and primitive electronics encouraged the AAF to fly at lower altitudes with heavier bomb loads, where it achieved greater accuracy and encountered fewer mechanical problems than had been the case earlier at higher altitudes. The American Airmen went on to burn out Japanese cities and towns with conventional weapons. The reduced and bearable attrition resulted from Japanese flak deficiencies and employment of such American measures as saturating the searchlight defenses, ECM, desynchronizing the propellers of the bombers to inhibit Japanese sound-controlled searchlights, and use of high-gloss black paint. The rate of B-29 losses to flak and flak plus fighters decreased steadily after peaking in January 1945 at 1.06 percent of sorties. Tokyo was the most bombed (4,300 of 26,000 sorties) and the best defended of the Japanese targets. Its defenses accounted for 25 of the 55 flak losses of the Twentieth Air Force and for 14 of its 28 losses to flak plus fighters. As would be expected, American losses were much lighter at the less-defended targets. Specifically, in flying 4,776 night sorties at low and medium altitudes against major Japanese cities, the Twentieth Air Force lost 83 bombers (1.8 percent) as compared with seven lost (.1 percent) under similar conditions against secondary cities.[99]

The Lessons of World War II

As in all major wars, World War II provided many lessons. World War II is even more important to the Airman as it was not only the first full-scale air war but also the only total air war and the only American air war against a peer competitor. Airmen of all countries tended to overlook or disregard flak. Although the war indicated the value and lethality of flak, the Airmen looked instead to lessons that better fit their preconceptions and future intentions. The Airmen's attitude changed little from the interwar years when they considered flak to be of little use and not worth the effort. The result of this disdain would be evident in the wars that would follow.

In retrospect, at least six flak lessons emerged from World War II. First, flak proved to be lethal and effective—downing more US aircraft than any other enemy weapon. Clearly, it was the big killer from early 1944 on. Concentrations of guns demonstrated the ability to seriously inhibit or nullify aerial operations such as the case of the V-1 campaign, the fall-winter 1944 oil campaign, and operations against the Remagen Bridge.

Second, flak made low-level operations very costly. Flak downed most of the American fighters lost during the war, the bulk of these in strafing attacks.[100] A number of missions emphasized the dangers of low-level operations; the most notable were the Ploesti mission of August 1943, flak suppression at

Arnhem, the Netherlands, in September 1944, and the German attack on Allied airfields in January 1945.

A third lesson that can be gleaned from the war is that the Airmen came up with countermeasures to AAA that would be standard for the future. The Airmen attempted to avoid areas of flak concentrations by flying irregular courses in the face of ground fire, by flying only one pass over the target, and by using both the sun and terrain for maximum protection. They also employed chaff and jammers to degrade radar equipment, especially during the night or in poor weather. Finally, the Airmen attacked the guns directly. However, in most aircraft-versus-gun duels, the gunners held the advantage. Combat experience indicated that pitting a highly trained pilot and an expensive aircraft against a less-trained crew and less-valuable gun made little sense.

Fourth, rapidly evolving technology tilted the offensive-defensive balance in favor of the defense. Radar was the first and most important piece of equipment. It overturned the theories of Douhet and others (such as instructors and students at the Air Corps Tactical School), who believed that the bomber would always get through, cause decisive damage, and suffer sustainable losses. Electronic countermeasures somewhat nullified defensive radar, but radar still gave the defenders early warning and more accurate aiming information than was previously available. Radar gave the defenders much greater capabilities in night and bad weather conditions as well. The proximity fuze gave another big boost to the defenders, increasing the effectiveness of the guns by a multiple of five or so. One technological advance that was in the development stage but did not see service during the war was the flak rocket. This device was capable of reaching altitudes well above that of the highest-flying World War II bombers, and, fitted with a proximity fuze, would have inflicted heavy casualties on the bomber formations.

Fifth, flak proved very cost-effective, downing hostile aircraft at a relatively low cost. However, flak effectiveness should be measured by more than kills. Ground fire complicated the Airman's task, forcing him to fly more sorties, carry additional equipment, and adopt additional procedures, all of which detracted from his primary job. Flak defenses also decreased bombing accuracy. The best measure, therefore, is the cost (effort and losses) required to put bombs on target.

A sixth and final lesson of the war concerned the difficulty of correctly identifying aircraft: the gunners never were able to adequately sort out the friendlies from the foes. Not only did friendly fire down friendly aircraft—most dramatically demonstrated by the loss of Allied troop carriers over Sicily in July 1943 and German fighters on 1 January 1945—but also frequently, friendly fire did not engage hostile aircraft. Despite electronic equipment, codes, procedures, briefings, and restricted zones, the problem persisted and accidents happened.

The end of the war brought two other developments that seemed to override these advantages gained by the defense. The first was jet propulsion that greatly increased aircraft performance, further complicating the defender's task. The other was the atomic bomb that extended the prospect that one aircraft and one bomb could destroy one city, which was very different from the massive formations of hundreds of aircraft returning day after day. This development overturned the attritional concept of defense that dominated the air war. This, then, was the air defense situation in the immediate post–World War II era.

Notes

1. Edward Westermann, *Flak: German Anti-Aircraft Defenses 1914–1945* (Lawrence, Kans.: University Press, 2001), 9.

2. Ibid., 10–16.

3. The Germans fielded almost 2,800 antiaircraft guns at the end of the war with 30 percent geared for homeland defense. See P. T. Cullen, "Air Defense of London, Paris, and Western Germany" (paper, Air Corps Tactical School, Maxwell Field, Alabama, n.d.), 7, 9, 28, 99, table 5, Air Force Historical Research Agency (HRA), Maxwell Air Force Base (AFB), Ala.; "Antiaircraft Defences of Great Britain: 1914 to 1946," appendix A, Royal Artillery Institute (RAI), Woolwick, United Kingdom; "Antiaircraft Gun Trends and Scientific and Technical Projection: Eurasian Communist Countries," July 1981, 1–1; N.W. Routledge, *History of the Royal Regiment of Artillery: Anti-Aircraft Artillery, 1914–55* (London: Brassey's, 1994), 22; and Westermann, *Flak*, 26.

4. Westermann, *Flak*, 27.

5. Another source lists the rounds per claim as United States, 1,055; British, 1,800; and French, 3,225. See Ian Hogg, *Anti-Aircraft: A History of*

Air Defence (London: MacDonald and Jane's, 1978), 67; US Army Air Defense School, "Air Defense," 21, 29, 30; Cullen, "Air Defence of London," 94; extracts from Conference on Antiaircraft Defense, Military Intelligence Division, France, no. 8312, 26 December 1923, HRA; A. F. Englehart, "Antiaircraft Defenses: Their Development During the World War" (paper, Air Corps Tactical School, circa 1934), 6, 9, HRA; V. P. Ashkerov, "Anti-Aircraft Missile Forces and Anti-Aircraft Artillery," translation from *Zenitnyye Raketnyee Voyska I Zenitnaya Artilleriya* (1968), 5–6, HRA. American machine gunners got another 41 German aircraft. See Charles Kirkpatrick, *Archie in the A.E.F.: The Creation of the Antiaircraft Service of the United States Army, 1917–1918* (Fort Bliss, Tex.: Air Defense Artillery Museum, 1984), 85–86.

6. Sound locators were fickle and unreliable. Under the best of conditions, they had a range of five to 10 miles. See Hogg, *Anti-Aircraft*, 64; and [British] *Manual of Anti-Aircraft Defence, Provisional*, March 1922, 164, RAI.

7. Maj Gen B. P. Hughes and Brig N. W. Routledge, Woolwick, United Kingdom, interviewed by author, October 1982; "Antiaircraft Artillery," Air Corps Tactical School, 1, 1 November 1932, HRA; Louis Smithey and Charles Atkinson, "Development of Antiaircraft Artillery," *Coast Artillery Journal*, January–February 1946, 70–71; William Wuest, "The Development of Heavy Antiaircraft Artillery," *Antiaircraft Journal*, May–June 1954, 23.

8. Theodore Ropp, *War in the Modern World* (Durham, N.C.: Duke University Press, 1959), 289.

9. "Antiaircraft Defences of Great Britain"; and Frederick Pile, *Ack-Ack* (London: Harrap, 1949), 73. One American wrote in his 1929 Air Corps Tactical School thesis that flak was not worth the effort, which was the view of bomber proponents on both sides of the Atlantic. See Kenneth Walker, "Is the Defense of New York City from Air Attack Possible?" Research report, Air Corps Tactical School, May 1929, 30, HRA.

10. From the German, *Flieger Abwehr Kanone*, for antiaircraft cannon.

11. Pile, *Ack-Ack*, 100, 157, 181, 183; "Antiaircraft Defences of Great Britain"; Hughes interview; "Air Defense," 2:122–24; Frederick Pile, "The Anti-Aircraft Defence of the United Kingdom from 28th July, 1939 to 15th April, 1945," supplement to the *London Gazette*, 16 December 1947, 5978, Air University Library (AUL), Maxwell AFB, Ala.; and "History of A. A. Command," n.d., 14, RAI.

12. Pile, *Ack-Ack*, 115; Pile, "Antiaircraft Defence of UK," 5975; and "History of A. A. Command," 14–15.

13. Routledge, *Royal Regiment of Artillery*, 400.

14. The British developed a two-inch rocket (that carried a .3-pound warhead) and a three-inch rocket that weighed 54 pounds, including its 4.5-pound warhead. The latter was successfully test-fired in Jamaica in 1938–39 and went into service in 1940. In July 1941, the British deployed 1,000 rocket tubes. Almost 6,000 were deployed by July 1943; most of which were twin-barrel devices. But rocket units registered few claims. See Routledge, *Royal Regiment of Artillery*, 56, 79.

15. Pile, *Ack-Ack*, 155–56, 186–93, and 379; Pile, "Anti-Aircraft Defence of UK," 5982; "History of A. A. Command," 123–24, plates 45, 49; "Antiaircraft Defences of Great Britain," appendix B; and Routledge, *Royal Regiment*, 338, 399.

16. Routledge, *Royal Regiment*, 108–12, 124, 144–53.

17. Guns larger than 50-55 mm are considered "heavy"; those less than this size are considered "light."

18. US Army Air Defense School, "Air Defense," 2, 127–28, 131–32; H. E. C. Weldon, "The Artillery Defence of Malta," *Antiaircraft Journal*, May–June 1954, 24, 26, 27, 29; Charles Jellison, *Besieged—The World War II Ordeal of Malta, 1940–1942* (Hanover, N.H.: University Press of New England, 1984), 166–67, 170, 205, 258; Christopher Shores, *Duel for the Sky* (London: Blandford, 1985), 88, 90, 92; and Routledge, *Royal Regiment*, 166–74.

19. Pile, *Ack-Ack*, 266, 301, 303, 305; Pile, "Anti-aircraft Defence of UK," 5984; and "Survey of Antiaircraft Defenses of the United Kingdom," 1, pt. 3:52, 53, 118, RAI.

20. Pile, *Ack-Ack*, 323–44; and "Fringe Targets," RAI.

21. For a more detailed discussion of the V-1 and its operations in World War II, see Kenneth Werrell, *The Evolution of the Cruise Missile* (Maxwell AFB, Ala.: Air University Press, 1985), chap. 3; Basil Collier, *The Battle of the V-Weapons, 1944–1945* (London: Hodder and Stoughton, 1964), 56–59; Roderic Hill, "Air Operations by Air Defence of Great Britain and Fighter Command in Connection with the German Flying Bomb and Rocket Offensives, 1944–45," supplement to the *London Gazette*, 19 October 1948, 5587–89; Basil Collier, *The Defence of the United Kingdom* (London: Her Majesty's Stationery Office, 1957), 361, 365; and British Air Ministry, "Air Defence of Great Britain, The Flying Bomb and Rocket Campaign: 1944 to 1945," first draft of report, 7:42–43, HRA.

22. Collier, *V-Weapons*, 69, 71–75, 79; Hill, "Air Operations by Air Defence," 5591–92; Rowland Pocock, *German Guided Missiles of the Second World War* (New York: Arco Publishing, Inc., 1967), 48; Jozef Garlinski, *Hitler's Last Weapons* (London: Times Book, 1978), 168; David Irving, *The Mares Nest* (London: Kimber, 1969), 233, 236, 240; and M. C. Helfers, *The Employment of V-Weapons by the Germans during World War II*, monograph (Washington, D.C.: Office of the Chief of Military History, Department of the Army, 1954), 18–30, HRA.

23. Hill, "Air Operations," 5594; Collier, *Defence of the UK*, 374; Mary Welborn, "V-1 and V-2 Attacks against the United Kingdom during World War II," technical report ORO-T-45 (Washington, D.C.: Johns Hopkins University Press, 16 May 1950), 9, HRA; "Minutes and Related Data Scientific Sub-Committee of Crossbow Committee, V-1, vol. 2," Operations Research Section (ADGB) Report 88, n.d., HRA; Report of the British Air Ministry, "Points of Impact and Accuracy of Flying Bombs: 22 June–28 July," 29 July 1944, HRA; "The Speed of Air-Launched Divers," HRA; Report of the General Board, US Forces, European Theater, "Tactical Employment of Antiaircraft Artillery Units Including Defense against Pilotless Aircraft (V-1)," study no. 38, 39, HRA; "Minutes and Related Data Scientific Sub-Committee of Cross-

bow Committee, V-1, vol. 2," 7 August 1944, S.B. 60093, HRA; Report of British Air Ministry, "Air Defence of Great Britain Tactical Memoranda I.G. no. 9675," 24 November 1944, HRA; British Air Ministry, "Air Defence of Great Britain," 126; Hillery Saunders, *Royal Air Force, 1939, 1945*, vol. 3, *The Fight Is Won* (London: Her Majesty's Stationery Office, 1954), 165.

24. Hill, "Air Operations," 5592, 5594; "Air Defence of Great Britain," 121, 151, 179; Saunders, *Royal Air Force*, 165; and Collier, *Defence of the UK*, 380.

25. AC/AS Intelligence, "Flying Bomb," 8, HRA; Mary Welborn, "Over-all Effectiveness of First US Army Antiaircraft Guns Against Tactical Aircraft" (working paper, Johns Hopkins University, Washington, D.C., 18 January 1950), 6, AUL; Report of Supreme Headquarters Allied Expeditionary Forces (SHAEF), Air Defense Division, "Notes on German Flying Bomb," 22 August 1944, HRA.

26. A related but almost entirely overlooked issue is that of the ground damage caused by the antiaircraft artillery shells. In one instance during World War I, for example, the shells caused one-third more damage than did German bombs. See James Crabtree, *On Air Defense* (Westport, Conn.: Praeger, 1994), 17.

27. Friendly fire also downed British fighters. In the first week, flak shot down two Tempests. See Bob Ogley, *Doodlebugs and Rockets: The Battle of the Flying Bombs* (Brasted Chart, Westerham, U.K.: Froglets, 1992), 83; and Pile, *Ack-Ack*, 330–33.

28. Hill, "Air Operations," 5592, 5594; SHAEF notes, 26 July 1944, HRA; and Collier, *Defence of the UK*, 375.

29. Hill, "Air Operations," 5596–97; and British Air Ministry, "Air Defence of Great Britain," 133–35. For another suggestion for a coastal belt, see Lt Gen Carl Spaatz to supreme commander, SHAEF, letter, subject: The Use of Heavy Anti-Aircraft against Diver, 11 July 1944, HRA.

30. Collier, *Defence of the UK*, 381–83; and Collier, *V-Weapons*, 91–95.

31. Pile, *Ack-Ack*, 334–35; Hill, "Air Operations," 5597; Collier, *Defence of the UK*, 523.

32. British Air Ministry, "Air Defence of Great Britain," 130; "Flying Bomb," 8; and SHAEF notes, 15 August 1944, HRA.

33. British Air Ministry, "Air Defence of Great Britain," 106; and Ralph Baldwin, *The Deadly Fuze* (San Rafael, Calif.: Presidio Press, 1980), 261–66.

34. Collier, *Defence of the UK*, 523; Welborn, "V-1 and V-2 Attacks," table 2; Hill, "Air Operations," 5599.

35. Collier, *Defence of the UK*, 523; and Welborn, "V-1 and V-2 Attacks," 10.

36. Hill, "Air Operations," 5599, 5601; "Air Launched 'Divers' September and October 1944," HRA; British Air Ministry, "Air Defence of Great Britain," 113; Collier, *Defence of the UK*, 389, 391, 522; Saunders, *Royal Air Force*, 167–68; Seventeenth report by assistant chief air staff (Intelligence), "War Cabinet Chiefs of Staff Committee Crossbow," 22 July 1944, HRA; and Collier, *V-Weapons*, 119, 131.

37. Air Ministry Weekly Intelligence Summary, 289, HRA; Benjamin King and Timothy Kutta, *Impact: The History of Germany's V-Weapons in World War II* (Rockville Centre, N.Y.: Sarpedon, 1998), 291.

38. Antiaircraft artillery cost a third of what fighters cost and about 25 percent more than the balloons. Collier, *Defence of the UK*, 523; Hill, "Air Operations," 5603; and British Air Ministry, "The Economic Balance of the Fly-Bomb Campaign," summary report, 4 November 1944, HRA.

39. Memorandum 5-7B by US Strategic Air Forces, Armament and Ordnance, "An Analysis of the Accuracy of the German Flying Bomb (V-1) 12 June to 5 October 1944," 144, HRA; British Air Ministry, "Air Defence of Great Britain," 123; and Collier, *Defence of the UK*, 523.

40. Collier, *Defence of the UK*, appendix L.

41. King and Kutta, *Impact*, 3, 211.

42. European Theater report no. 38, 40–41, 45, HRA; Operations Report of Headquarters Antwerp X Forward, no. 2J, 1 May 1945, annex A, HRA; SHAEF, "Report of 'V' Section on Continental Crossbow (September 1944–March 1945)," 28, HRA; and United States Strategic Bombing Survey (USSBS), *V-Weapons (Crossbow) Campaign*, January 1947, 2d ed., 15.

43. Report of Headquarters Antwerp X Forward, no. 2H, 4 March 1945, HRA; Antwerp X report no. 2J, annex A; European Theater report no. 38, 40–45; and King and Kutta, *Impact*, 274.

44. Peter G. Cooksley, *Flying Bomb* (New York: Scribner, 1979), 185. For a good secondary account, see R. J. Backus, "The Defense of Antwerp Against the V-1 Missile" (master of military arts and sciences thesis, US Army Command and General Staff College, 1971).

45. US Army Air Defense School, "Air Defense," 2:36; and Welborn, "Over-all Effectiveness," table 8.

46. US Army Air Defense School, "Air Defense," 2:37; and US Army, "Antiaircraft Artillery" note no. 8, 4, US Army Command and General Staff College, Fort Leavenworth, Kans.

47. "The GAF 1 January Attack," United States Strategic Air Forces in Europe, Air Intelligence Summary 62 (week ending 14 January 1945), 5, HRA; "Airfield Attack of 1 January," HRA; SHAEF Intelligence Summary 42, 30 [USACGSC]; Daily Air Action Summary, Office of Assistant Chief of Staff, Intelligence Headquarters, Army Air Forces, Washington, D.C., 3 January 1945, HRA; Duty Group Captain's Daily Resume of Air Operations, serial no. 1843, Air Ministry, Whitehall, 2 January 1944, HRA; Saunders, *Royal Air Force*, 209; Roger Freeman, *The Mighty Eighth War Diary* (New York: Jane's Publishing Co. Ltd., 1981), 412–13; History and Statistical Summary, IX Air Defense Command, January 1944–June 1945, 80; Werner Gerbig, *Six Months to Oblivion* (London: Allan, 1973), 74, 76–79, 110, 112; USAF Credits for the Destruction of Enemy Aircraft, World War II, USAF Historical Study 85 (Maxwell AFB, Ala.: USAF Historical Division, Air University, 1978), 286; and Air Staff Operational Summary Report nos. 1503, 1504, Air Ministry War Room, 2, 3 January 1945, HRA. The most detailed, but not necessarily

most accurate, account is Norman Franks, *The Battle of the Airfields* (London: Kimber, 1982).

48. Gerbig, *Oblivion*, 99–103, 116; USAF Historical Study 85, 286; IX Air Defense Command, 78–79; History, 352d Fighter Group, January 1945, HRA; History, 366th Fighter Group, January 1945, HRA.

49. US Army Air Defense School, "Air Defense," 2:158–63; and Welborn, "Over-all Effectiveness," 9, 29.

50. See notes 30 and 33; US Army, Antiaircraft Artillery [USACGSC]; and US Air Forces in Europe, "Air Staff Post Hostilities Intelligence Requirements on German Air Defenses," report, vol. 1, sec. 4 (14 September 1945): 17, HRA.

51. Walter Grabman, "German Air Force Air Operations Defense: 1933–1945," circa 1957, 3, 18, 40a, 81, 83–84, HRA; D. von Renz, "The Development of German Antiaircraft Weapons and Equipment of all Types up to 1945," study, 1958, 102, HRA; and Westermann, *Flak*, 84, 285.

52. Ian Hogg, *German Artillery of World War II* (London: Arms and Armour, 1975), 162, 167; R. A. Devereux, "German Experience with Antiaircraft Artillery Guns in WWII," study, 19 July 1946, AUL; and US Air Forces in Europe (USAFE), "Post Hostilities Investigation," 1:3.

53. Hogg, *German Artillery*, 115, 170, 172; USAFE, "Post Hostilities Investigation," 1:5; Peter Chamberlain and Terry Gander, *Antiaircraft Guns* (New York: Arco Publishing, Inc., 1975), 22.

54. The Germans cancelled efforts to build a 150 mm flak gun in 1940. See Hogg, *German Artillery*, 173–78; Chamberlain and Gander, *Antiaircraft Guns*, 23–24; USAFE, "Post Hostilities Investigation," 1:10, 22; and Westermann, *Flak*, 69.

55. Matthew Cooper, *The German Air Force, 1933–1945* (London: Jane's Publishing Co. Ltd., 1981), 185; Samuel Morrison, *History of US Naval Operations in World War II*, vol. 9, *Sicily-Salerno-Anzio: January 1943–June 1944* (Boston, Mass.: Little, Brown and Co., 1954), 215–16; Albert Garland and Howard Smyth, *The US Army in World War II: The Mediterranean Theater of Operations, Sicily and the Surrender of Italy* (Washington, D.C.: Office of the Chief of Military History, 1965), 375, 379, 412; and John Terraine, *A Time for Courage: The Royal Air Force in the European War, 1939–1945* (New York: Macmillan Publishing Co., Inc., 1985), 579.

56. Assistant Chief of Air Staff, Intelligence Historical Division, "The Ploesti Mission of 1 August 1943," USAF Historical Study 103 (Maxwell Field, Ala.: Historical Division, June 1944), 16, 50, 99, HRA; Report of Army Air Forces Evaluation Board, "Ploesti," 15 December 1944, vol. 6:7–8, HRA; and Report of Mediterranean Allied Air Forces (MAAF), "Ploesti: Summary of Operations Results and Tactical Problems Involved in 24 Attacks between 5 April–19 August 1944," 13 January 1945, 1–3, HRA.

57. AAF Evaluation Board, "Ploesti," 2, 4, appendix E; MAAF, "Ploesti," 2; History, 1st Fighter Group, June 1944, 2, HRA; and History, 82d Fighter Group, June 1944, 2, HRA.

58. Between 1939 and 1944, the Germans captured and used 9,500 anti-aircraft guns and 14 million rounds of ammunition. See Westermann,

German Flak, 325; MAAF, "Ploesti," 1–3; AAF Evaluation Board, "Ploesti," ii; Fifteenth Air Force, "The Air Battle of Ploesti," report, n.d., 83, HRA.

59. Von Renz, "Development of German Antiaircraft Weapons," 380; USAFE, "Post Hostilities Investigation," 8:11; USSBS report, *European War*, no. 115, "Ammoniakwerke Merseburg, G.M.B.H., Leuna, Germany," March 1947, 7–16, 21, AUL; and Frank Anderson, "German Antiaircraft Defenses in World War II," *Air University Quarterly Review* (Spring 1954): 85.

60. USAFE, "Post Hostilities Investigation," 5:2; Report of Army Air Forces Evaluation Board European Theater of Operations, "Flak Defenses of Strategic Targets in Southern Germany," 20 January 1945, 25, HRA; Report of Mediterranean Allied Air Forces, "Flak and MAAF," 7 May 1945, 9, HRA; and Report of Fifteenth Air Force, "Comparative Analysis of Altitudes and Flak Experienced during the Attacks on Vienna 7 and 8 February 1945," 3–4, HRA.

61. Westermann, *Flak*, 110–11.

62. A gram weighs .035 ounces.

63. Von Renz, "Development of German Antiaircraft Weapons," 257; USAFE, "Post Hostilities Investigation," 7:7, 37; USSBS, "The German Flak Effort Throughout the War," 13 August 1945, 16, 19, HRA; Johannes Mix, "The Significance of Anti-Aircraft Artillery and the Fighter Arm at the End of the War," *Flugwehr und Technik*, February–March 1950, 5, 10; Thomas Edwards and Murray Geisler, "Estimate of Effect on Eighth Air Force Operations if German Antiaircraft Defenses Had Used Proximity Fuzed (VT) Ammunition," report no. 1, Operations Analysis, AC/AS-3, Headquarters Army Air Forces, Washington, D.C., 15 February 1947, HRA; and USAFE, Walter von Axtheim, "Interrogation Report," vol. 12 (1945): 26–27, HRA.

64. Von Renz, "Development of German Antiaircraft Weapons," 340–43, 353; Ernst Klee and Otto Merk, *The Birth of the Missile—The Secret of Peenemünde* (New York: E. P. Dutton, 1965), 65; and Westermann, *Flak*, 164, 196–97, 209, 227.

65. Von Renz, "Development of German Antiaircraft Weapons," 257; USAFE, Von Axthelm, "Interrogation Report," 24; and USAFE, "Post Hostilities Investigation," 3:43–44.

66. Von Renz, "Development of German Antiaircraft Weapons," 357; USAFE, "Post Hostilities Investigation," vol. 12, figs. 61, 8, 9, and 1:23; Willy Ley, *Rockets, Missiles and Space Travel* (New York: Viking Press, 1951), 222–23, 393.

67. There are various accounts of these missiles, as the citations indicate. I have relied primarily on Military Intelligence Division, "Handbook on Guided Missiles: Germany and Japan," no. 461, 1946 (hereafter cited as MID 461). It is a single source, has the most detailed technical data, and is a postwar publication. Also, see Von Renz, "Development of German Antiaircraft Weapons," 362; Von Axthelm, "Interrogation Report"; USAFE, "Post Hostilities Investigation," 12:7, fig. 60; Klee and Merk, *The Birth of Missiles*, 68, 86; and Ley, *Rockets, Missiles and Space Travel*, 395.

68. MID 461; USAFE, "Post Hostilities Investigation," 12:8, fig. 61; and Ley, *Rockets, Missiles and Space Travel*, 223, 394.

69. MID 461; Von Renz, "Development of German Antiaircraft Weapons," 362; USAFE, "Post Hostilities Investigation," 8:10, 12:7, fig. 61; Ley, *Rockets, Missiles and Space Travel*, 395; Klee and Merk, *Birth of Missiles*, 68; and Georgia Institute of Technology, *Missile Catalog: A Compendium of Guided Missiles and Seeker Information*, April 1956, 110, 124, Redstone Scientific Information Center, Huntsville, Ala. One source states that the HS 117 was capable of a slant range of 24,000 yards and 35,000-foot altitude and that the Germans fired 80 of these. See USAFE, "Post Hostilities Investigation," 1, 12:6.

70. The V-2 was almost 47 feet long and had a takeoff weight of 28,229 pounds. See Ley, *Rockets, Missiles and Space Travel*, 390, 393.

71. Ibid.; USAFE, "Post Hostilities Investigation," 12:5–6; and Klee and Merk, *Birth of Missiles*, 66–68, 125.

72. MID 461; USSBS, "German Flak," 1, 2, 5, 6, 19; Von Axthelm, Interrogation Report, 44; Mix, "Significance of Anti-Aircraft Artillery," 22; and Westermann, *Flak*, 234, 292–93.

73. *Army Air Forces Statistical Digest: World War II* (Washington, D.C.: Office of Statistical Control, December 1945), 255–56; and Hogg, *Anti-Aircraft*, 115.

74. Thomas Edwards and Murray Gelster, "The Causes of Bombing Errors as Determined from Analysis of Eighth Air Force Combat Operations," report no. 3, *Operations Analysis, AC/AS-3, Headquarters Army Air Forces*, 15 July 1947, 3, 19, HRA; "Report by Mr. Butt to Bomber Command on His Examination of Night Photographs, 18 August 1941," in Charles Webster and Noble Frankland, *The Strategic Air War against Germany, 1939–1945*, with four annexes and appendices (London: Her Majesty's Stationery Office, 1961); and minutes of the Flak Conference conducted at Headquarters United States Strategic Air Forces in Europe (A-2), London, 1–11 June 1945, HRA.

75. A tighter formation might appear counterintuitive as it puts more aircraft in one location, seemingly a better target. Operations analysis found, however, that in fact the key was how fast the aircraft crossed over the flak as the guns could only fire so many rounds in a given period. The quicker the aircraft passed over the guns meant fewer rounds could be fired at them.

76. German sources indicate a three-fourths reduction, while US sources use more modest figures ranging between one-fourth and two-thirds. See USSBS, "German Flak," 19; Harry Smith, "Flak Evasion," *Electronic Warfare*, April–May 1970, 18–19, 36; Eighth Air Force, "Reduction of Losses and Battle Damage," operational research report, 12 February 1944, 15, 50, HRA; and Daniel Kuehl, "The Radar Eye Blinded: The USAF and Electronic Warfare, 1945–1955" (PhD diss., Duke University, 1992), 30.

77. Eighth Air Force, "Special Report of Operations in Support of First Allied Airborne Army: 17–26 September 1944," 9–13, HRA.

78. Albert Davis et al., *56th Fighter Group in World War II* (Washington, D.C.: Infantry Journal Press, 1948), 79–81; History, 56th Fighter Group, summary report, 18 September 1944, HRA; John Tussell Jr., "Flak versus Fighters," *Coast Artillery Journal*, July–August 1946, 43; and Eighth Air Force, "Special Report of Operations in Support of First Allied Airborne Army," 18, HRA.

79. "Special Report of Operations in Support of First Allied Airborne Army," 43–44.

80. Headquarters US Strategic Air Forces in Europe, Office of the Director of Operations, "Neutralizing German Anti-Aircraft Defenses," study, 14 November 1944, 1–3, HRA.

81. Fifteenth Air Force, "High Altitude Bombing Attacks on Flak Batteries," 31 March 1945, HRA.

82. Ibid.; Historical Division, Department of the Army, *Utah Beach to Cherbourg (6 June–27 June 1944)* (Washington, D.C.: Government Printing Office [GPO] 1947), 171–73.

83. Joint report no. 4, "German Flak and Allied Counter-Flak Measures in Operation Varsity," RAI; "History of Air Defense," *Air Defense Magazine*, April–June 1977, 22. Little information is available on Soviet flak defenses. James Hansen writes that the Soviets increased their antiaircraft weapon by a factor of eight between 1941 and 1945. He asserts that the Soviets credit flak with 40 percent of their 7,000 aircraft claims. See James Hansen, "The Development of Soviet Tactical Air Defenses," *International Defense Review*, May 1981, 53.

84. Elwood Quesada, "Effect of Antiaircraft Artillery on IX Tactical Air Command Operations," *Coast Artillery Journal*, September–October 1946, 29.

85. Kirkpatrick, *Archie in the A.E.F.*, 93, 100, 179.

86. Garland and Smyth, *The US Army in World War II*, 175–82; and Charles Shrader, "Amicicide: The Problem of Friendly Fire" (paper, Combat Studies Institute, Fort Leavenworth, Kans., 1982), 67–68.

87. A British source states that 14 of 100 aircraft were downed, 19 others turned back, while the rest scattered their loads across the countryside. Routledge, *Antiaircraft Guns*, 262; and Shrader, "Amicicide," 69.

88. Just as the subject of fratricide is neglected, so too is the issue of enemy aircraft not engaged. Only one example should be required to make the point: American radar detected aircraft flying toward Pearl Harbor before the attack but could not identify them. See Aircraft Identifiers, Gree, 2757, and Brentrall, 2759, to commandant, subject: "Aircraft Identifiers Aboard Merchant Ships, 9 June 1944," HRA; "Analysis of Reports Concerning the Engagement of Friendly Aircraft by Our Own Ground or Shipborne Forces and Also All Reports Covering the Engagement of Our Own Ground Forces by Friendly Aircraft," item no. 4, "Attacks on Friendly Aircraft by Ground and Naval Forces," annex A to 21 Army Group/225/Ops, 29 July 1944, HRA; History, 65th Fighter Wing, "Light, Intense and Accurate: US Eighth Air Force Strategic Fighters versus German Flak in the ETO," 89, HRA; US Army Air Defense School, "Air Defense," 2:38, 169; War Diary of Brig Gen Richard E. Nugent, November 1944, 12, HRA; Shrader, "Amicicide," 34, 45, 66, 70; and David Mets, *Master of Airpower* (Novato, Calif.: Presidio Press, n.d.), 268.

89. Report of General Board, US Forces, European Theater, "Antiaircraft Artillery Techniques," 10, HRA.

90. Stephen McFarland and Wesley Newton, *To Command the Sky: The Battle for Air Superiority over Germany, 1942–1944* (Washington, D.C.: Smithsonian Institution, 1991), 81n, 261; US Fleet, "Antiaircraft Action Summary–October 1944," Information Bulletin no. 27, 9-2, HRA.

91. Shrader, "Amicicide," 70–71.

92. Buford Rowland and William Boyd, *US Navy Bureau of Ordnance in World War II* (Washington, D.C.: GPO, n.d.), 219–20, 231, 235, 238, 245–47, 258, 266; and Robert Sherrod, *History of Marine Corps Aviation in World War II* (Washington, D.C.: Combat Forces, 1952), 401.

93. Rowland and Boyd, *US Navy Bureau*, 221–34, 266; Chamberlain and Gander, *Antiaircraft Guns*, 40; US Fleet, Information Bulletin no. 27, 1–5; Hogg, *Anti-Aircraft*, 80; and Routledge, *Royal Regiment*, R52–53.

94. Rowland and Boyd, *US Navy Bureau*, 220, 266, 283, 286; US Fleet, Information Bulletin no. 27, 1–5.

95. US Army Air Defense School, "Air Defense," 2:192.

96. Ibid., 197–98; Chamberlain and Gander, *Antiaircraft Guns*, 34; Report of General Headquarters, United States Army Forces Pacific, Antiaircraft Research Board, "Survey of Japanese Antiaircraft Artillery," 3–5, 59, 65–66, 72, USACGSC; and United States Pacific Fleet and Pacific Ocean Areas Flak Intelligence Memorandum no. 4, "Japanese Antiaircraft Materiel," 11 April 1945, Naval Historical Center (NHC), Washington, D.C.

97. *AAF Statistical Digest*, 221–27, 255–61; A. H. Peterson, R. G. Tuck, and D. P. Wilkinson, "Aircraft Vulnerability in World War II" (working paper, RAND Corporation, Santa Monica, Calif., rev. 12 July 1950), table 8, AUL; Office of Information, Document, 3 May 1967, in "Korean Combat Statistics for Three-Year Period," 19 June 1953, NHC; and Kuehl, "The Radar Eye Blinded," 31.

98. US Army Air Defense School, "Air Defense," 2:293; AAA Research Board, "Survey of Japanese AAA," 192, HRA; and Chief of Naval Operations, Air Intelligence Group, Flak Information Bulletin no. 10, June 1945, 28, HRA.

99. *AAF Statistical Digest*, 226, 261; Air Intelligence report no. 8, 15–17; Twentieth Air Force, "Flak Damage on Various Types of Missions," and "Final Analysis of Flak Loss and Damage for Operations against Japan," Air Intelligence report, vol. 1, nos. 26–27, November–December 1945, 3–7, HRA. See also Kuehl, "The Radar Eye Blinded," 37–38.

100. Flak downed a number of the top aces. In World War I, ground fire downed the top ace, the Red Baron, Manfred von Richthofen (80 credits). In World War II, the leading American ace in Europe, Francis Gabreski (28 credits), crashed while attacking an airfield; US flak killed George Preddy Jr. (26.8 credits); and German flak downed others such as Hubert Zemke (17.8 credits) and Duane Beeson (17.3 credits). Japanese AAA killed Robert Hanson (25 credits), the third-ranking Marine ace. Flak also got two of the top British aces, Brendan Finucane (32 credits) and Robert Tuck (29 credits).

Chapter 2

From Guns to Missiles, 1945–1965

Rapid demobilization of the American military followed the war's end. As the magnificent US war machine disappeared, not much was left in its place. Americans thought little of either war or the military as they engaged in their peacetime pursuits, thereby leaving the US armed forces with minimal tangible strength. The two driving forces of national policy during this period were tight budgets and trust in the atomic bomb. America based its defense on confidence in overall American superiority and distance, but most of all, on the bomb. Specifically, the United States had the atomic bomb and a means to deliver it; the Soviet Union had neither.

The offensive problem seemed relatively simple to American Airmen, compared to what they had just faced in World War II. Instead of vast formations of aircraft, now only one aircraft (with the equivalent bomb load of thousands of World War II bombers) needed to be employed. The penetration problem also appeared easier; for, in contrast to dense German defenses covering a target area of hundreds of miles, the Soviet Union had relatively sparse defenses to cover thousands of miles. Another factor favoring the offensive was that jet aircraft offered performance superior to that of World War II aircraft. Probably most important, instead of opposing a foe with essentially equivalent technology and the potential to develop superior technology, the United States now faced a nation considered to be years behind its own development. The most serious problems for the American Airmen appeared to be those of range and basing.

American technological superiority delayed the Airmen's defensive concerns. Few Airmen thought the Soviets would get nuclear weapons in short order, so certainly they would be slow to master the problem of weapons delivery over intercontinental distances. Consequently, American antiaircraft defenses shrank along with the entire American military to the extent that by late 1947, the US Army had only two battalions of AAA. Active

American air defense took three directions in the late 1940s. The most expensive of these, air defense aircraft, falls beyond the scope of this study. The other two directions were antiaircraft guns and missiles.

The postwar story of antiaircraft guns is primarily that of phase out and false starts. At first, postwar budget cuts and the existence of World War II equipment disguised the gun's fate. The Army did attempt to replace the .50-caliber machine gun and develop an effective low-altitude weapon. In June 1948, the Ordnance Corps began development of the Stinger, four .60-caliber guns (radar-directed and mounted on a vehicle). In 1951, the Army terminated the project when the developer conceded that the .60 guns could not satisfy the slant range requirement of 14,000 feet (ft).[1] The Army did field two new pieces of antiaircraft equipment. To upgrade its 40 mm antiaircraft gun, the Army authorized a model in July 1951 and named it Duster (fig. 35). Mounted on a light tank (M41) chassis, the Army planned to link the guns to a second vehicle with

Figure 35. Duster. The Duster was one of a number of failed Army antiaircraft projects. It mounted two 40 mm guns on a tracked vehicle. (Reprinted from http://www.militaryhistorymuseum.org/gallery.html.)

radar fire-control equipment. Cost killed the radar portion in 1952, but the Army adopted the M42 Duster in October 1952. A later Army attempt to add range-only radar called Raduster failed by 1956. The Army then tried to develop a 37 mm Gatling gun known as Vigilante for this role in both a self-propelled and trailer version. By 1957, the Army concluded that Vigilante could not provide all-weather capability, would have a low-kill probability against the expected opposition, lacked ruggedness and reliability, and would create mobility and logistics problems.

The United States did develop and field two antiaircraft guns in the postwar period. The first was the 75 mm Skysweeper (fig. 36). The pilot model appeared in 1948, and the weapon went into service in March 1953.[2] Despite its many capabilities, it was soon replaced by SAMs. The other gun had a longer and more distinguished career.

The 20 mm cannon was based on the mid-19th century Gatling gun and German experiments of World War II. In June 1946, the US government awarded General Electric a contract for a rapid-fire cannon that became known as the Vulcan. The

Figure 36. Skysweeper. The 75 mm Skysweeper was the last American antiaircraft gun. (Reprinted from USAF Army Air Defense Museum.)

company delivered a .60-caliber version in 1950, and two years later, a more advanced model appeared in three calibers: .60 mm, 20 mm, and 27 mm. The Air Force and Army adopted the 20 mm as the M61 Vulcan. Its six barrels were electrically rotated and could fire at a maximum rate of 7,200 shots per minute. The cannon was produced in a number of calibers. Not only mounted aboard fixed- and rotary-wing aircraft, the weapon was also adapted by the Navy (Phalanx) and initially deployed in 1979 (fig. 37). The Army began development of its version in 1964 and mounted the M61 on an M113 armored personnel carrier as a daytime, clear-weather, air-defense

Figure 37. Vulcan Phalanx. The Navy fitted a number of its ships with the fast-firing Vulcan Phalanx for close-in protection against aircraft. (Reprinted from http://www.bb62museum.org/images/phalanx.jpc.)

weapon designated M163 (fig. 38). Deliveries of the Army version began in 1968. In 1984, the ground service began to upgrade many of these cannons in the Product Improved Vulcan Air Defense System project that added a digital computer and range-only radar. These modifications increased effectiveness and simplified operations. Another improvement was new ammunition (armor piercing discarding sabot) that increased maximum effective antiaircraft range from 1,600 to 2,600 meters. The Army also fielded another version mounted on a trailer (M167 Vulcan Air Defense System).[3]

Army efforts to replace the Vulcan with a more advanced gun system ended in disaster. The Army's concern over the Vulcan centered on its short range, its slow reaction times, and the absence of both crew protection and the ability to distinguish friend from foe. The success of the Soviet ZSU-23-4 23 mm guns mounted on a tank chassis in the Middle East wars

Figure 38. Vulcan M163. The Army mounted the 20 mm Vulcan gun with radar guidance on an M163 armored personnel carrier. (Reprinted from http://www.relli.com/weapons.htm.)

(discussed later in chap. 4) and the rising threat of Soviet helicopter gunships were additional factors. In the early 1980s, the Army sought a mobile, all-weather system that would overcome these shortcomings. After rejecting the German Gepard, the Army believed that it could get what it wanted quickly and cheaply by combining several bits of existing equipment. After competing with General Dynamics, Ford Aerospace won a contract in May 1981 for the Division Air Defense or M247 Sergeant York. It would use an M48A5 tank chassis, twin 40 mm Bofors guns, and radar (APG-66) from the F-16. Problems with manufacturing, weight, reliability, and radar increased both time and cost. It also drew a host of critics, both from inside the Army (SAM and helicopter advocates) and outside (an unsympathetic media). Poor, or at least questionable, test results did not help. Most of all, the threat increased beyond what the system could handle. As a result, Secretary of Defense Caspar Weinberger cancelled the project in August 1985. It cost the United States $1.8 billion.[4]

To drop back in the chronology somewhat, antiaircraft guns proved useful as ground-support arms, despite the almost utter lack of air opposition in the Korean War. In the military buildup prompted by the Korean War, the Army deployed 66 battalions of American aircraft (AA) guns for continental defense. Nevertheless, the Army began to phase out its antiaircraft guns. Following tests in 1955, the Army dropped its quadruple .50-caliber guns. The dual 40 mm guns lingered on in service into the early 1960s before being transferred from the Regular Army into the National Guard. Army studies in the mid-1950s indicated that guns could not provide adequate protection against the expected threat and that guided missiles would be more effective for the role of air defense in forward areas. The Army phased out its last antiaircraft guns used in continental defense in mid-1960. In this way, the Hawk (Homing All the Way Killer) missile, although considered a medium- and high-altitude weapon, took over the job of the 40 mm, 75 mm, and 120 mm guns.[5] This ends the story of AAA employed by the US air defenders, but not the end of AAA. American Airmen had a different perspective—they would continue to face guns in combat.

Antiaircraft Returns to Combat: The Korean War

The Korean War was far different from what the planners anticipated: unlike their experience of World War II or their forecasts of World War III. In the Korean War, American Airmen did not face dense, technically advanced, ground-based anti-aircraft defenses or an extensive air-to-air threat; nor did they conduct strategic nuclear operations against a major power. Instead, both sides limited the Korean War politically and militarily. The United States (through the United Nations) fought a second-rate and third-rate power, albeit with major power backing, without nuclear weapons, and with few strategic targets. American Airmen waged an air war primarily of close air support (CAS) and interdiction against weak and obsolete antiaircraft defenses. American flyers engaged modern fighters but in action geographically remote from the main theater of operations.

Compared to air defenses the Allies encountered in World War II, Communist ground-based defenses in Korea proved weak in both numbers and technology. American intelligence estimated that initially the North Koreans were poorly equipped with antiaircraft guns. While their forward units used 12.7 mm (.50-caliber) machine guns, the defense of rear areas was left to about 20 76 mm guns, which lacked radar direction. But, these weapons multiplied when the Communist Chinese entered into the war in late 1950. By May 1951, the Communists were estimated to have in action 252 heavy flak pieces and 673 light pieces, increasing and peaking at 786 heavy and 1,672 light guns in early 1953. Nevertheless, these totals barely exceeded the numbers the Germans deployed around some of their key targets late in World War II. The equipment itself was vintage World War II. Although the Airmen faced a few 76 mm guns, the Communists' principal heavy flak weapon was the Soviet 85 mm Model 1939 gun that later was supplemented by the 85 mm Model 1944. In the later stages of the war, some of these guns were controlled by radar. The main light flak piece was the 37 mm automatic weapon. The Communists also used large numbers of 12.7 mm machine guns. Beginning in October 1951, Allied airmen reported unguided

75

flak rockets that reached 10,560 feet. But there are no indications of any successes with this weapon, and reports of its firing faded out by December 1952.[6]

How effective was Communist flak in the Korean War? It did not prevent air operations, but it did make them more expensive. Hostile fire forced airmen to fly higher and thus reduced bombing accuracy. The USAF estimated that dive-bombing accuracy declined from a 75-foot circular error probable (CEP) in 1951 to 219 feet in 1953, which meant that more sorties were required to destroy a target.[7] Likewise, B-29s that earlier had attacked in what one writer describes as an "almost leisurely fashion" as low as 10,000 feet with multiple passes, now operated at 20,000 feet or above.[8] Nevertheless, despite increasing Red flak, USAF loss rates declined during the course of the war from 0.18 percent per sortie in 1950 to 0.07 percent in 1953. Overall, American (Air Force, Marine Corps, and Navy) combat losses of 1,230 aircraft on 736,439 sorties amounted to a rate of .17 percent. The airmen believed that all but 143 of these were claimed by ground fire (flak and small arms fire).[9]

A further breakdown reveals that USAF losses were not evenly distributed. That is, fighter-bombers sustained 58 percent of aircraft losses, although they logged only 36 percent of sorties. Jets suffered less than did propeller-powered aircraft, as they operated at higher speeds and altitudes. The Navy's piston-powered F4U Corsair took hits at twice the rate of the jet-powered F9F and was considered 75 percent more vulnerable. Similarly, the USAF's famous propeller-powered F-51 Mustang was much more vulnerable than the jet-powered F-80 Shooting Star (fig. 39).[10] In the period July through November 1950, the Mustang had a loss rate of 1.9 percent of sorties compared with the Shooting Star's loss rate of .74 percent.[11] The Air Force assessed the loss rate of prop aircraft to be triple that of jet aircraft. A breakdown of losses in August 1952 indicated that light flak was the main problem. In that month, flak destroyed 14 Fifth Air Force aircraft and damaged 153 others. During the entire war, the Air Force credited light flak with 79 percent of the downed aircraft and 45 percent of the damaged aircraft, small arms with 7 and 52 percent, and heavy flak with 14 and 3 percent.[12]

Figure 39. F-51 Mustang. The North American Mustang, the P-51 of World War II fame, saw action as the F-51. It suffered the highest number of USAF losses to enemy action, of which 95 percent of the known losses were to ground fire. (Reprinted from USAF.)

In early 1952, American losses to ground fire prompted remedial action. One factor in the equation involved how close the aircraft flew to the ground; but, despite the wealth of data from World War II, it apparently took an operations analysis study in early 1952 to bring this fact to the attention of the decision makers. One study indicated that in the first four months of 1952, Fifth Air Force aircraft sustained half of their ground-fire hits below 2,500 feet.[13] Following a Communist flak success on 10 July 1952, Fifth Air Force ordered a minimum recovery altitude of 3,000 feet. Similarly, in reaction to B-26 losses, Fifth Air Force established a 4,000-foot attack altitude for light bombers with only selected crews permitted to operate lower. In August, the Navy adopted a 3,000-foot minimum pullout altitude. As a result, losses to AAA declined.[14] In the first four months of 1952, Fifth Air Force studies concluded that ground fire destroyed or damaged 21.6 aircraft per 1,000 sorties; whereas, in the period 1 September 1952 through 30 April

1953, the rate decreased to 11.1 aircraft per 1,000 sorties. Analysts attributed 19 percent of the decrease to the altitude policy and a further 32 percent to target diversification. As a counterpoint, the Fifth Air Force removed the altitude restriction for two weeks in June 1953 and suffered the consequences. During that month, the unit suffered its highest 1953 monthly losses—18 aircraft to ground fire, including 12 of its newest jet fighter-bombers, the F-86F.[15]

Another policy adopted by the Fifth Air Force in June 1952 limited the time over the target. It mandated that, with the exception of air defense and F4U aircraft, pilots were to make only one run over a target for each type of external ordnance carried; and it forbade strafing. In August 1952, the Fifth Air Force modified the policy by restricting general support and interdiction missions to one pass and CAS to two passes.[16]

American Airmen also employed more direct methods against enemy AAA. The Marines tried flak-suppression tactics in late 1951 or early 1952, with spotter aircraft temporarily diverting strike aircraft to hit flak positions. In June 1952, the Marines published a procedure that put suppressive fire on flak positions 30 seconds before their aircraft began dive-bombing runs. Thereafter, Marine aircraft losses dropped.[17]

At about the same time, the Army and Air Force adopted similar tactics, although there is no indication that there was any coordination between the three services. Before July 1952, the Army and Air Force operated under procedures established in plan NEGAT, which curtailed friendly artillery fire during an air strike and restricted almost all artillery fire within a 2,500-yard radius of the target. Friendly guns would mark targets with smoke or white phosphorous shells and, between the time the spotter aircraft left the area and the fighter-bombers arrived, would fire against known antiaircraft positions. Prompted by the loss of two C-119s to American artillery fire in June 1951, the policy emphasized safety from friendly fire. However, the policy satisfied neither Airmen nor soldiers and became even less acceptable to both as the Communists burrowed deeper into the ground, brought up more flak pieces, and learned American air-support procedures. Not only did fighter-bomber losses remain high, but the procedures left a large area along the front without artillery support for eight to 45 minutes during the air strike. Following a meeting between the two services in July 1952, the Army eased the restriction on artillery fire to a minimum time, although it retained prohibitions on the use of proximity-fuzed and high-angle fire when aircraft were in the area. The Airmen now believed that the danger from enemy guns exceeded the danger from friendly guns.

In their next step, the Americans actively engaged the flak. On 6 August 1952, the Air Force and Army produced a plan named SUPPRESS, which set out procedures to neutralize suspected and known antiaircraft positions. While retaining the July artillery restrictions, SUPPRESS permitted the fighter-bomber pilots either to accept or to reject artillery support. The gunners would hit suspected positions with proximity-fuzed fire before the strike and then signal the end of proximity-fuzed fire with a radio call and a white phosphorous or colored smoke round. The artillery would continue the bombardment with impact-fuzed ammunition. During a one-month experiment (25 September 1952 through 25 October 1952) with these procedures in IX Corps, the USAF lost only one aircraft on 1,816 CAS sorties, compared with planning figures of one loss for every 380 CAS sorties. (Army artillery fired 679,000 rounds in connection with the air strikes.) This marked decline in aircraft losses came despite the tripling of Communist flak guns in the area facing the IX Corps.

The Eighth Army and Fifth Air Force adopted the policy that became effective on 2 December 1952. Under the slightly modified procedures, a light aircraft (T-6 Mosquito) led the fighter-bombers into the area, marked the target, and after the fighter-bomber pilots identified the target, called in artillery fire. Friendly artillery would hit all known enemy antiaircraft guns within 2,500 yards of the target first with proximity-fuzed shells and finally with a white phosphorous or colored smoke round. The barrage continued with impact-fuzed shells for three minutes, as the aircraft attacked. Despite such problems as fighter-bomber pilots not always being ready to exploit the suppression fire and increased numbers of Communist flak guns, fighter-bomber losses remained acceptable. CAS sorties per fighter-bomber loss rose from 917 in December 1952

79

to 1,285 in January 1953, to 2,981 in late March and early April, then dropped to 1,281 in June, and, finally, rose to about 1,515 in July.[18]

The United States Air Force reluctantly and belatedly introduced electronic countermeasures (ECM) in the Korean air war because of fears that its use would reveal both US tactics and equipment to the Communists. While this policy risked Airmen's lives, there was another issue. Although Korea was a real war, it was secondary to the buildup stateside and in Europe and preparations for a nuclear strike in the event of World War III. Not only were the newest Air Force aircraft not sent to Korea (for example, B-47s and B-36s), at first ECM was not used, although this equipment and its associated tactics had been employed in World War II. However, the Communist introduction of the MiG-15 that savaged B-29s in daylight operations pushed the USAF to begin ECM operations in April 1951 and night-bomber operations in October. Increasing losses at night forced the Air Force to use chaff, a World War II technology, in September 1952. ECM was effective. A postwar USAF study concluded that during the night-bombing campaign, ECM cut losses and damage by two-thirds. More specifically, during the last six months of the war, in 78 percent of the cases where the bombers were illuminated by radar-directed searchlights, the bombers' ECM broke the lock.[19]

Another defensive tactic used by the USAF in night operations was the direct attack. In two separate night attacks on the crucial strategic targets in September and October 1952, the Airmen used B-26s at low level to suppress Communist searchlights illuminated by flares dropped by B-29s. Although the bombers knocked out a number of the lights, the USAF judged the tactic unsuccessful as only one-quarter of the lights was destroyed, and the flares made the attacking bombers more visible to the gunners.[20]

Clearly, the Americans had forgotten much of their experience with flak in World War II. The Airmen's flak countermeasures came as a response to losses and not from any study of the situation or from previous experience. Not until late in the war, after almost two years, did the Army and Air Force establish effective coordination tactics. No one attempted to compare notes with the other services. But even having done all of this, the question is how much did the American Airmen learn from the war? In a study of the lessons from the air war in Korea that included about 100 items covering such areas as heckling attacks, rescue operations, and Communist passive defense, the US Air Force did not mention enemy flak. Surely, flak was more important and more costly to the US Air Force than that. This attitude led Air Force chief of staff Thomas D. White to tell his top commanders in October 1957 that the USAF had never respected flak but that it could no longer ignore it. He insisted that the airmen find out more about antiaircraft defenses, and find it out quickly.[21]

Antiaircraft Missiles

At the same time US military forces were enduring the post–World War II reduction and then the trauma and frustrating limited war in Korea, a new weapon was evolving (fig. 40). This weapon that would greatly improve air defense and radically change air warfare, was, of course, the SAM. A number of countries attempted to follow up on the German efforts in the field, but for 20 years, these first-generation missiles were notable more for their promise than their performance. The large and unwieldy missiles demonstrated limited mobility, poor reliability, and questionable lethality. Initially, they used liquid fuel that presented problems of handling, reliability, reaction time, and storage. The early missiles were guided by command systems in which one radar unit acquired and tracked the target, a second tracked the missile, and a computer made missile corrections to enable interception. Although this awkward system could down aircraft flying at relatively high altitudes, steady courses, and moderate speeds, it had little ability to kill fast-moving, low-flying, maneuvering targets. (It must be remembered, however, that air defenders saw formations of high-flying aircraft as the threat.) The command guidance system was also vulnerable to electronic countermeasures.

A number of projects emerged from American designers. The US Army sponsored the widest variety of missiles. These missiles can probably best be divided generically into three fami-

Figure 40. Army SAMs. The US Army fielded an impressive number of both surface-to-air missiles and surface-to-surface missiles. From left to right: Hercules (SAM), (front) Hawk (SAM), (rear) Sergeant, Zeus (SAM), Pershing, LaCross, and Ajax (SAM). The soldiers from left to right are holding LAW, Redeye (SAM), and Entac. (Adapted from Redstone Arsenal.)

lies based on the missile's mobility: large, immobile SAMs; mobile missiles; and man-portable systems. The earliest of these Army projects was the Nike family, begun in 1945 by Bell Laboratories. The original Nike requirement was to knock down an aircraft flying at 600 miles per hour (mph), between 20,000 and 60,000 feet, maneuvering at three Gs at a 60,000-foot ground range. From the outset, the Army decided to keep the missile simple and more reliable by emplacing the complicated aspects (guidance and fuzing) on the ground. The Nike initially used liquid fuel for the missile and solid fuel for the booster. The Army froze the design in mid-1946.[22]

The Army tested eight unguided missiles between late September 1946 and late January 1947. Although the first of these reached an altitude of 140,000 feet and a speed of Mach 2.7, quite impressive for that day, the series was beset by problems that should have been expected with a new technology. There were difficulties with the motor, but the more serious ones included booster malfunctions (separation, explosions, and misfires). This led the developers in 1948 to adopt a unitary booster positioned underneath the missile that replaced the four boosters clustered around it and increased the system's length. More importantly, this arrangement offered advantages of cost, assembly, handling, reliability, and the tactical advantage of smokelessness. The newness of the technology also was evident in that initially the testers relied on recovering a 25-channel flight data recorder by parachute until telemetry was demonstrated in early 1947.[23] Other changes included moving the position of the control fins and increasing the size and location of the warhead.[24]

The Army vigorously tested Nike. Systems tests began in November 1951 and consisted of 23 guided shots, all but three against a drone aircraft. Ten were unsuccessful because of a missile component failure, with another four considered partially successful despite a missile component failure. The remaining nine averaged a miss distance (metal to metal) of 15 feet, and two hit the drone. While most of these tests used pyrotechnic devices in lieu of a real warhead, in April 1952 the Army fired five live warheads against drones (QB-17, radio-controlled World War II B-17 bombers). Although these were low-performance targets when compared to the threat, they were real aircraft and did yield dramatic photos. Two of the test missiles malfunctioned (one attributed to the missile, the other to its beacon), one inflicted heavy damage on the target, while the other two destroyed the drones.[25] There were additional live firing tests in early 1953; six were aimed at QB-17s and 10 at QF6F drones (radio-controlled World War II naval fighters). The testers concluded that 43 percent of the 49 shots were completely successful, and another 23 percent achieved "qualified" success. Six of the seven live warhead rounds were successful. The tests continued. Between June 1953 and December 1958, the Army fired 3,225 Nikes, two-thirds of which were considered successes.[26]

In November 1956, the Nike I became known as the Nike Ajax (fig. 41). The Army deployed the first Ajax unit to Fort Meade, Maryland, in March 1954 and received its last production missile in April 1958. Eleven other countries also deployed the Ajax. In all, the United States spent $1.2 billion for the system consisting of more than 13,700 missiles.[27]

The Army placed the missiles near the major cities they were to protect because of their short (just over 25 miles) range. Originally, the Army wanted 119 acres for each Ajax battery, but the cost of real estate in an urban area forced a different arrangement. This led to a January 1954 decision to use underground storage and launch facilities for all US installations, which cut the requirement to 40 acres per missile site. But even this did not stem public opposition. This included fears that the Nike boosters would land on people and property, that the sites would reduce real estate values, and that locating missiles, fuel, and (conventional) warheads in an urban location was unsafe.

Figure 41. Nike Ajax. The Nike Ajax was America's first operational SAM. (Reprinted from US Army Air Defense Museum.)

The safety issue was driven home when in May 1958 an explosion of seven Nikes near Middletown, New Jersey, killed six soldiers and four civilians and caused property damage for miles.[28] The reason the Army phased the Ajax out of service in 1964 had little to do with safety; it was replaced by a more advanced version.

In 1953, the US Army Ordnance Corps, Bell Laboratories, Western Electric, and Douglas began work on the Nike Hercules (fig. 42). One reason for the development of a successor to Ajax was that by early 1952, it was clear that its radar had difficulty dealing with aircraft that flew in formation. One solution was to use a nuclear warhead. Because of the size of the proposed nuclear warhead (30-inch diameter), the Army decided it was more efficient, albeit more time consuming, to develop a new missile rather than modify the Ajax. There was, of course, also a desire to improve the system's performance. The second-generation Nike was to employ an atomic warhead against formations of aircraft flying as fast as 1,000 mph at a maximum altitude of 60,000 feet and at a horizontal range of 28 miles. Hercules could be fitted with a conventional fragmentation warhead as well. It would build on the existing Ajax technology and be compatible with the Ajax ground equipment.[29]

The proposed missile was somewhat larger than its predecessor. The Model 1810 Hercules was seven feet longer, considerably wider, and four times heavier than the Ajax. The Army made good use of its experience with missiles in general and the Nike in particular as it was able to begin deployment of the Hercules in June 1958.[30] Flight tests with research and development missiles began in early 1955 and extended through June 1956. In sharp contrast to the Ajax record, Hercules had few difficulties with the booster but did encounter problems with the sustainer (main) engine: 12 of the first 20 flight tests in 1955 were terminated, half by sustainer problems. In addition, the program suffered a setback in September 1955, when a Hercules blew up on a test stand, killing one civilian and injuring five others. This led the Army to adopt a solid-fuel sustainer engine in 1956, which proved to be more reliable without a loss of performance.[31] The Army began to test the Hercules against drone aircraft (again the QB-17) in 1956, achieving its

85

Figure 42. Nike Hercules. The Nike Hercules was larger, heavier, and better performing than its predecessor. (Adapted from US Army Air Defense Museum.)

first kill with the conventional warhead in April 1957. Early on, the program was hobbled by test failures (76 percent of attempts through April 1958) mainly attributed to malfunctions of the guidance beacon, auxiliary power, and warhead circuitry. The missile improved, and, in its first public launch on 1 July 1958, it intercepted a simulated target flying at a speed of 650 knots (kts) at 100,000 feet. In tests later that month, Hercules showed it could single out a target when it destroyed three drones with fragmentation warheads. (It should be further noted that these targets were more challenging than the tried-and-true QB-17.) The Army never tested the Hercules with an atomic warhead, although it had scheduled such a demonstration for August 1958. (The nuclear warhead entered service in 1958.) Later tests showed a greatly improved missile success rate of 71 percent on 75 attempts in July through October 1958.[32]

The Army was not content with the Hercules missile. From the outset of the Hercules program in October 1954, overall direction called for modernization, research, and development. The Army's specific concern was to defeat such higher-performing aircraft (expected in the 1960–70s timeframe) as low-flying aircraft and to increase kill effectiveness and target-handling ability. While the Nike Zeus program (see below) was designed to combat enemy ballistic missiles, the Army initiated improvements to Hercules to combat aircraft. Principal improvements were made to the system's radars to extend detection and tracking ranges to the ground-based units. Testing of these improvements against flying targets began in early 1960 and by midyear demonstrated successes against both drones and ballistic missiles (Corporal and Hercules). The Army began to deploy the improved Hercules in June 1961 and by May 1964 had phased out all of its stateside-based Ajax missiles. Total Hercules production exceeded 25,500 missiles. Hercules served in six countries in addition to the United States.[33]

The Airmen also engaged in SAM work. In April 1946, the Army Air Forces (AAF) had three SAMs under development out of 28 missile projects. Boeing designed the ground-to-air pilotless aircraft (GAPA) missile system to defend against aircraft with a range of 35 miles and an altitude of 60,000 feet. The

Airmen test-fired about 100 of these missiles. Two other AAF projects were the University of Michigan's Wizard and General Electric's Thumper, both designed to reach ranges of 550 miles and altitudes of 500,000 feet. In 1947, the USAF relegated the two antiballistic missile projects to "prolonged study" status. By March 1948, the Air Force canceled Thumper. Wizard continued as a study, but Boeing replaced the GAPA project with Bomarc (Boeing, University of Michigan Aeronautical Research Center) in 1949 (fig. 43).[34]

These efforts emersed the Army and Air Force into a roles and missions battle.[35] While the missile field had been divided along the lines of ballistic missiles (Army) and aerodynamic missiles (Air Force), this arrangement mutated into a division according to range, point or tactical defense (Army), and area or long-range defense (Air Force). As a result, the Navy's Talos missile, which the USAF was adopting for ground-based point defense, was given to the Army. This was formalized by Secretary of Defense Charles E. Wilson in November 1956.[36] Bomarc fit into this scheme, as it was powered by ramjets that required atmosphere air, had wings and aerodynamic controls, and had a longer range than the Nike series. In January 1950, the Air Force killed GAPA and replaced it with the Bomarc project. It was essentially an unmanned aircraft. In fact, the Airmen initially designated the missile XF-99 (later changed to IM-99 [Interceptor Missile]) as it would any experimental fighter. Bomarc had the appearance, size (46.8-foot length, 18-foot span), and weight (15,500 pounds). It was radio-controlled with an active radar-homing device.

The USAF began testing the IM-99A in 1952 but did not accomplish its first successful launch, without ramjets, until October 1954. The missile's test record was poor, as fewer than 40 percent of 134 Bomarc A launches met their objectives. Nevertheless, in 1958 a Bomarc completed an interception located 1,500 miles away from its controllers. Two years later, the missile became operational. Bomarc employed a solid fuel booster and two ramjet sustainer engines to reach Mach 2.5 and a 125-mile range. The USAF first fired the B model, boosted by a solid fuel booster, in May 1959. The B had better performance (increased range and improved low-altitude ca-

Figure 43. Bomarc. The Air Force Bomarc was only in service a brief period of time. (Reprinted from Smithsonian Institution.)

pability), greater reliability, and superior guidance than its predecessor. Although 1.7 feet shorter than the A model, it weighed 532 pounds more and could reach slant ranges of 400 nautical miles and almost Mach 4.0. In its most memorable flight, it intercepted a Regulus II target drone at 100,000 feet, 446 miles from its launch point. That July, the IM-99B became operational. It carried a nuclear warhead and remained in service until October 1972. The Air Force deployed just under 500 Bomarcs in eight sites (of the 40 planned) in the northeastern United States, and the Canadians deployed a number at two sites. In all, Boeing built 700 Bomarcs at a cost of $1.6 billion.[37]

Bomarc failed for several reasons, including rising costs and slipping schedules. The threat changed from bombers before 1955 to intercontinental ballistic missiles in the late 1950s or bomber-launched, air-to-surface missiles, weapons that surpassed the Bomarc's capabilities. In addition, the United States adopted a strategy of offensive deterrence; that is, building up American nuclear offensive capabilities at the expense of defense. Finally, the improved performance of the Nike missiles duplicated, if not surpassed, the capabilities of Bomarc.[38]

Other countries also engaged in designing, building, and testing SAMs (fig. 44). The British put their first SAM, the Bloodhound, into service in 1958; the Thunderbird in 1960; and the Seaslug in 1962 (fig. 45). These first-generation missiles had command guidance systems and were large (about 20 feet in length).[39] The French worked on the PARCA and the

Figure 44. Thunderbird. Thunderbird was an early Royal Navy SAM. (Reprinted from http://www.nms.ac.uk/.../the%20collection/rockets_missiles. htm.)

Figure 45. Seaslug. The Seaslug was an early Royal Navy SAM that served in the Falklands War but earned no victory credits. (Reprinted from Imperial War Museum.)

MATRA R422-B, and the Swiss (Oerlikon) built the RSD 58, again all first-generation missiles.

Meanwhile, the Soviets were also making progress with SAMs. Their Soviet antiaircraft missile evolved from German World War II programs. The first Soviet SAM, the SA-1, was a German Wasserfall with ground (command) guidance. It became operational in early 1954, the same year the US Army deployed the Nike Ajax. The West first saw its successor, the SA-2, in 1957. The Soviets designed this missile to defend against high-flying, essentially nonmaneuvering, strategic bombers. The SA-2 first achieved prominence by knocking down an American U-2 over the Soviet Union in the spring of 1960 and downing another over Cuba in October 1962.[40] SAMs introduced a new element into air warfare, shifting the advantage back toward the defense.

Despite knowledge of the SA-2 since 1957 and its potential (similar to the Nike Ajax), the United States made only mixed progress with countermeasures. Tight budgets in the late 1950s hampered these efforts. Airmen assigned high priority to countermeasures against the SA-2 in budgets for fiscal years 1964 and 1965, but this was too late. The American Airmen had nothing effective to use when the need arose. Because of a joint Air Force–Army exercise in 1964, using the Hawk missile, some Airmen concluded that aircraft could not operate in SAM-protected areas. (It should be noted that Hawk was a more capable SAM than was the SA-2.)

Although it is easy and partially correct to blame tight funding, it is also true that the Airmen underestimated the requirement for countermeasures. Although the USAF equipped strategic bombers with electronic warning and jamming devices in the late 1950s, it did not similarly equip tactical fighters and bombers. Initially, the US Navy did a better job. Whatever the reason—money, obsession with nuclear weapons delivery, electrical power requirements, trust in fighter maneuverability or speed—the USAF's tactical air forces were unprepared for the style of combat they would face in Vietnam.[41]

The United States developed two other families of missiles that were considerably smaller and much more mobile. The 1946 Stilwell Board saw the need for lightweight, man-carried equipment for US soldiers and concluded that the existing .50-caliber machine gun was inadequate. It sought an antiaircraft machine gun capable of engaging aircraft flying up to 1,000 mph at ranges of 200 to 2,500 yards. Four years later, the Army requested a family of weapons to counter aircraft flying up to 1,000 mph at altitudes from zero to 60,000 feet and at horizontal ranges up to 27,000 yards. From these studies came the formal requirement in early 1951 for a surface-to-air guided missile to protect forward combat units from low-altitude aerial attack.[42]

The United States began development of Hawk in 1952 (fig. 46). Progress was relatively rapid. The Army awarded Raytheon a development contract in July 1954, began flight-testing in June 1956, started production in 1957, and activated the first missile unit in August 1960.[43] To better defend against low-flying aircraft, in 1964, the Army began an upgraded

Figure 46. Hawk launch. The Hawk went into service (1959) only a year after the Nike Hercules. Whereas the Nike family was only employed from fixed installations, the Hawk was mobile. (Reprinted from US Army Air Defense Museum.)

program that became known as Improved Hawk or I-Hawk. The changes included better electronics (including solid-state), an improved warhead, and a more powerful engine. Using the same basic airframe, the weight increased from about 1,250 pounds to 1,380 pounds. While speed was about the same or perhaps somewhat faster (Mach 2.5 or Mach 2.7), the I-Hawk increased its range (from 20 to 25 miles) and altitude (from 45,000 to 58,000 feet) capabilities and its lethality with a 20 percent heavier warhead. The Hawk was air transportable and quite mobile and was mounted on either a three-round trailer or a self-propelled unit (fig. 47).[44] The most notable aspect of the Hawk, however, is its adaptability. It has been modified, improved, and fielded in a number of advanced variants, some of which remain first-line equipment today in the Marine Corps, Army National Guard, and several foreign countries.[45]

The Army's success with the Hawk tends to obscure its other less successful efforts. In addition to the various investigations with machine guns and cannons, the Army also studied missiles. One of these was Porcupine, a system proposed in the mid-1950s that consisted of 2.75-inch rockets. A battery of

Figure 47. Hawk intercepting an F-80. The Hawk was the Army's first mobile SAM. It had a long and distinguished career, although it did not down any aircraft for the United States. This sequence shows what it could do against an F-80 drone. (Reprinted from Redstone Arsenal.)

64 launching tubes would have the capability of firing at a rate of 6,000 shots per minute. But the Army terminated this project in February 1956.[46]

Mauler was another system that failed to become operational (fig. 48). In the mid-1950s, the Army desired a radar-guided missile system that would be highly mobile and provide short-range, all-weather, low-altitude air defense protection. It ran into funding and technical problems, and as its historian explains, Murphy's Law prevailed. Weight grew as requirements increased. The Army wanted the entire system mounted on one lightly armored vehicle that could be carried by a C-123, C-130, or Chinook helicopter. As one Army colonel put it: "We are essentially compressing a Hawk system into 1/30th of the

Figure 48. Mauler. The Mauler was another Army antiaircraft missile system that failed to reach operational status. (Reprinted from Redstone Arsenal.)

Hawk volume."[47] It couldn't be done, at least not within a reasonable time and at a reasonable cost. By late 1964, the program had lost support at the Department of the Army and Office of the Secretary of Defense levels. Although Mauler was assessed to be superior to Hawk on measures of mobility, reaction time, and fewer vehicles and personnel, it was "exceedingly expensive." The historian of the project defends the Mauler, stating that it had no more problems than other complex missile programs. He summarizes that "the project was plagued by inadequate funding, a lack of a firm and timely guidance from higher headquarters, changes and compromises in military requirements, unsolved technical problems, and a gradual loss of confidence in both the contractor and the weapon system."[48] Perhaps a more balanced assessment is that the goals were too ambitious, the available technology was inadequate, and the program lacked clear direction and support. The record shows that development costs had risen from the original $78 million to $380 million, and the readiness date slipped six years. The secretary of defense killed Mauler in July 1965. The

Army decided to terminate Mauler and employ other weapons instead: Hawk and Hercules (followed by SAM D) as long-range weapons, and, at the front, Hawk, Chaparral, and the 20 mm rapid-fire Vulcan.[49]

Two systems were acquired in Mauler's place. The first was an extremely rapid-firing cannon adapted from aircraft use (see the Vulcan above). The other was a missile system the Army initially wanted to fill the gap in its antiaircraft coverage until the Mauler was deployed. This interim system was intended solely for fair-weather use, only for the North Atlantic Treaty Organization (NATO) arena, and for a brief two to four years until the Mauler appeared. The system was to be based on existing (off-the-shelf) technology. More specifically, the Army investigated two air-to-air missiles already developed, the Air Force's Falcon and the Navy's Sidewinder.[50] The Army eliminated the former in January 1964 and awarded a contract for the latter the next year. The Army thought it would be a relatively cheap and simple system, as it used components already developed, mounting four of the proven infrared-guided Sidewinder air-to-air missiles atop an M113 armored personnel carrier.[51]

As with so many other attempts, this concept, which became known as Chaparral, proved easier in theory than in practice (fig. 49). Although the air-to-air and surface-to-air missiles were 95 percent common, a host of problems emerged. The vehicle was too high for transit through the critical Berne Tunnel, too large for airlift, and yet too small for the crew and the eight spare missiles. The M45 mount and LAU-7A launch rails proved unsatisfactory, and there were problems with the ground launch and the seeker. In addition, questions of priority and coordination issues with the Navy also surfaced.[52] Testing uncovered further problems with lethality, detection and identification of targets, and smoke that obscured the gunner's vision and that revealed the Chaparral's position. These technical problems forced major changes that included a new prime mover, rocket motor, and warhead. The seeker was also upgraded. A small radar (Forward Area Alerting Radar [FAAR]) served both the Vulcan and Chaparral and helped in other areas (and had its share of problems also).

Figure 49. Chaparral. The Chaparral consisted of a Sidewinder air-to-air missile adapted for surface-to-air operations. Intended as an interim, short-term measure, it saw much longer service, including—as seen here—in the first Gulf War. (Adapted from Defense Visual Information Center.)

Chaparral began overseas deployment in November 1969, and FAAR was fielded in December 1972. The historian of the system summarizes that: "What originally appeared to be a fairly routine task of providing a quick-fix, interim Chaparral/FAAR capability by January 1968 turned into a nightmare of funding shortages, performance deficiencies, changes in military requirements, cost overruns, and schedule delays . . . further complicated by the fragmented management structure, manpower deficiencies, and a lack of timely guidance from higher echelons."[53] Nevertheless, Chaparral continued to soldier on. Later improvements included adding a forward-looking infrared device that gives the system night capability. Other versions of the Chaparral include trailer systems (M85) and a nautical version (Sea Chaparral) used by the Taiwanese navy. The United States and other countries manufactured over 700 systems and 21,700 missiles for service in eight countries.[54]

The third family of antiaircraft missiles, man-portable ones, also resulted from this post–World War II Army effort to obtain more effective and mobile antiaircraft protection. In 1954, the Army Equipment Development Guide recommended that first priority be given to the low-altitude (below 10,000 feet) air threat. It went on to note the need to research infrared techniques to enable operations in poor visibility conditions. In 1955, Convair began its own feasibility studies of a lightweight, man-transportable, low-altitude missile system, as there was no formal military requirement for such a weapon. The company named it Redeye, a system built around a small infrared guided missile that could be carried and fired by one man. In November 1956, the company presented the concept to Army and Marine representatives.[55]

The shoulder-launched system looked like a World War II bazooka (fig. 50). Its launching tube weighed less than four pounds, while the rocket weighed 14.5 pounds and measured 43 inches in length and 2.75 inches in diameter. A boost rocket would push the missile out about 25 feet, where the main motor would ignite, safely away from the operator. The infrared homer was designed to guide the device and its 1.2-pound warhead into the target for an impact explosion. The company estimated a maximum range of two nautical miles and a probability of kill of 0.35 to 0.40.[56]

The Army responded with a requirement in July 1957 that called for a one-man system that could destroy aircraft flying at low altitudes with speeds up to 600 knots at a maximum range of 4,100 meters. The Army also wanted an antitank capability and the system operational by fiscal year 1961. Two other companies besides Convair bid on the contract, Sperry (Lancer) and North American (Shoulder-Launched Antiaircraft Missile), but the Army rejected both because of excessive weight. The Army had some doubts about Convair's Redeye proposal, specifically its seeker and weight, and sought further research. But, the Marines, with one million dollars in research and development money to use or lose, pushed the Army to begin development. Thus, in April 1958, Convair received a one-year contract for a feasibility study and demonstration from the Army and Marine Corps.[57]

Figure 50. Redeye launch. The Redeye gave the individual American soldier a weapon that could down aircraft. This first-generation missile was limited by its inability to identify friend from foe and restricted engagement envelope. (Reprinted from Redstone Arsenal.)

The military characteristics were refined and approved by the secretary of the Army in February 1959. Redeye was designed to destroy aircraft flying up to 600 kts, up to 9,000 feet, at horizontal ranges out to 4,500 yards, and maneuvering up to six Gs. The one-man system was not to exceed 20 pounds in weight but was to have a reliability of 90 percent and a single shot-kill probability of 0.5. The Army set specific priorities in case of competing characteristics for (1) weight, (2) simplicity, and (3) effectiveness.[58] The program encountered technical problems in meeting these requirements relative to inadequate speed, inability to maneuver soon enough, and inadequate discrimination. It appeared that the Redeye would only be effective against targets up to 400 kts and would have difficulty with both less intense infrared targets presented by small helicopters and liaison aircraft and larger aircraft at certain angles. Kill probability against high-performance aircraft would be less than the 0.5 requirement, later reduced to 0.3. In addition, weight increased to 29 pounds due to the steel motor case and a more complex launching system. Thus, Army doubts were confirmed by various problems the project encountered. The result was that estimated research costs tripled, and the schedule stretched so that it took almost seven years to field an interim system (in October 1967).[59]

The Army recognized these problems and in May 1961 agreed to accept a less-capable weapon on an interim basis. Various failures in what was intended as a demonstration of the system in July and August 1961 dampened hopes for the Redeye and forced delays to remedy the deficiencies. Nevertheless, on 12 October 1961, the Army introduced the missile to the public in a demonstration to 300 onlookers, including Pres. John F. Kennedy and Secretary of Defense Robert S. McNamara. But the Redeye's problems were not solved as shown later that month, when six of seven missiles missed target drones by more than 200 feet. The contractor solved some of the aerodynamic problems but a year later still had not solved the seeker difficulties: insufficient guidance accuracy and nontarget infrared (IR) radiation. Nevertheless, the Army stuck with the project and even began funding an improved weapon, initially named Redeye II, later known as Stinger.[60]

The contractor made good progress with Redeye's major technical problems with the exception of background rejection and weight (exceeding the 22-pound requirement by a third). Nevertheless, in late 1963, the Army decided to push Redeye into limited production because of the need for this weapon.[61] Difficulties continued, in this case both reliability and production problems stalled the missile in limited production until December 1968. In February 1967, the Army issued Redeye to the troops. The system was making progress with the problem of background rejection but still lacked a lightweight IFF system. Costs and continued problems created some congressional resistance to the program.[62] But, by 1970, Redeye met or exceeded all military requirements except weight. Production stopped in 1974 after the delivery of more than 33,000 systems. About 10 countries purchased the system, while small numbers were sent to such hot spots as Chad, Nicaragua, Somalia, and Sudan.[63] The Redeye gave a man on the ground unprecedented ability to defend himself against aircraft—the power to down an aircraft with a single round. But, while the missile blazed a trail for other man-portable, infrared-guided missiles, Redeye's development record was mixed. As one writer noted, the Redeye required "a protracted development programme, and has never proved entirely successful."[64] It should be emphasized that these first-generation man-portable systems were limited by their short range, lack of identification friend or foe capability, vulnerability to simple countermeasures, low speed aircraft, and agility against only tail-chase engagements. Nevertheless, they did give attacking pilots considerable reason for pause.[65]

The developers made several efforts to adapt the Redeye for more diverse roles. In the late 1960s, the Air Force investigated using the missile in an air-to-air mode (Redeye air-launched missile [RAM]). It also looked at helicopter-launched Redeyes directed at both enemy helicopters and trucks. These missiles were successfully flight-tested but dropped because of launch restrictions, cost, and nonavailability. The Navy also saw the possibility of using Redeyes to defend small craft and in 1966 conducted Redeye firing from 85-foot boats. Further tests through 1969 were successful, but no firm military requirement emerged.[66]

Meanwhile, the Army sought a more capable weapon to handle the threat postulated for the 1970s. Specifically, it was looking for a system transportable by a two-man team and weighing no more than 30 pounds to defeat 660-knot aircraft using infrared and ECM at ranges from 2,500 to 5,000 meters. The ground service also wanted the ability to identify the aircraft. In 1971, the Army selected the improved Redeye—Redeye II or Stinger—for this role. It looked like a Redeye, but it was a much more sophisticated and higher-performing missile system. Compared to the Redeye, it featured an improved seeker, warhead, and fuzing. However, it also was larger (10 inches longer) and heavier (three pounds).[67] Following tests that fired over 130 missiles, the Army authorized production in 1978. Stinger reached the troops in February 1981. By 1985, Stinger was superseded by a version fitted with a more advanced seeker, Passive Optical Seeker Technology. This system has the added advantage of IFF and a range of 10 kilometers. Production of a third improvement version, Reprogrammable MicroProcessor, began in 1987. It features a removable software module that can be upgraded.[68] The Stinger has superior performance to the Redeye in speed (Mach 2.2 versus Mach 1.6), range (4,800 meters versus 3,000 meters), and altitude (3,800 meters versus 3,000 meters) (fig. 51). It also has several capabilities absent in the Redeye: IFF on the launch tube and sensor countermeasures to aircraft ECM.[69]

Although designed as a man-portable system, the Army acquired Stingers on a variety of platforms. First production missiles of an air-to-air version went to the Army in mid-1986 and can be fitted to a number of Army helicopters. Another Stinger application is Avenger (fig. 52). The ubiquitous High-

Figure 51. Stinger launch. The Stinger was the successor to the Redeye missile. (Reprinted from Redstone Arsenal.)

Figure 52. Avenger. The Avenger consisted of a turret with Stinger missiles mounted on the ubiquitous Hummer. (Reprinted from Redstone Arsenal.)

Mobility Multipurpose Wheeled Vehicle (HMMWV or Hummer) mounts a turret armed with eight Stingers. The Army awarded Boeing a contract to manufacture the system in August 1987. It received its first production system in November 1988 and by January 1997 had received over 900 units. Current plans call for the Army to get just over 1,000 Avengers and the Marines almost 240. It is the first Army antiaircraft system that has the capability to shoot on the move. Another self-propelled version of Stinger is the M6 Bradley Linebacker (fig. 53). It consists of a four-round Stinger pod mounted on a Bradley fighting vehicle. The Army awarded the initial contract in 1995, which now consists of converting 260 Bradleys to this configuration. Besides being fielded by the United States, Stinger serves 17 other countries.[70]

Figure 53. Bradley Linebacker. The Bradley Linebacker mounted four Stinger missiles atop a Bradley fighting vehicle. (Reprinted from internet: army-technology.com.projects/linebacker1.htm.)

Several other countries have fielded similar man-portable SAMs. These include the French Matra, Swedish Bofors RBS-70, the British Blowpipe and Javelin, but most importantly, the Russian SA-7 (the Russian Strela, NATO code-named Grail). Prompted by the development of the Redeye, the SA-7 project began in 1959 but entered service in 1966 before the appearance of the US system (fig. 54). The SA-7 was limited in a number of ways: strictly a tail-chase system for use against aircraft flying less than 574 mph and preferably below 287 mph. It was also very sensitive to IR sources other than the target; that is, it could not be aimed within 20 degrees of the sun, or at elevations of less than 20 to 30 degrees, as it could home on these heat sources. Its small (1.15 kilograms) warhead had limited lethality. An improved version (Strela-2M) appeared in 1971. This version provided a wider engagement envelope, with greater range and speed, as well as devices to

Figure 54. SA-7 Grail. The Soviets quickly developed and fielded man-portable SAMs. The North Vietnamese first used the SA-7 in 1972, and it proved especially effective against slow-moving and low-flying aircraft. (Reprinted from USAF.)

detect aircraft radars. The SA-7 has performance similar to the Redeye but has been in service with far more countries, perhaps as many as 56 in all. About 35,000 were built.[71]

Just as the Stinger replaced the Redeye, the SA-14 (NATO code-named Gremlin) replaced the SA-7. It has an improved motor, warhead, and seeker, giving it not only head-on firing capability but also better performance than the SA-7. The SA-14 entered operational service in 1974.[72]

The two-decade period following World War II saw great progress in aircraft. The world's major air forces transitioned from prop to jet propulsion, which increased speeds from 400 mph to 1,400 mph and ceilings from just over 30,000 feet to more than 50,000 feet. This performance advance gave the offense an increasing advantage over the defense. While the jet transition took place rapidly, jet-powered fighters engaged in combat during the Korean War (1950–53); the corresponding improvement in defensive equipment, the surface-to-air missile, took longer. During this period, air defenders phased out heavy AAA, retained light guns, and gradually equipped their forces with SAMs. Some SAMs were fielded in the 1950s, but the first combat use did not take place until U-2s were shot down over the Soviet Union in 1960 and Cuba in 1962. Now the defender had a potential counter to the jets, at least high-flying jets. The first wide-scale combat test came in Southeast Asia in the mid-1960s.

Notes

1. This Stinger should not be confused with the surface-to-air missile bearing that same name that is discussed below. See Mary Cagle, "History of the Mauler Weapon System," December 1968, 4, R.

2. The 20 mm gun would fire a two-ounce projectile at 2,870 feet per second (fps) out to a vertical range of 5,100 yards and a horizontal range of 5,200 yards. Vigilante was designed to defend against jet aircraft up to 10,000 feet and out to slant ranges of 14,000 feet. The Skysweeper could fire at a rate of 45 to 55 shots per minute (spm) with a muzzle velocity of 2,825 fps and could reach a vertical altitude of 18,600 feet. See Cagle, "Mauler," 5, 9–10, 19, 55; Robert Frank Futrell, "United States Air Force Operations in the Korean Conflict: 1 July 1952–27 July 1953," USAF Historical Study 127 (Maxwell AFB, Ala.: USAF Historical Division, Air University, 1956), 87; and US Army Air Defense School, "Air Defense: A Historical Analysis," June 1965, 3:30–33, AUL.

3. The Army version has two rates of fire, 1,000 and 3,000 spm, either of which quickly exhausts the 2,300 rounds of ammunition carried aboard the vehicle. See Tony Cullen and Christopher Foss, eds., *Jane's Battlefield Air Defence, 1988–89* (London: Jane's, 1988), 64–65; "M163 20 mm Vulcan," blokadvies.www.cistron.nl/m163.htm; Federation of Atomic Scientists, "GAU-4 20 mm Vulcan M61A1/M61A2 20 mm Automatic Gun"; Federation of Atomic Scientists, "M167 VADS Vulcan Air Defense System"; and US Army TACOM-RI, "The Gatling Gun," 6 www-acaka1rai.army.mil/LC/cs/csa/aagatlin.htm.

4. The system had an estimated unit cost of $6.6 million, about 2.4 times the cost of the tanks it was to protect. Its 4 kilometer (km) range was out-distanced by Soviet helicopter missiles at 6 km. See O. B. Koropey, *"It Seemed Like a Good Idea at the Time": The Story of the Sergeant York Air Defense Gun* (Alexandria, Va.: US Army Materiel Command, 1993), 44, 46, 66, 104–5, 131, 183, 185; and George Mauser, "Off the Shelf and into the Trash Bin: Sgt York, NDI Integration and Acquisition Reform" (thesis, US Army War College, 1996), AUL.

5. Cagle, "Mauler,"13–14, 19; US Army Air Defense School, "Air Defense," 3:33–34; James Eglin, *Air Defense in the Nuclear Age* (N.Y.: Garland, 1988), 190; Max Rosenberg, "The Air Force and the National Guided Missile Program: 1944–1954," study, 1964, 36, 42, HRA; and Joseph Russo, "ADA in Retrospect," *Air Defense Trends* (July–September 1975): 12.

6. The 85 mm Model 1939 was capable of firing 15 to 20 20-pound shells per minute at 2,625 fps to an effective ceiling of 25,000 feet, while the 85 mm Model 1944 had an additional muzzle velocity of 325 fps and an increased altitude capability of 4,000 feet. The 37 mm could fire a 1.6-pound projectile at a rate of 160 spm up to an effective ceiling of 4,500 feet. See Futrell, Historical Study 127, 41, 43; "Far East Air Forces Intelligence Roundup," 12–18 January 1952, 2:11–12; "Far East Air Forces Intelligence Roundup," 29 December 1951–4 January 1952, 3:8; "Far East Air Forces Intelligence Roundup," 28 February–6 March 1953, no. 31, II-1, II-2, II-10, HRA; and Andrew T. Soltys, "Enemy Antiaircraft Defenses in North Korea," *Air University Quarterly Review* 7, no. 1 (Spring 1954): 77–80.

7. Circular error probable is the radius of a circle within which one-half of a missile's projectiles are expected to fall. See Futrell, Historical Study, 165.

8. Robert Jackson, *Air War over Korea* (N.Y.: Scribner's, 1973), 99.

9. Commander in chief, US Pacific Fleet, *Korean War: (25 June 1950–27 July 1953) US Pacific Fleet Operations,* chap. 3, NHC; "Carrier Operations Evaluation Report No. 6, interim, 1 February 1953–27 July 1953," 44, 68, reproduced in William Hodge et al., "Theater Air Warfare Study" (thesis, Air War College, Maxwell AFB, Ala., 1977), 39, AUL; "Far East Air Forces Report on the Korean War," study, bk. 1:63, 82, 97, HRA; Futrell, Historical Study 127, 80; and US Navy Office of Information, "Korean Combat Statistics for Three-Year Period," NHC. A Chinese source states that more than 90 percent of US aircraft were downed by AAA during the war. See Jon Halliday, "Air Operations in Korea: The Soviet Side of the Story," 156–57, in William Williams, ed., *A Revolutionary War: Korea and the Transformation of the Postwar World* (Chicago: Imprint, 1993).

10. The US Air Force knew the F-51 was vulnerable to ground fire because of its liquid-cooled engine and the air scoop beneath the fuselage. One World War II study of fighters in the European theater indicated that the P-51 (as it was then designated) was three times as vulnerable to flak as was the P-47. The author was told the decision to employ the F-51, not the more rugged P-47, in Korea was based primarily on the availability of parts. See

107

A. H. Peterson et al., "Aircraft Vulnerability in World War II," RAND Report RM-402, rev. July 1950 (Santa Monica, Calif.: RAND, 1950), fig. 13, AUL.

11. Pacific Fleet Evaluation Group, research memorandum, "The Relative Risk to Anti-Aircraft Fire for Jet and Propeller Driven Ground Attack Aircraft in Korea," March 1952, NHC; Robert Futrell, "United States Air Force Operations in the Korean Conflict: 25 June–1 November 1950," USAF Historical Study 71 (Maxwell AFB, Ala.: USAF Historical Division, Air University, 1952), 57, HRA.

12. "FEAF Report on Korean War," 128; and Fifth Air Force Intelligence Summary, 15 September 1952, 26, HRA.

13. Futrell, Historical Study 127, 152; Fifth Air Force, Operations Analysis Office, operations analysis memorandum, "A Survey of Fighter Bomber Tactics and Flak Losses," January 1952, 7, HRA; Pat Meid and James Yingling, US Marine Corps Operations in Korea 1950–1953, vol. 5, Operations in West Korea (Washington, D.C.: Historical Division, US Marine Corps, 1972), 64, 69.

14. Futrell, Historical Study 127, 152; and Meid and Yingling, US Marine Corps Operations, 5:70.

15. Futrell, Historical Study 127, 152–53.

16. Meid and Yingling, US Marine Corps Operations, 5:70, 492n.

17. Ibid., 70–72.

18. Futrell, Historical Study 127, 219–22; History, Far East Air Forces, July–December 1952, vol. 1:58, HRA; and "FEAF Report on Korean War," 39.

19. Another reason for the nonuse of ECM was that insufficient jamming power could be generated by the relatively small number of B-29s involved and the shortages of both trained operators and equipment. See Daniel Kuehl, "The Radar Eye Blinded: The USAF and Electronic Warfare, 1945–1955" (PhD diss., Duke University, 1992), 131, 134, 151–52, 157–58.

20. Another problem was that the targets were located very close to the Yalu River and thus were covered by Chinese guns that could not be suppressed. See Kuehl, "The Radar Eye Blinded," 150–51; and A. Timothy Warnock, ed., The USAF in Korea: A Chronology, 1950–53 (Maxwell AFB, Ala.: Air Force History and Museums Program, 2000), 75.

21. Futrell, Historical Study 71, 116; "FEAF Report on Korean War," 39–41, 128–33; memorandum from Thomas Power to Gen James Knapp, subject: Commanders' Conference, Patrick Air Force Base, Fla., 30 September–1 October 1957, 4 October 1957, 2; and "Strategic Air Command Participation in the Missile Program from March 1957 through December 1957," USAF Historical Study 70, vol. 2, HRA.

22. The missile had two sets of fins: the forward four spanning 23 inches and the rearward four measuring 52 inches. Overall, the missile measured 19.5 feet in length and had a maximum diameter of 12 inches that tapered to 8 inches at the base. See Bell Laboratories and Douglas Aircraft, "Project Nike: History of Development," April 1954, 1, 2, 7, 13, 16, R; and Mary Cagle, "Development, Production, and Deployment of the Nike Ajax Guided Missile System, 1945–1959," June 1959, 3–5, 30, R.

23. Bell Labs, 17, 20, 29–30, 76; and Cagle, "Nike Ajax," 37–39, 54.

24. The warhead was the most changed component. It was increased from the original 200 pounds to 312 pounds and changed in concept from using large, slow-moving fragments to smaller, faster-moving ones. Initially, each of the two main charges (150 pounds each) was designed to fragment into 30,000 pieces each weighing 30 grains (.087 ounces). Later, this was changed to 60-grain fragments in a 179-pound center and 122-pound aft warhead. The warhead was designed to "deliver a high order of tactical damage within a 20-yard radius." See Cagle, "Nike Ajax," 87, 89, 154.

25. Bell Labs, 43, 91, 108, 111, 129; and Cagle, "Nike Ajax," 81, 103–17.

26. Bell Labs, "Project Nike," 78; and Cagle, "Nike Ajax," 160, 177–78.

27. Another source gives 15,000 as the total produced. See Tony Cullen and Christopher Foss, eds., *Jane's Land-Based Air Defence: Ninth Edition, 1996–97* (London: Jane's, 1996), 290; and Cagle, "Nike Ajax," 122, 179–81.

28. Cagle, "Nike Ajax," 167, 182–99.

29. Mary Cagle, "History of the Nike Hercules Weapon System," April 1973, v, 8–9, 15, 35, 39–40, R.

30. Cagle, "Nike Hercules," 42–43, 53.

31. Ibid., 57–59, 97.

32. Ibid., 97–99, 102–6; Christopher Chant, *Air Defence Systems and Weapons: World AAA and SAM Systems in the 1990s* (London: Brassey's, 1989), 93.

33. Cagle, "Nike Hercules," 161–64, 171–72, 187, 192n; and Cullen and Foss, *Jane's Land-Based Air Defence, 1996–97*, 290.

34. US Army Air Defense School, "Air Defense," vol. 3:48–50; and Rosenberg, *The Air Force*, 71, 75, 76, 79, 83, 117–18, 150.

35. See Clayton Chun, "Winged Interceptor: Politics and Strategy in the Development of the Bomarc Missile," *Air Power History* (Winter 1998): 48.

36. Eglin, *Nuclear Age*, 103, 114, 135–37.

37. Another source states that the Air Force built 570 Bomarcs. See Chun, "Winged Interceptor," 50–51, 57; Mark Morgan and Mark Berhow, *Rings of Supersonic Steel: Air Defenses of the United States Army 1950–1979 and Introductory History and Site Guide* (San Pedro, Calif.: Fort MacArthur Museum Association, 1996), 22, 24; Kenneth Schaffel, *The Emerging Shield: The Air Force and the Evolution of Continental Air Defense, 1945–1960* (Washington, D.C.: Office of Air Force History, 1991), 236–38; and Eglin, *Nuclear Age*, 179.

38. Chun, "Winged Interceptor," 46, 52–53, 55–57.

39. British SAMs are addressed in chap. 4 in a discussion of the Falklands War.

40. The SA-2 measured 35 feet in length and weighed 4,875 pounds with its booster. It could carry a 288-pound warhead at Mach 3.5 out to a slant range of 24–25 miles and was effective between 3,000 and 60,000 feet. Apparently, the Soviets fired 14 SA-2s at Francis Gary Powers in 1960: 12 missed, one destroyed a MiG-19, and one got the U-2. See R. A. Mason, ed., *War in the Third Dimension: Essays in Contemporary Air Power* (London: Brassey's, 1986), 105; John Taylor, ed., *Jane's All the World's Aircraft, 1967–68* (New York: McGraw-Hill Book Co., 1967), 521–22; C. M. Plattner,

"SAMs Spur Changes in Combat Tactics, New Equipment," *Aviation Week,* 24 January 1966, 26, 30; US Army, "Air Defense Artillery Reference Handbook," study, 1977, 18–19, AUL; Lon Nordeen, *Air Warfare in the Missile Age* (Washington, D.C.: Smithsonian Institution, 1985), 15; and Laurence R. Jensen, "Use of Intelligence Information to Determine Countermeasures Requirements for the SA-2" (thesis, Air Command and Staff School, Maxwell AFB, Ala., 1966), 9–10, AUL.

41. Marshall Michel, *Clashes: Air Combat over North Vietnam, 1965–1972* (Annapolis: Naval Institute, 1997), 33; Jensen, "Use of Intelligence Information," 28–42; Richard Rash, "Electronic Combat, Making the Other Guy Die for His Country!" (thesis, Air War College, Maxwell AFB, Ala., March 1983), 7, 92, AUL; William Momyer, *Air Power in Three Wars* (Washington, D.C.: Department of the Air Force, 1978), 138; and Wayne Thompson, *To Hanoi and Back: The US Air Force and North Vietnam, 1966–1973* (Washington, D.C.: Smithsonian Institution, 2000), 48.

42. Mary Cagle, "History of the Redeye Weapon System," May 1974, 1–3, R.

43. Cullen and Foss, *Jane's Land-Based Air Defence, 1996–97,* 292.

44. Chant, *Air Defence Systems,* 100; Tony Cullen and Christopher Foss, eds., *Jane's Battlefield Air Defence, 1988–89* (Coulsdon, Surrey, U.K.: Jane's, 1988), 201–2, 205; and Cullen and Foss, *Jane's Land-Based Air Defence, 1996–97,* 298.

45. Morgan and Berhow, *Rings of Supersonic Steel,* 24.

46. Cagle, "Redeye," 4.

47. In December 1958, the Army increased the Mauler requirement to defeat targets of a one meter square radar cross section to the much more difficult requirement of .1 meter square, which would allow engagement of ballistic missiles. This increased cost and complexity by about 75 percent. See Cagle, "Mauler," 80, 105, 107, 168.

48. Ibid., 35, 227, 232, 243–44, 251, 255.

49. Ibid., 245, 251; and Chant, *Air Defence Systems,* 125.

50. The Navy began the Sidewinder project in the late 1940s and test-flew the first missile in 1953. It was in service by 1956. See Duncan Lennox, ed., *Jane's Air-Launched Weapons* (London: Jane's, 2000), 82.

51. Mary Cagle, "History of the Chaparral/FAAR Air Defense System," May 1977, 3–5, 10, 18.

52. Cagle, "Chaparral," 20, 36–37, 44, 66.

53. Ibid., 91–92, 109, 111, 114, 116, 129, 193–94; and Chant, *Air Defence Systems,* 126.

54. Chant, *Air Defence Systems,* 127; and Tony Cullen and Christopher Foss, eds., *Jane's Land-Based Air Defence, 1999–2000* (Coulsdon, Surrey, U.K.: Jane's, 1999), 168, 170.

55. Cagle, "Redeye," 5–8.

56. Ibid., 8, 13. Probability of kill is the estimate of the chances of one missile downing a target, in this case, a 35 to 40 percent chance.

57. The contract was for $1.58 million. See Cagle, "Redeye," 14–18.

58. Ibid., 44–45.

59. Ibid., 18, 28.
60. Ibid., 85, 96–98, 102–5, 112–13, 198.
61. Ibid., 117–19, 133.
62. Ibid., 121, 127–28, 139.
63. These requirements included target speed, altitude, slant range, maneuver, reliability, and warm-up time. Single-shot probability against jets was set at 0.3 but was estimated at 0.4 against a MiG-21 and calculated at 0.51 against an F9F drone flying at 300 feet and 430 kts. See Cagle, "Redeye," 147, 155; and Cullen and Foss, *Jane's Battlefield Air Defence, 1988–89*, 23–24.
64. Chant, *Air Defence Systems*, 105.
65. Ibid.
66. Cagle, "Redeye," 157, 159–61.
67. Ibid., 198, 203–4; and Chant, *Air Defence Systems*, 129.
68. Cullen and Foss, *Jane's Battlefield Air Defence, 1988–89*, 20, 22; and Cullen and Foss, *Jane's Land-Based Air Defence, 1999–2000*, 36.
69. Cullen and Foss, *Jane's Battlefield Air Defence, 1988–89*, 25; and Cullen and Foss, *Jane's Land-Based Air Defence, 1999–2000*, 39.
70. Cullen and Foss, *Jane's Battlefield Air Defence, 1988–89*, 22, 23; and Cullen and Foss, *Jane's Land-Based Air Defence, 1999–2000*, 162–63.
71. Cullen and Foss, *Jane's Battlefield Air Defence, 1988–89*, 4–19; and Steven Zaloga, *Soviet Air Defence Missiles: Design, Development and Tactics* (London: Jane's, 1989), 177, 184, 237.
72. Cullen and Foss, *Jane's Battlefield Air Defence, 1988–89*, 10–11; and Cullen and Foss, *Jane's Land-Based Air Defence, 1999–2000*, 22–23.

Chapter 3

Airmen versus Guerrillas: Vietnam

The Vietnam conflict was another war that pitted Western armies and high-technology arms against numerous tenacious foes in primitive terrain. The technology brought with it many advantages, the most significant of which were firepower and mobility. Air power was the most important and visible manifestation of this technology. In response, the guerrillas relied on dispersion, camouflage, mobility, and night operations to neutralize the impact of air power, airfield attack, and ground-based weapons to directly defend themselves.

French Operations

Compared to the later American involvement in Indochina, the French conducted smaller military operations with less-modern equipment. One compensating factor was that initially the Communists offered little direct defense against air attack, not fielding their first antiaircraft opposition until January 1950.[1] During the decisive 1954 battle of Dien Bien Phu, the French had only 107 World War II–vintage combat aircraft (fighters, fighter bombers, and bombers). Here, the French attempted to duplicate their 1953 success at Na San, where they used some of their best troops to lure the guerrillas into the open to be cut down by air and artillery fire.

The Vietminh, however, learned the lessons from their previous defeats and increased their antiaircraft protection. The Communist AAA forced French aircraft, which had initially flown at 600 to 1,800 feet, to fly at 2,700 to 3,000 feet, which decreased French effectiveness. The guns also took a toll on French aircraft. During attacks on the Vietminh supply lines, for two weeks after 24 November 1953, Communist AAA hit 45 of 51 French aircraft and downed two. Not surprisingly, flak and air power played a vital role in the actual siege. The Communists opened the battle by attacking French airfields throughout Indochina with artillery and infiltrators and damaged a number of the scarce French aircraft. A Vietminh artillery bombardment on 10 March 1954 initiated the direct attack on Dien Bien Phu and within four days closed the garrison's airstrips. Meanwhile, the Communists assaulted the French positions as they fended off French air attacks.

The air portion of the battle saw French aircraft duel Communist flak. Communist antiaircraft guns, 16 Vietminh and 64 Chinese, forced French aircraft higher and higher and disrupted the accuracy of both weapons and supply delivery. Thus, the Vietminh countered French aerial firepower and forced more than 50 percent of French air-dropped supplies to miss their mark and fall to the Communists. Radar-directed guns hit aircraft flying as high as 10,000 feet. During the battle, the Vietminh downed 48 French aircraft and damaged another 167. More importantly, they cut off the fortress from the outside and neutralized one of its most potent weapons. Thus, AAA played a critical role in the decisive battle of the first Indochina War.[2]

America Enters the War

American involvement in Indochina began in the 1950s, with the dispatch of advisers and equipment. Again, the insurgents, this time called Vietcong (VC), lacked air power. The South Vietnamese used American helicopters, which gave them a tactical advantage over the guerrillas; however, the Communists employed discipline and .50-caliber machine guns to counter the choppers, as they demonstrated during the December 1962 battle at Ap Bac. Despite the advantages of superior numbers and helicopters in this encounter, the South Vietnamese suffered heavy losses, including five helicopters destroyed and 14 others hit. The VC continued to exact a steady toll on the aircraft attacking them. On 24 November 1963 in An Xuyen province, for example, Communist ground fire hit 25 aircraft and downed five.[3]

The American presence and air activity steadily increased, and with this increase came losses. The United States suffered its first combat aircraft loss on 2 February 1962, when a C-123 flying a low-level training mission failed to return. The United States lost 11 aircraft to hostile causes in 1962 and 23 aircraft the next year. The first US Navy loss, one of 60 American aircraft lost in combat in Indochina in 1964, occurred in Laos in June 1964.

The air war expanded in May 1964 as the United States began a continuing program of Air Force and Navy reconnaissance flights over Laos. Nevertheless, the Gulf of Tonkin incident of August 1964 marked the "official" start of the American air war in Vietnam, as it led to the first air strike against North Vietnam. Two of the 80 attacking Navy planes involved in the reprisal attack went down. Considering the meagerness of the North Vietnamese defenses in terms of quantity and quality at this point, these losses should have been a warning signal to the decision makers of what was to come. The air war escalated further with armed reconnaissance and fixed-target strikes in Laos in December 1964. In February 1965, American reprisal strikes on North Vietnam resumed on a tit-for-tat basis.

The full-scale bombing offensive against North Vietnam, code-named Rolling Thunder, began in March 1965.[4] On the first mission, 2 March 1965, North Vietnamese gunners downed four of the 130 attacking US and South Vietnamese aircraft. The North Vietnamese lacked the most modern equipment—they had no surface-to-air missiles and few jets—but they did have numerous conventional AAA weapons. So, while they could not stop the air attacks, they could make them costly (fig. 55).

From the start, America used air power against the north as a political tool: first, during the reprisal raids and second, during the Rolling Thunder campaign. The objectives of the latter were to stiffen the morale of the South Vietnamese, interdict Communist supplies, inflict punishment and cost on the North Vietnamese, and demonstrate American will.[5] But many, then and now, adamantly proclaim the operation was restricted, some say decisively, by the civilian decision makers. Sortie levels were controlled, areas of North Vietnam were put off-limits to air attack, bombing halts were frequent, and targets were carefully selected from Washington. For example, MiG airfields were off-limits until 1967, as were missile sites until they downed an American aircraft. In addition, the campaign was graduated, robbing the Airmen of the elements of shock and surprise and permitting the North Vietnamese to build and adjust their defenses.[6]

Figure 55. Captured North Vietnamese antiaircraft gun. The Communists had a plentiful supply of AAA and ammunition. (Reprinted from USAF.)

The Airmen were also hindered by other factors, the most significant was their unpreparedness to fight a sustained, conventional air campaign.[7] First, American aircraft were unsuited for these operations. Paradoxically, "strategic" bombers such as the B-52 were used against "tactical" targets in the south, while tactical fighters such as the F-105 were used against strategic targets in the north.[8] The limited numbers of all-weather aircraft presented a considerable burden in the air war against North Vietnam, especially in the winter monsoon season (December through mid-May). The only American all-weather aircraft were the Marine and Navy A-6s and Air Force B-52s and F-111s, the first two types entered action in 1965, the latter in 1968. Second, America fought a conventional air war with tactics and aircraft designed for nuclear warfare. The best example of this mismatch was the F-105. A fighter with an internal bomb bay—a contradiction in terms—it was the US Air Force's workhorse, flying many of the missions over the north and suffering the most damage.[9]

The United States, for its entire technological prowess, was ill equipped in other areas as well. At the beginning of the air war, the United States was still using unguided (dumb) munitions, just as Airmen had used in World War I! Thus, aircrews had to overfly their targets, which proved dangerous and often fatal.[10] Second, the United States had inadequate electronic ECM. Although Strategic Air Command (SAC) B-52s were reasonably equipped, TAC fighters were not. The irony therefore is that, until late in the war, the better-equipped B-52s operated unopposed over South Vietnam, while throughout the war, fighters flew against the growing and increasingly lethal defenses in North Vietnam.

Another factor, perhaps the most important, was that the Americans underestimated the power of the defense and the abilities of the North Vietnamese. The Airmen focused on the weapons on which Airmen always focus, where the glamour and glory are, fighters and air-to-air combat. It is true that the North Vietnamese built up their air force. But, this air force proved as elusive as the Vietcong, using guerrilla tactics of hit-and-run and fighting only when circumstances were favorable. With the major exception of Operation Bolo in January 1967, when US fighter pilots ambushed the North Vietnamese fighters and destroyed seven MiGs without a loss, American Airmen did not engage in major air battles and thus were unable to rack up scores as they had in World War II and Korea.[11] While glamorous as always, a matter of pride, and a symbol of success, air-to-air combat was neither frequent nor important in the Vietnam air war. The principal Communist weapon against US aircraft was AAA. American Airmen not only underestimated North Vietnamese defenses, they especially underestimated the impact of flak. Both were serious mistakes.

The North Vietnamese fielded a formidable ground-based air defense system. In early 1965, the North Vietnamese manned about 1,200 antiaircraft guns, which they increased to almost

2,000 guns within six months. In 1967, Pacific Air Forces estimated that there were 9,000 antiaircraft weapons in North Vietnam, while a Headquarters Air Force estimate put the number at 3,100 medium (37 mm or 57 mm) and 1,300 heavy (85 mm or 100 mm) guns. With better intelligence, the estimate was lowered to 2,000 guns by the end of 1969 and to less than 1,000 guns (37 mm and larger) in 1972. Whatever their numbers, their impact was significant.[12]

The farther north the Airmen operated, the more intense were the defenses. Although only 20 percent of US sorties over Indochina in 1965 were against North Vietnam, 62 percent of its combat losses were there. The following year, 1966, proved only a little better, with about 30 percent of the total Indochina sorties and fewer than 60 percent of losses occurring over the north. The area north of 20 degrees latitude, especially around the Hanoi-Haiphong area, proved most dangerous. In the period September 1966 through July 1967, the United States flew fewer than 30 percent of its North Vietnam attack sorties north of 20 degrees yet lost 63.5 percent of its aircraft in that area.[13]

In all, the United States lost just over 2,400 fixed-wing aircraft in flight to enemy defenses during the Vietnam War (through 15 August 1973). Of the known causes of loss, gunfire caused 89 percent; SAMs, 8 percent; and MiGs, 3 percent. In addition, the United States lost approximately 2,400 helicopters in flight to enemy action, all but nine (two to MiGs and seven to SAMs) to AAA (fig. 56). The Communists downed about 1,100 American planes over North Vietnam, 72 percent to gunfire, 19 percent to SAMs, and 8 percent to MiGs.[14]

The American Airmen initially used nuclear delivery tactics that they had practiced in the late 1950s and early 1960s: high-speed, low-altitude approaches and a rapid climb (pop-up) to bombing altitude just before reaching the target. One adjustment with conventional ordnance was to make multiple passes over the target, but intense ground fire and the resulting losses forced a change. Therefore, the Airmen raised approach altitudes to 15,000 to 20,000 feet, from which the aircraft dive-bombed their targets and limited attacks to a single pass. This reduced losses, but, as a consequence, it also reduced

Figure 56. North Vietnamese gunners. North Vietnamese gunners scramble to their guns. Communist guns downed three-quarters of US aircraft lost in the war. (Reprinted from USAF.)

accuracy, one author asserts, from under 300 feet to over 500 feet.[15]

SAMs Join the Fight

The air war changed dramatically on 24 July 1965 when a Soviet SA-2 missile downed an Air Force F-4 and damaged three others. Proving this shootdown was no fluke, an SA-2 destroyed an American drone two days later. US reconnaissance spotted construction of the first SAM site in early April and watched it and three other sites progress throughout the spring. But, the civilian decision makers would not permit the Airmen to attack the missile sites, another of the many political restrictions on the air war. Secretary of Defense Robert S. McNamara argued that if the Airmen attacked the SAM sites, they must also attack the MiG bases, which would be a major escalation of the air war.

The leaders also feared that such attacks might cause Soviet casualties. Besides, one of McNamara's chief assistants, John McNaughton, believed that the SAMs only represented a bluff and would not be used.[16]

The potential SAM threat grew as the North Vietnamese incorporated more missiles into their inventory (fig. 57). North Vietnamese SAM battalions increased from one in 1965 to 25 the next year, to 30 in 1967, and to 35–40 in 1968. This growth in units permitted the North Vietnamese to increase their missile

Figure 57. SA-2 position with missiles. The introduction of the SAM changed the dynamic of the air war. Although responsible for only 9 percent of total aircraft losses, the SA-2 forced American aircraft lower and into the sights of Communist gunners. (Reprinted from USAF.)

firings from 30 per month in the first 11 months of air operations over the north to 270 per month between July 1966 and October 1967. SAM firings peaked in the latter month when the North Vietnamese launched 590 to 740 SAMs, the most fired until the Linebacker II operations of 1972. From October 1967 to the bombing halt on 1 April 1968, SAM firings averaged 220 each month. During this period, the American Airmen observed 5,366–6,037 SAMs, which downed 115–28 aircraft.[17]

Despite the increase in SAM firings, their effectiveness diminished. In 1965, it took almost 18 SAMs to down each American aircraft, a figure that rose to 35 in 1966, to 57 in 1967, and to 107 in 1968. A number of factors contributed to this decline.[18]

The Airmen quickly learned that the SA-2 could be outmaneuvered. The Soviets designed the SA-2 to destroy high-flying, nonmaneuvering, strategic bombers; but until 1972, it engaged primarily low-flying, maneuvering, tactical fighters. On clear days, alert Airmen could spot SA-2 launches, as the missile was large, appeared to most flyers as a flying telephone pole, and left a visible smoke trail (fig. 58). The pilots would rapidly dive toward the missile, and when it changed direction to follow the aircraft, the pilot would pull up as abruptly and as sharply as possible. The SA-2 could not follow such maneuvers. However, such action required sufficient warning, proper timing, and, of course, nerve and skill. To give pilots adequate time to maneuver, procedures prohibited the pilots from flying too close to clouds between them and the ground. Later, the Airmen received electronic devices that gave a visual and aural warning when SAM radar was tracking them.[19]

In addition, the American Airmen directly took on the missiles. On 27 July, 46 US Air Force fighter-bombers attacked two missile sites and met disaster. The Central Intelligence Agency reported that they hit the wrong targets. Worse, North Vietnamese gunners downed three aircraft while a midair collision accounted for two others. Naval aviators had a similar experience, as they were unable to find one SAM site and lost six aircraft. Nevertheless, the anti-SAM attacks continued. In the first nine months of 1966, the Airmen launched 75 strikes against 60 sites and claimed to have destroyed 25 and damaged 25. Such attacks proved unprofitable because of the tough de-

Figure 58. SA-2 launch. American Airmen could avoid the Soviet SA-2 if they were alert and spotted them in time. (Reprinted from USAF.)

fenses and the mobility of the SAMs, which could be relocated within hours.[20]

One effort to counter North Vietnamese SAMs was standoff ECM—aircraft crammed with electronics gear that orbited a distance from the defenses and interfered with Communist radar and SAM signals. The Marines employed EF-10Bs in this role between April 1965 and 1969. The Douglas Skyknight was ancient, having first flown in 1948, and it saw action in the Korean War as a night fighter. It was joined in the ECM role in late 1965 by another Douglas product, the Skywarrior, which first flew in 1952. The Navy employed the twin-engine jet bomber as an electronics warfare aircraft designated as the EKA-3B.

The Air Force adopted the Navy aircraft and used it in the ECM role as the RB-66, later EB-66 (1966). It carried a crew of seven, including four ECM operators in a crew compartment fitted in the bomb bay (fig. 59). The US Air Force fielded three versions in Vietnam, each model with different equipment and

Figure 59. EB-66. One counter to North Vietnamese radar was standoff electronic jamming. The EB-66 was the chief USAF platform for such activity. (Reprinted from USAF.)

capabilities. The EB-66 served well throughout the war, but its operations were limited by its small numbers, old airframe, inadequate engines, fuel leaks, and restricted operator training. The Communists countered the jamming by moving their SAMs forward, forcing the EB-66 in turn to move away from North Vietnam to orbits over both Laos and the Gulf of Tonkin, farther from their radars and thus making them less effective. They also directly attacked the jammers with both MiGs and missiles, downing six EB-66s over the course of the war.[21] In late 1966, the Marines introduced the EA-6A into the jamming role.

A third American measure against the SAMs was code-named Wild Weasel. The Air Force installed radar homing and warning—electronics equipment that could detect SAM radar and indicate its location—into F-100Fs, the two-seat trainer version of its fighter-bomber. Wild Weasel I went into action in November 1965, flying with and guiding conventionally armed

F-105s against SAM positions. These operations, known as Iron Hand (SAM suppression), preceded the main force by about five minutes, attacked and harassed the SAMs, and thus permitted operations at 4,000–6,000 feet above the light flak into which the SAMs had forced the American aircraft.[22]

The Airmen also used a new version, antiradiation missiles (ARM), in the battle against enemy radars. In April and May of 1966, American Airmen first used the Navy's AGM-45A Shrike missiles that homed in on the SAM's radar signal (fig. 60). It was a great concept; however, the Shrike had limited range and maneuverability and could become confused. These liabilities reduced the ARM's effectiveness, as did Communist countermeasures. North Vietnamese crews soon learned that by limiting emissions and coordinating several radars, they could still operate the SAMs and yet limit their vulnerability to the Wild Weasels. Just as the North Vietnamese used decoys to neutralize and ambush American air strikes, SAM operators sometimes turned on their radar to provoke an ARM launch and then turned it off before missile impact. The Shrike's kill rate declined from 28 percent of those launched by Air Force

Figure 60. Navy A-4 firing Shrike. An active counter to Communist radar was the Navy's Shrike antiradiation missile that homed in on radar signals. It was also used by the US Air Force. (Reprinted from USAF.)

124

and Navy crews in 1966 to 18 percent in the first quarter of 1967. In the fall of 1967, SA-2 crews began using optical aiming, which rendered American ECM efforts useless; however, optical aiming required favorable visual conditions, which also reduced SAM effectiveness. In March 1968, the Americans introduced the more capable AGM-78 Standard ARM. Although it was constrained by reliability and size problems, the AGM-78 gave American Airmen another and better weapon against the SAM. Compared to the earlier Shrike radar homing missile, it had a heavier warhead, greater range, and a memory feature that allowed it to home in on the last signal it received from its radar target, even if that radar was turned off.[23]

In the summer of 1966, Wild Weasel III appeared; it was a modification of the two-seat F-105 trainer, redesignated F-105G. Iron Hand operations were now easier, as compatible aircraft were flying together. In late 1966, US Airmen began using cluster bomb units (CBU) antipersonnel munitions against North Vietnamese positions. However, in the period following the 1968 bombing halt, 1969 until summer 1972, free-fall munitions were removed from Iron Hand aircraft, degrading their effectiveness.[24]

Before leaving this discussion of Iron Hand, one point requires amplification. Wild Weasel crews were the first over enemy territory and the last to leave (fig. 61). They actively sought out danger and found it. Losses were substantial. Noting that two Air Force and one Navy pilot who flew these missions earned the Medal of Honor best sums this up.[25]

The United States developed external pods mounted under the aircraft to jam Communist electronics. In July 1965, the US Air Force tested the devices on the reconnaissance versions of the F-101 and F-4 without success. Later that year, the Navy tested an internally mounted ECM package that did not work much better. Both services were more successful when the Navy in mid-1966 and the US Air Force in September or October tested ECM pods carried beneath the fighters. A formation of fighters using the pods—the Navy's ALQ-51 and the Air Force QRC-160 (redesignated ALQ-71)—seriously inhibited radar-directed defenses. The various jamming devices forced SAM operators to adopt a new procedure—track-on jamming.

Figure 61. Wild Weasel. The USAF employed special units, called Wild Weasel, to attack Communist radar. This two-seat F-105G is carrying two Shrike antiradiation missiles. (Reprinted from USAF.)

They fired the SA-2s at the jamming signal, but as this gave azimuth and not range information, this technique was much less accurate than the normal method. Thus, the pods permitted operations from 10,000 to 17,000 feet, above the reach of light and medium flak. The Air Force put the pods into service in January 1967. There were, of course, drawbacks to using ECM pods. The tighter formations that were best suited for ECM results made the aircraft more vulnerable to MiG attack. Another penalty was that the increased altitude of operations decreased the weapon's accuracy.[26] The Navy did not adopt the pods and paid a price. In the first nine months of 1967, the US Air Force pod-equipped forces lost five aircraft in the heavily defended Route Package VI, while at the same time, the Navy lost about 20 aircraft in that area. In the previous year, SAMs accounted for 50 percent of Air Force losses in that area; now they claimed only about 16 percent. During these times, SAMs were credited with one-half of Navy aircraft losses.[27]

American Air Operations through Linebacker I

The 1968 Tet offensive changed the war for the United States. As a result, Pres. Lyndon B. Johnson capped American troop levels, stopped American bombing of North Vietnam above 20 degrees north latitude, and then, just before the November election, stopped all bombing of the north. In the fall, Americans elected Richard M. Nixon president. He began to withdraw US troops and turn more of the burden of the war over to the South Vietnamese. Because of the bombing halt, American aircraft losses, especially fixed-wing machines, declined.[28]

The air war raged in other areas besides North Vietnam; however, losses were proportionally the greatest in the north. American combat losses on a per sortie basis were next highest over Laos, then South Vietnam, and lowest over Cambodia. However, because American Airmen flew most of their sorties over the south, this became the area where most of the aircraft fell. Between 1961 and 1968, the United States lost 859 aircraft to hostile action over the north compared with about 1,709 over the south. One sharp difference was the proportion of helicopters destroyed in the two areas. Only 11 went down in North Vietnam, but about 1,073 helicopters (or about 63 percent of all aircraft lost in the south) were lost in South Vietnam.[29]

The helicopter proved to be vulnerable even in the less-lethal antiaircraft environment of South Vietnam. The vulnerability of the chopper is highlighted by the deaths associated with it. During most of the war (1961–71) in all of Southeast Asia, about 62 percent of the deaths from combat aircraft losses and 66 percent of noncombat aircraft losses were associated with helicopters. These numbers may overemphasize the point, however, as helicopters were employed in large numbers as troop carriers near the ground, where ground fire was intense, all of which led to high personnel losses. Helicopter vulnerability was dramatically demonstrated in the 1971 South Vietnamese invasion of Laos (Lam Son 719). Although official figures put helicopter losses at 107–22 and the number damaged at 600, some put loss figures much higher, as many as one-third of those engaged. The same doubt clouds the official

127

Army figures, which acknowledge 2,166 helicopters lost in combat and 2,075 lost to noncombat causes during the entire war. There are allegations that the Army disguised the magnitude of their chopper losses by repairing many damaged machines that did not deserve such efforts. One source states that the Communists downed 5,600 Army helicopters, but the Army successfully retrieved two-thirds of these. One critic puts total helicopter losses at 10,000.[30]

In March 1972, the North Vietnamese attempted to knock the South Vietnamese out of the war with a massive conventional invasion. The Communists used weapons heretofore not seen in the war in the South: tanks, 130 mm artillery, and the SA-7. The latter was a shoulder-launched, man-portable, heat-seeking missile with a range of just under two miles and able to reach almost 10,000 feet. The SA-7 gave the guerrillas a potent weapon against air power and put the slow-moving, low-flying aircraft, especially helicopters and propeller aircraft, at considerable risk. It knocked down a number of helicopters, observer aircraft, and, in June, an AC-130. Between 29 April and 1 September, the Communists fired 351 SA-7s at American aircraft in 221 incidents and downed 17 fixed-wing and nine rotary-wing aircraft. It took 1.8 missiles to down each helicopter—as compared to 10 required for each slow-moving fixed-wing aircraft kill—and 135 missiles to destroy one F-4. The American Airmen used flares to decoy the SA-7, but most effective of all, they increased both their speed and altitude. Thus, although the number of aircraft downed was not great, SA-7s had a major impact, forcing American aircraft to fly higher where they were less effective and to put some aircraft, such as the A-1, out of business.[31]

The Communists employed their SA-2s differently during the 1972 campaign. Before their invasion, they deployed SA-2s to cover the demilitarized zone and on 17 February 1972 fired 81 missiles there that downed three F-4s. In March, once the invasion started, SA-2s downed two AC-130s over Laos and the next month an EB-66. The SA-2s also took on B-52s, which now ventured further north (fig. 62). The Communists fired 23 SAMs on both 21 and 23 April in defense of Vinh and destroyed a B-52, the first loss to Communist fire. During Linebacker

Figure 62. Damaged B-52. The B-52s operated at high altitudes out of the reach of most North Vietnamese guns, but not from missiles. SAMs hit this Stratofortress and forced it to make an emergency landing at DaNang. (Reprinted from USAF.)

(later called Linebacker I), the code name for the renewed air attacks of the North in 1972, the Communists fired 2,750 SA-2s at US aircraft and downed 46 planes.[32]

Just as North Vietnam changed the rules of the game, so did the United States. Nixon's policy of détente gave him flexibility that his predecessor, who feared direct intervention by the Soviets or the Chinese, lacked.[33] In 1972, the president authorized the mining of North Vietnamese ports, long requested by the military, and used air power as it had not been used before. The Airmen employed air power more effectively also because they had fewer political restrictions, although some targets and areas continued to be denied to them.[34] US air power played a major role in stopping the invasion by inflicting terrific losses on North Vietnamese forces. As never before, American Airmen had targets they could see, hit, and destroy. The Airmen also had better weapons.

Although the Airmen had not introduced new aircraft since the 1968 bombing of North Vietnam, they did use other equipment that improved bombing effectiveness. These devices put more bombs on target, thus reducing the exposure of friendly aircraft to hostile fire. The Airmen began long-range aid to navigation (LORAN) bombing in 1970, which made it possible to operate in the worst weather conditions and still get bombs within hundreds of meters of the aiming point.[35] Although this was not precision bombing, it did permit bombing during bad weather.

The most important new equipment introduced was guided munitions (smart bombs), which could get bombs within meters of the target. A number of bridges that had withstood numerous and costly American strikes quickly fell to these new weapons. For example, on 13 May 1972, four flights of F-4s attacked the formidable Thanh Hoa Bridge with guided bombs, dropping its western span and causing other critical damage. There were no US losses in the attack, whereas the previous 871 sorties had cost 11 aircraft and had not neutralized the bridge. The Airmen considered the guided bombs to be 100 times more effective than unguided weapons against bridges and 100–200 times more effective against such hard targets as bunkers.[36] Greater accuracy meant fewer aircraft at risk and, thus, fewer losses.

The Americans also employed new ECM and anti-SAM tactics to combat the formidable Communist defenses. They introduced a new electronic jamming platform when in July 1972 US Marines thrust the EA-6B into action (fig. 63). Against North Vietnamese electronics, the Airmen employed more chaff, a World War II device that still worked. Chaff had seldom been used because the Navy feared its impact on their shipborne radar, and the US Air Force lacked a suitable dispenser. In June 1972, American Airmen introduced the ALE-38 chaff dispenser and, in August, chaff bombs. Both devices greatly enhanced US ECM capabilities and reduced the vulnerability of chaff-dispensing aircraft. The Airmen created chaff corridors within which attackers were almost immune from North Vietnamese radar-guided SAMs and AAA. Seventh Air Force commander Gen William W. Momyer noted that only one of seven losses to SAMs during Linebacker I occurred in a chaff corridor. One author called the use of chaff corridors "the most significant tactical change instituted by the Air Force for its 1972 bombing campaign."[37] In August, the US Air Force also changed its anti-SAM tactics (Wild Weasel) from Iron Hand—four F-105s

Figure 63. EA-6B Prowler. The EA-6B Prowler carried a four-man crew to jam enemy radars. (Reprinted from USAF.)

using antiradiation missiles—to hunter-killer teams consisting of two F-105 hunters armed with ARMs and two F-4 killers armed with CBUs.[38]

If the Airmen operated successfully over North Vietnam, they nevertheless paid a price. During the April through October 1972 bombing, the US Air Force flew 9,315 sorties, dropped 155,500 tons of bombs on the north, and lost 63 planes. In all, the United States lost 111 fixed-wing aircraft in combat, apparently in equal proportions to AAA, MiGs, and SAMs. In addition to aircraft losses, the Airmen paid another price: only 2,346 of the total sorties directly attacked enemy installations; the others were in support of missions. The ratio of support aircraft was even higher than these numbers indicate (3.4:1), as they do not include tanker and reconnaissance aircraft.[39]

As the bombing took its toll in the north and the Vietnamese invasion of the south stalled and then was pushed back, negotiations prompted Henry A. Kissinger's "peace-is-at-hand" comment on 26 October. But as close as the peacemakers got to an agreement, they did not get a treaty.

Linebacker II

On 14 December President Nixon gave the North Vietnamese 72 hours to get back to serious negotiations "or else." The "or else" was a three-day bombing offensive against North Vietnam, which Nixon ordered that day and then changed on 19 December to an indefinite period. The object of Linebacker II—the code name for the December bombing—was to restart negotiations.[40]

US Airmen returned to the home of the SAMs, AAA, and MiGs on the night of 18 December.[41] For three consecutive days, the script was about the same. First, F-111s began with attacks on airfields and various other targets at 1900, kicking off an operation that lasted about nine and one-half hours.[42] About 20 to 65 minutes later, the first of three waves of B-52s unloaded their bombs. The second wave followed about four hours later and was in turn followed by the third wave about five hours later. Each wave consisted of 21 to 51 B-52s supported by 31 to 41 other aircraft, and each wave flew exactly the same pattern: the same heading from the west and, after a sharp turn after bombing, the same exit heading to the west. There were also daylight attacks by Air Force, Marine, and Navy aircraft.

The bombing rocked Hanoi, but the aircraft losses jolted the Airmen as well. During the first three days of the operations, 12 aircraft went down, not a large number and seemingly bearable; however, B-52 losses—three on the first night and six on the third—were shocking. B-52s were, after all, America's primary strategic nuclear bomber, the foundation of the air-breathing leg of the Triad. Up to this point, the US Air Force had lost only one B-52 to enemy fire, although 17 had been lost to other causes. While the overall B-52 loss rate of 3 percent of effective sorties on the three missions appeared acceptable, the loss rate on the third mission was 6.8 percent, and the nine B-52s lost to this point in Linebacker II represented almost 5 percent of the 170 to 210 B-52s the US Air Force had deployed in Southeast Asia and over 2 percent of the 402 in service in 1972.[43] This was reminiscent of the summer and fall of 1943 over Germany.

The B-52 losses highlighted a number of problems. First, the B-52 fleet was of mixed quality, consisting of 107 of the older but modified D models and 99 of the later G models. Only half of the G models had upgraded ECM equipment, which proved to be one of the critical factors in determining which aircraft the SAMs hit, the big killers of the B-52s.[44] Although the defenders fired more SAMs at the B-52Ds, more B-52Gs were hit and downed, with five destroyed on the first three missions.

A second problem was that the B-52s were controlled, or better put, overcontrolled, from SAC headquarters in Omaha. SAC formed the basic battle plan and tactics literally thousands of miles from the actual combat. Initially, SAC had a policy of no maneuvers on the bomb run, although such maneuvers often permitted aircraft to elude the SAMs.[45] SAC also mandated a "press-on" procedure, which dictated that bombers continue their missions despite the loss of engines, computers, and most critically, ECM equipment.[46] Not surprisingly, with one headquarters controlling the bombers and another the support aircraft, there were coordination problems between the bombers and their escorts, including two instances in which B-52s fired on US aircraft.[47] Other coordination difficulties included US radios jammed by EB-66 ECM and friendly radar severely degraded by B-52 ECM.[48]

Losses indicated that the ECM was inadequate. First, B-52 ECM protection markedly declined in the 100-degree turn immediately after bomb release, as the bombers' bank reduced the effectiveness of the spot jammers.[49] Second, winds that differed from forecasts in direction and speed upset the ECM protection of the chaff corridors. For example, on 20 December, only four of 27 B-52 cells received chaff protection at the bomb-release line, and all of the B-52s downed were 5 to 10 miles from chaff cover. Third, the North Vietnamese gunners surprised the American Airmen by using radar designed and deployed for gun control (designated T8209) to guide the SA-2s. American Airmen lacked equipment to both warn of and jam this "new" I-band radar.[50]

The North Vietnamese took advantage of the stereotyped tactics by salvoing barrages of SAMs at the point where the B-52s executed their post-target turns. SAM operators limited radar guidance to the last five to 10 seconds of intercept, which made the tasks of the ECM operators and Wild Weasels difficult.[51] The losses forced the Airmen to modify their operations.

Thus, the Air Force formed a tactics panel and changed tactics.[52] Although most US aircraft continued to fly their missions about the same way, this was not true for B-52s. On the four missions between 21 and 24 December, the US Air Force employed only 30 B-52Ds in a single wave. In addition, the planners varied the timing, headings, and altitudes. The Airmen increased the amount of chaff, attempting to lay a chaff blanket instead of a chaff corridor. Thus, instead of 15 percent of the bombers receiving chaff protection at the bomb release point, now 85 percent did. In all, US Airmen dropped 125 tons of chaff during Linebacker II. Night hunter-killer teams were first used on 23 December to nullify the SAM threat; however, bad weather permitted only marginal results. The Air Force also quickly installed jammers and modified ARMs for use against the I-band radar that had surprised them.[53] But the American Airmen initially lacked the AGM-45 A-6 version suitable for this job and did not get these missiles until 27 December. The AGM-78, which also could be used against this band of radar, was in short supply even before the start of Linebacker II.[54]

The Airmen hit Hanoi with these new tactics on 21 December and lost two B-52s and one A-6A. During the next three nights, bombs fell on targets in Haiphong and north of Hanoi. The new tactics and new targets paid off as the Airmen lost only three aircraft on these three missions. There was no bombing on 25 December, a gallant and certainly a diplomatic gesture that allowed North Vietnamese defenders to rearm.

The attack on 26 December was one of a kind. The United States sent 120 B-52s, the most on any of the Linebacker missions, against targets in Hanoi and Haiphong. Although supported by 99 aircraft, two B-52s went down. Both followed SAC's "press-on" procedures, attacking in broken cells—formations of two rather than the normal three bombers—and thus lacked adequate ECM power. The remaining three missions (27–29 December) employed 60 B-52s each night, but otherwise fit the same pattern. Five aircraft (two B-52s) went down on 27 December. There were no losses on the last two days.

In all, during Linebacker II, B-52s dropped about 15,000 tons of bombs, while tactical aircraft added another 5,000 tons of bombs.[55] Because there were only 12 hours of visual conditions during the 12-day operation, the Airmen aimed the bulk of their ordnance by nonvisual techniques using radar and LORAN.[56]

Despite North Vietnamese claims of 81 aircraft destroyed (38 B-52s), Linebacker II cost 27 aircraft, 15 of which were B-52s.[57] Compared to the 3 percent expected losses, the overall loss rate of below 2 percent and a B-52 loss rate slightly above 2 percent were acceptable.[58] Thus, Airmen favorably compared the loss rates in Vietnam and especially those of Linebacker II with those in World War II and Korea. Such a comparison, however, overlooks the fact that Vietnam-era aircraft were much more expensive than their predecessors, while inventories and aircraft production were much smaller.[59]

The American Airmen throttled two parts of the North Vietnamese air defenses. The small Communist air force launched 32 aircraft, attempted interceptions with 20, but scored no hits on the B-52s, and downed only two F-4s for the loss of six MiGs.[60] American tactics of airfield suppression, fighter escort, ECM, night attacks, high-altitude operations, and bad weather nullified the MiGs. All but the first two tactics were also successful in neutering North Vietnamese AAA, which damaged only one B-52 and downed three tactical aircraft.[61] But, if the American Airmen adequately handled the fighter and flak threats, the same cannot be said of the SAMs.

During Linebacker II, the North Vietnamese fired 1,285 SAMs, which downed all 15 B-52s lost and three other aircraft.[62] The American Airmen, however, did not target the SAM sites until the sixth day of operations (23 December) and did not attack them again until 27 December, when B-52s and F-111s attacked the most effective single SAM site.[63] US Air Force hunter-killer units also attacked this site, designated by the Americans as VN 549, with at least nine AGM-45s and two AGM-78s. But VN 549 survived, and, therefore, on 27 December briefers instructed the American bomber crews to fly well clear of it. Rumors circulated that it was manned by Chinese gunners. The B-52 and F-111 attacks on SAM sites continued on the last two days of the operation, along with F-4 attacks on SAM storage facilities. Despite these efforts, intelligence estimated that only two sites were 50 percent damaged, eight were undamaged, and results against three were unknown.[64] It should be noted that only 3 percent of the bombs dropped during Linebacker II fell on SAM targets as compared with 5.3 percent that fell on airfields.[65] The redeeming feature was that by 29 December, the north Vietnamese had run out of SAMs, leaving North Vietnam essentially defenseless (fig. 64).[66]

Clearly, Linebacker II was an outstanding feat of arms. After years of restrictions and frustrations, American Airmen were able to directly take on and defeat a formidable air defense system. For the United States, and especially the Airmen, this was a proud, satisfactory way to end the war, or at

Figure 64. Talos. During the Vietnam War, the Navy's Talos missiles downed one MiG in 1968 and another in 1972. This Talos is aboard the USS *Galveston*. (Reprinted from USAF.)

least an end to American involvement. The US Air Force saw Linebacker II as a validation of air power and a demonstration of what it could do if unencumbered by political restrictions (fig. 65). Yet, the tactical aspects, the victory, should not obscure the fact that strategic bombing did not achieve decisive ends in Vietnam; the final treaty was substantially the same as the agreements made in October.[67]

Conclusions

The American Airmen were unprepared for the war fought in the skies over Southeast Asia—unprepared in terms of the political restrictions levied on them, the scant targets they had to attack, and the nature of the long conventional war they had to fight. As the realities of battle forced them to change both their tactics and equipment, the Airmen had to relearn the lessons of the past, and in the process, suffer substantial losses. They again found that enemy antiaircraft defenses, SAMs rather than aircraft, presented the major obstacle to air operations. They again learned how dangerous it was to fly close to the

Figure 65. Terrier. A Terrier downed a MiG in 1972, one of three MiGs destroyed by Navy SAMs. This Terrier is mounted on the USS *McCormick*. (Reprinted from USAF.)

ground in the face of intense ground fire. They again realized that attacking enemy antiaircraft positions (SAM and AAA) was dangerous and of dubious value. Most of all, they again saw that the tactics used in World War II and Korea were relevant for modern air warfare.

SAMs greatly enhanced the power of the defense and presented new difficulties to the Airmen. The SA-2s were the first challenge. They did not destroy that many aircraft and became less effective as the war continued, but they did force the Airmen to lower their altitudes and put their aircraft into the teeth of the guns. Another disturbing weapon introduced was the man-portable SAM. Although not possessing great lethality, it was easily concealed, highly mobile, and gave one man the power to down a multimillion-dollar aircraft. It proved especially effective against low-flying, slower (prop-powered) aircraft and helicopters. Second, to counter the missiles, the Airmen had to expand the total number of support sorties, a requirement that increased as the war progressed. The effectiveness of the defense is much more than the total aircraft destroyed by the air defense system but must include the cost for the attacker to get bombs on target. SAMs made aerial attack more complicated, dangerous, and expensive. Clearly, the cost of conducting the air offensive rose as the Vietnam War continued.

Countermeasures helped to keep American aircraft losses to a manageable rate. One Air Force officer estimated that ECM reduced losses by 25 percent, while a Navy officer put the figure at 80 percent (fig. 66).[68] Nevertheless, air operations were expensive in both losses and effort. Communist gunners proved a worthy and resourceful foe, although limited by second-rate Soviet equipment. Yet, despite the able Communist air defense tactics and their adaptation to the changing tactical situation, the American Airmen gradually increased their edge. The big improvement for the offensive side came with the use of ECM along with antiradiation, "smart," and standoff weapons. These weapons increased accuracy and decreased losses. In the full-scale operations of Linebacker II, the American Airmen showed that massive application of modern aircraft with modern equipment could succeed against defenses limited in numbers and quality.[69]

Figure 66. RF-4C. More F-4s were lost than any other USAF aircraft in Vietnam. The Air Force attributed 80 percent of these losses to ground fire, 10 percent to MiGs, 7 percent to SAMs, and 2 percent to ground attack. (Reprinted from USAF.)

Notes

1. Victor Flintham, *Air Wars and Aircraft: A Detailed Record of Air Combat, 1945 to the Present* (New York: Facts on File Yearbook, Inc., 1990), 256.

2. The Vietminh used American 105 mm guns captured in the Korean War so the errant French ammunition drops were important supply channels for the Communists. See Bernard Fall, *Hell in a Very Small Place: The Siege of Dien Bien Phu* (Philadelphia, Pa.: J. P. Lippincott, 1966), 31–34, 49, 133, 144, 454–55; William Leary, "CAT at Dien Bien Phu," *Aerospace Historian*, September 1984, 178–80, 183; Robert Frank Futrell, *The United States Air Force in Southeast Asia: The Advisory Years to 1965* (Washington, D.C.: Office of Air Force History, 1981), 19–20, 116; and V. J. Croizat, trans., *A Translation from the French: Lessons of the War in Indochina*, vol. 2, RAND Report RM-5271-PR (Santa Monica, Calif.: RAND, 1967), 292, 302.

3. Futrell, *USAF in Southeast Asia to 1965*, 158–59, 163, 196.

4. Benjamin Schemmer, "Vietnam Casualty Rates Dropped 37% after Cambodia Raid," *Armed Forces Journal*, 18 January 1971, 30; Michael McCrea, "U.S. Navy, Marine Corps, and Air Force Fixed-Wing Aircraft Losses and Damage in Southeast Asia (1962–1973)," Center for Naval Analyses (CNA), study, August 1976, 2-1, 2-13, 2-19, 2-20, AUL; and Futrell, *USAF in Southeast Asia to 1965*, 116.

5. *The Pentagon Papers*, ed., the Senator Gravel edition (Boston, Mass.: Beacon Press, 1975), 3:269; and Lon Nordeen, *Air Warfare in the Missile Age* (Washington, D.C.: Smithsonian Institution Press, 1985), 11.

6. *The Pentagon Papers*, 3:294–95; Nordeen, *Air Warfare*, 15, 18; U. S. Grant Sharp, *Strategy for Defeat: Vietnam in Retrospect* (San Rafael, Calif.: Presidio Press, 1978), xiii–xiv, 271; Lou Drendel, . . . *And Kill MiGs: Air to Air Combat in the Vietnam War* (Carrollton, Tex.: Squadron Signal Publishers, 1984), 8; David Halbertstam, *The Best and the Brightest* (New York: Random House, 1972), 367–68; and Richard Kohn, chief of Air Force History, interviewed by author, June 1986.

7. For especially sharp criticism of the Airmen, see Hanson Baldwin, "Introduction," in Jack Broughton, *Thud Ridge* (Philadelphia, Pa.: J. P. Lippincott, 1969), 12–13; and Dana Drenkowski, "Operation Linebacker II," *Soldier of Fortune*, September 1977, 32–37, 60–61.

8. A number of factors help explain this situation. Communist air defenses over the south were minimal when compared with those over the north, and no one wanted to risk the nuclear-capable B-52s. In addition, the decision makers feared that the use of the large strategic bombers would send the wrong signal to the various warring, unfriendly, neutral, and friendly powers and generate hostile publicity.

9. This aircraft was poorly designed, having essentially no backup for its vital hydraulic controls. Of 617 US Air Force aircraft lost over North Vietnam, 280 were F-105s. See McCrea, "Fixed-Wing Aircraft Losses and Damages," 6–47. In addition to 334 F-105 combat losses in Southeast Asia, there were 63 operational losses. See John Granville, "Summary of USAF Aircraft Losses in SEA," Tactical Air Command study, 1974, 22, 36, 57, HRA.

10. Broughton, *Thud Ridge*, 22, 96; and William W. Momyer, *Air Power in Three Wars* (Washington, D.C.: Department of the Air Force, 1978), 126.

11. This was one-half of North Vietnam's MiG-21 force. See R. Frank Futrell et al., eds., *Aces and Aerial Victories: The United States Air Force in Southeast Asia, 1965–1973* (Washington, D.C.: GPO, 1976), 35–42. The Navy's MiG kill-to-loss ratio in Vietnam was 3.9:1 (54 MiGs destroyed) and the Air Force's was 2.2:1 (129 MiGs destroyed). See "Southeast Asia Air-to-Air Combat," *Armed Forces Journal International*, May 1974, 38. In World War II, USAAF fighters had a 3.6:1 edge in air-to-air combat against Germany and 4.3:1 against Japan. The Navy and Marine Corps' ratio against Japan was 13:1. See United States Army Air Forces, *Army Air Forces Statistical Digest: World War II* (Washington, D.C.: Office of Statistical Control, 1945), 255–61, 263–68; and Adm Louis Denfeld, chief of Naval Operations, US Navy, address on the 37th anniversary of naval aviation, 9 May 1949, NHC. In the Korean War, US Air Force fighter pilots ran up a 6.9:1 score of victories to losses in air-to-air combat. See Larry Davis, *MiG Alley: Air to Air Combat over Korea* (Carrollton, Tex.: Squadron Signal Publishers, 1978), 70; and Maurer Maurer, *USAF Credits for the Destruction of Enemy Aircraft, Korean War*, USAF Historical Study no. 81 (Maxwell AFB, Ala.: Albert F. Simpson Historical Research Center, Air University, 1975).

12. John Kreis, *Air Warfare and Air Base Air Defense, 1914–1973* (Washington, D.C.: Office of Air Force History, 1988), 285–86; Nordeen, *Air Warfare*, 13; Paul Burbage et al., "The Battle for the Skies over North Vietnam," in *Air*

War Vietnam (Indianapolis, Ind.: Bobbs-Merrill Co., Inc., 1978), 224; Schemmer, "Vietnam Casualty Rates," table 351; Institute for Defense Analyses (IDA), Jason Study, "The Bombing of North Vietnam," December 1967, 2:49, LBJ; and Wayne Thompson, *To Hanoi and Back: The U.S. Air Force and North Vietnam, 1966–1973* (Washington, D.C.: Smithsonian Institution, 2000), 40, 242.

13. Report of the Central Intelligence Agency (CIA), "The Effectiveness of the Rolling Thunder Program in North Vietnam: 1 January–30 September 1966," November 1966, A-2, A-16, LBJ; CIA, "Report on Rolling Thunder," 1966, 6, LBJ; IDA, Jason Study, "The Bombing of North Vietnam," 3:49–50; and Raphael Littauer and Norman Uphoff, eds., *The Air War in Indochina*, rev. ed. (Boston, Mass.: Beacon Press, 1971), 283.

14. Rene Francillon, *Vietnam: The War in the Air* (New York: Arch Cape Press, 1987), 208; and McCrea, "Fixed-Wing Aircraft Losses and Damages," 6-2, 6-11, 6-20.

15. McCrea, "Fixed-Wing Aircraft Losses and Damages," 2–3; Futrell, *Aces and Aerial Victories*, 4; and Thompson, *To Hanoi and Back*, 49.

16. Cable to White House Situation Room, 12/16437 May, 1; Intelligence memorandum, subject: Status Report on SAMs in North Vietnam, 29 June 1965, 1–2; and memorandum, subject: CIA Appreciation of SA-2 Activity in North Vietnam during Late July, 1 August 1965, 1, in *CIA Research Reports: Vietnam and Southeast Asia, 1946–1976*, ed. Paul Kesaris (Frederick, Md.: University Publications, 1983); Futrell, *Aces and Aerial Victories*, 5; Notes of Lyndon B. Johnson, White House meeting, 16 May 1965, 3, LBJ; and Thomas D. Boettcher, *Vietnam: The Valor and the Sorrow* (Boston, Mass.: Little, Brown and Co., 1985), 232.

17. McCrea, "Fixed-Wing Aircraft Losses and Damages," 2–10; Granville, "Summary of USAF Aircraft Losses," 10–11; and US Pacific Fleet, "An Analysis of SA-2 Missile Activity in North Vietnam from July 1965 through March 1968," staff study 8–68, October 1968, 2, NHC.

18. Momyer, *Air Power in Three Wars*, 136.

19. Nordeen, *Air Warfare*, 16; Peter Mersky and Norman Polmar, *The Naval Air War in Vietnam* (Annapolis, Md.: Nautical and Aviation, 1981), 61; Bryce Walker, *Fighting Jets* (Alexandria, Va.: Time-Life Books, 1983), 112; and M. J. Armitage and R. A. Mason, *Air Power in the Nuclear Age*, 2d ed. (Urbana, Ill.: University of Illinois, 1985), 108.

20. Marshall Michel, *Clashes: Air Combat over North Vietnam, 1965–1972* (Annapolis: Naval Institute, 1997), 32; Nordeen, *Air Warfare*, 18; CIA, "Effectiveness of Air Campaign," B-22; and Paul Burbage et al., "Air Superiority Tactics over North Vietnam" (thesis, Air Command and Staff College, Maxwell AFB, Ala., 1975), 13, AUL.

21. Giles Van Nederveen, "Sparks over Vietnam: The EB-66 and the Early Struggle of Tactical Electronic Warfare," CADRE paper, 2000, 11, 14, 19, 38–44, 62, 70, 74, 76, 99; Futrell, *Aces and Aerial Victories*, 4–5; Nordeen, *Air Warfare*, 13; Gordon Swanborough and Peter Bowers, *United States Navy Aircraft since 1911* (New York: Funk and Wagnalls Co., 1968), 177–78; Gordon Swanborough and Peter Bowers, *United States Military Air-*

craft since 1908, rev. ed. (London: Putnam, 1971), 267–69; Julian Lake and Richard Hartman, "Air Electronic Warfare," US Naval Institute *Proceedings*, October 1976, 46; and "US Marine Corps Forces in Vietnam: March 1965–September 1967, Historical Summary," 2:36.

22. Nordeen, *Air Warfare*, 16; and Burbage, "The Battle for the Skies," 240.

23. McCrea, "Fixed-Wing Aircraft Losses and Damages," 2-24, 2-29; Michel, *Clashes*, 225; USAF Pacific Command Scientific Advisory Group, "Shrike Missile Effectiveness under Rolling Thunder Operations" (Working paper 1-67, Headquarters of the Commander in Chief Pacific, Scientific Advisory Group, January 1967), 1, AUL; USAF Pacific Command Scientific Advisory Group, "Shrike Effectiveness under Rolling Thunder Operation, First Quarter, 1967," (Working paper 7–67, assistant for operations analysis, Headquarters Pacific Air Forces, April 1967), 1, AUL; Nordeen, *Air Warfare*, 18–19; Military Assistance Command, Vietnam, uncoordinated draft, "Linebacker Study," staff study, January 1973, 7, HRA; and Burbage, "The Battle for the Skies," 247.

24. Report of Tactical Air Command (TAC), Directorate of Fighter Operations, "SEA Tactics Review Brochure," April 1973, 2:77–79, AUL; Nordeen, *Air Warfare*, 19, 22; Swanborough and Bowers, *United States Military Aircraft*, 471; and Momyer, *Air Power in Three Wars*, 130.

25. Ivan Rendall, *Rolling Thunder: Jet Combat from World War II to the Gulf War* (New York: Free Press, 1997), 151–54.

26. McCrea, "Fixed-Wing Aircraft Losses and Damages," 2–24; Michel, *Clashes*, 37–38, 62; Nordeen, *Air Warfare*, 23–24; Burbage, "Battle for the Skies," 240; Momyer, *Air Power in Three Wars*, 127; and Lake and Hartman, "Air Electronic Warfare," 47.

27. Michel, *Clashes*, 127.

28. Littauer and Uphoff, *The Air War in Indochina*, 283.

29. Schemmer, table 351.

30. Ibid.; Carl Berger et al., eds., *The United States Air Force in Southeast Asia: 1961–1973* (Washington, D.C.: Office of Air Force History, 1977), 116; Armitage and Mason, *Air Power in the Nuclear Age*, 2; James Coath and Michael Kilian, *Heavy Losses: The Dangerous Decline of America's Defense* (New York: Penguin Books, 1985), 136–37; Warren Young, *The Helicopters* (Alexandria, Va.: Time-Life Books, 1982), 140; and Peter Mersky, *US Marine Corps Aviation: 1912 to the Present* (Baltimore, Md.: Nautical and Aviation, 1987), 244. In Vietnam, on average, one helicopter was hit on every 450 sorties, one downed on every 7,000, and one lost on every 20,000. See Peter Borgart, "The Vulnerability of Manned Airborne Weapon Systems, pt. 3: Influence on Tactics and Strategy," *International Defense Review*, December 1977, 1065.

31. Claude Morita, "Implication of Modern Air Power in a Limited War," Report of interview with Gen John Vogt Jr., commander, Seventh Air Force, Office of Pacific Air Forces History, 29 November 1973, 23–24, AUL; John Doglione et al., *Airpower and the 1972 Spring Invasion*, monograph 3 in USAF Southeast Asia Monograph Series, ed., Arthur J. C. Lavalle (Washington

D.C.: Department of the Air Force, 1975–1979), 142, 197; Nordeen, *Air Warfare*, 64; G. H. Turley, "Time of Change in Modern Warfare," *Marine Corps Gazette*, December 1974, 18; CNA, "Documentation and Analysis of US Marine Corps Activity in Southeast Asia: 1 April–31 July 1972," 1:110, 1:111, Marine Corps Historical Center; and Lake and Hartman, "Air Electronic Warfare," 47.

32. Doglione, *Airpower and the 1972 Spring Invasion*, 132; Berger et al., *The USAF in Southeast Asia*, 168; Nordeen, *Air Warfare*, 64; House of Representatives, *Hearings before the Subcommittee of the Committee on Appropriations*, 93d Cong., 1st sess., 9 January 1973, 10; and CNA, "Summary of Air Operations in Southeast Asia: January 1972–31 January 1973," OEG/OP508N, January 1974, 4-17, 4-19.

33. Seymour Hersh, *The Price of Power—Kissinger in the Nixon White House* (New York: Summit Books, 1983), 506; and Richard Nixon, *RN: The Memoirs of Richard Nixon* (New York: Grosser & Dunlap, 1976), 606–7.

34. Guenter Lewy, *America in Vietnam* (New York: Oxford University, 1978), 410; and Hersh, *The Price of Power*, 526.

35. TAC, "SEA Tactics Review Brochure," 11, 68.

36. Guided weapons were expensive, limited by the weather, and few in number. See Directorate of Operations Analysis, Headquarters Pacific Air Forces, Project Contemporary Historical Examination of Current Operations Report, "Linebacker: Overview of the First 120 Days," 27 September 1973, 21, 27, AUL; and Nordeen, *Air Warfare*, 59, 63. One problem encountered with the ECM pods was that they created interference with the electro-optical guided bomb (EOGB) guidance system. A wire screen quickly solved that problem. See Patrick Breitling, "Guided Bomb Operations in SEA: The Weather Dimensions, 1 February–31 December 1972," Contemporary Historical Examination of Current Operations Report, 1 October 1973, 3, 24, AUL; Jeffery Rhodes, "Improving the Odds on Ground Attack," *Air Force Magazine*, November 1986, 48; Delbert Corum et al., *The Tale of Two Bridges*, monograph 1 in USAF Southeast Asia Monograph Series, ed., Arthur J. C. Lavalle (Washington, D.C.: Department of the Air Force, 1975–1979), 85–86; and Morita, "Implications of Modern Air Power," 6.

37. Michel, *Clashes*, 222; Momyer, *Air Power in Three Wars*, 129; Military Assistance Command, Vietnam, "Linebacker Study"; Nordeen, *Air Warfare*, 24; and Senate Committee on Armed Services, *Hearing on Fiscal Year 1974 Authorization*, 92d Cong., 2d sess., 13–20 March 1973, pt. 6:4275.

38. TAC, "SEA Tactics Review Brochure," 11, 78. During the period of 10 May through 10 September 1972, the United States lost 63 fixed-wing aircraft in combat over the north: 21 to AAA, 22 to MiGs, and 20 to SAMs.

39. Military Assistance Command, Vietnam, "Uncoordinated Draft," 7, chap. 8; Burbage, "Battle for the Skies," 267; Directorate of Operations Analysis, "Linebacker," 70–72; DOD, Office of the Assistant Secretary of Defense, "US Aircraft Losses in SE Asia," October 1973, table 351, 5; R. Mark Clodfelter, "By Other Means: An Analysis of the Linebacker Bombing Campaigns as Instruments of National Policy" (master's thesis, University of

Nebraska, 1983), 77; and CNA, "Summary of Air Ops in SEA: January 72–January 73," 4-1, 4-8, 4-19, 4-23.

40. Marvin and Bernard Kalb, *Kissinger* (Boston, Mass.: Little, Brown and Co., 1974), 412; Clodfelter, "By Other Means," 105, 111; W. Hays Parks, "Linebacker and the Law of War," *Air University Review* 34 (January–February 1983): 16; and Nixon, *RN: The Memoirs,* 734.

41. Broughton, *Thud Ridge,* 36.

42. Briefing Books IV, Headquarters US Air Force, details on the Linebacker II missions, 2 vols., December 1972, HRA.

43. Norman Polmar, ed., *Strategic Air Command—People, Aircraft, and Missiles* (Annapolis: Nautical & Aviation, 1979), 126; Granville, "Summary of USAF Aircraft Losses," 18; James McCarthy and George Allison, *Linebacker II—A View from the Rock* (Maxwell AFB, Ala.: Air Power Research Institute, 1979), 12; and Karl Eschmann, "The Role of Tactical Air Support: Linebacker II" (thesis, Air Command and Staff College, Maxwell AFB, Ala., 1985), 70–72, AUL.

44. "The Role of Tactical Support," 49, 70–72; and McCarthy and Allison, *Linebacker II,* 86. On these first three missions, 1.6 percent of the Ds and 4.9 percent of the Gs went down per sortie. In the entire 11-day campaign, the Ds suffered 1.8 percent and the Gs, 2.7 percent. About 10 percent of the missiles fired against the Gs impacted, whereas only 3 percent of those fired against the Ds impacted. See Headquarters US Air Force, briefing books, December 1972; briefing, Headquarters Pacific Air Forces, "Operations Analysis: Linebacker II Air Operations," 31 January 1973, HRA; McCarthy and Allison, *Linebacker II,* 70; and Eschmann, "The Role of Tactical Air Support," 49.

45. This policy quickly changed beginning with the second wave on the second day. See McCarthy and Allison, *Linebacker II,* 46–47.

46. Robert Clement, "A Fourth of July in December: A B-52 Navigator's Perspective of Linebacker II" (thesis, Air Command and Staff College, Maxwell AFB, Ala., 1984), 18, 49, AUL; and McCarthy and Allison, *Linebacker II,* 30, 32.

47. Headquarters USAF, "Linebacker USAF Bombing Survey," 1973, 35, HRA; TAC, "SEA Tactics Review Brochure," 11, 77; and Eschmann, "The Role of Tactical Support," 60.

48. Eschmann, "The Role of Tactical Support," 60, 63; and Clodfelter, "By Other Means," 121.

49. TAC, "SEA Tactics Review Brochure," 11, 76.

50. Strategic Air Command (SAC) Briefing, subject: Chaff Effectiveness in Support of Linebacker II Operations, March 1973, HRA.

51. TAC, "SEA Tactics Review Brochure," 11, 76.

52. "The Battle for the Skies over North Vietnam: 1964–1972," 94, HRA.

53. SAC, "Chaff Effectiveness," March 1973; and TAC, "SEA Tactics Review Brochure," 11, 76.

54. SAC, "Chaff Effectiveness," March 1973. For a general discussion of the changes, also see Clement, "A Fourth of July in December," 49; Eschmann, "The Role of Tactical Air Support," 75–76; McCarthy and Allison, *Linebacker II,*

97, 121; and History, 388th Tactical Fighter Wing, October–December 1972, 27, 32–33, HRA.

55. B-52s flew 708 effective sorties; F-llls, 148; A-7s, 226; and F-4s, 283. See Headquarters US Air Force, Briefing Books, II.

56. During periods of limited visibility, TAC fighters scored some remarkable successes, most notably hitting two especially difficult targets, the Hanoi thermal plant and Radio Hanoi. The latter, protected by a 25-foot high and 10-foot thick blast wall, had survived the bombing of 36 B-52s. F-4s got four laser-guided bombs inside the walls and destroyed the target. See Clodfelter, "By Other Means," 120; and Office of Assistant Chief of Staff, Intelligence (ACSI), "Lincbacker II: 18–29 December 72," supporting document III-KI, HRA.

57. History, Air Force Intelligence Service, 1 July 1972–30 June 1973: Linebacker Summary III, K2, HRA; CNA study, "US Navy, Marine Corps, and Air Force Fixed-Wing Aircraft Losses and Damage in Southeast Asia (1962–1973), Pt. 1: List of Aircraft Lost," report no. CRC 305 (Alexandria, Va.: Defense Documentation Center, 1977), 191–93, 223, 488–92, AUL; Eschmann, "The Role of Tactical Air Support," 103–4, lists 30 aircraft destroyed, including three lost in accidents. Futrell, *Aces and Aerial Victories,* 17, states that 27 US Air Force aircraft were lost. The North Vietnamese claimed 81 US aircraft (34 B-52s). See also Gareth Porter, *A Peace Denied—The United States, Vietnam, and the Paris Agreements* (Bloomington, Ind.: Indiana University, 1975), 161–62; and Richard Holloran, "Bombing Halt Brings Relief to B-52 Crews in Guam," *New York Times,* 2 January 1973, 3. Drenkowski, "Operation Linebacker II," pt. 2, 55, says that 22 to 27 B-52s were destroyed.

58. Clodfelter, "By Other Means," 108; and Clement, "A Fourth of July in December," 47.

59. Headquarters US Air Force, Briefing Books, I and II.

60. Eschmann, "The Role of Tactical Air Support," 108; Berger et al., *USAF in SEA,* 60; Drendel, *And Kill MiGs: Air to Air Combat,* 47, 73; SAC, "Chaff Effectiveness," March 1973; McCarthy and Allison, *Linebacker II,* 65, 116; and Futrell, *Aces and Aerial Victories,* 125.

61. Eschmann, "The Role of Tactical Air Support," 46.

62. CNA, "Summary of Air Ops SEA: January 72–January 73," 4-17. The North Vietnamese did not have the most modern equipment; in the 1973 Middle East War, Egyptians and Syrians inflicted heavy losses on Israeli aircraft with Soviet SA-3 and SA-6 missiles and ZSU-23-4 guns, equipment not employed in the Vietnam War. See chap. 4. The North Vietnamese may have improved and manned their defenses without the help or knowledge of the Soviets. See Porter, *A Peace Denied,* 161; and Jon Van Dyke, *North Vietnam's Strategy for Survival* (Palo Alto, Calif.: Pacific Books, 1972), 61, 217.

63. On the third day of the campaign, a SAC commander ordered a search for North Vietnamese SAM storage facilities. Within 18 hours, the intelligence people began to find them, whereupon SAC requested JCS permission to bomb them. Permission for all but one was forthcoming, although it took another 24 to 36 hours. As a result, these targets were not hit until

26 December. See McCarthy and Allison, *Linebacker II*, 97–98.

64. Ibid., 155; Eschmann, "The Role of Tactical Air Support," 94; and George Allison, "The Bombers Go to the Bullseye," *Aerospace Historian*, December 1982, 233; and History, 388th Tactical Fighter Wing, October–December 1972.

65. While several helicopters and transports were destroyed on the ground, intelligence claimed that only two to three MiG-21s were damaged. The bulk of the bombs fell on railroad yards (44 percent) and storage facilities (30 percent). See ACSI, "Linebacker II," Headquarters USAF, "Linebacker USAF Bombing Survey," 3, 14, 16–17, 40–43.

66. Clodfelter, "By Other Means," 127. The Airmen had also run out of worthwhile targets in the Hanoi-Haiphong area. See McCarthy and Allison, *Linebacker II*, 163.

67. It would be a historical mistake to maintain, however, that the same terms could have been reached in October. Some believe the Linebacker II bombing was as much aimed at the South Vietnamese (to reassure them of American support) as at the North Vietnamese.

68. Momyer, *Air Power in Three Wars*, 126; and Senate, *Hearing on Fiscal Year 1974 Authorization*, pt. 6:4253.

69. American antiaircraft gunners tracked very few targets during the course of the Vietnam War. There were at least two incidents of North Vietnamese aircraft attacking American ground or sea forces. Although some US Army AAA units served in the war, none fired their weapons against hostile aircraft. The Navy credits its gunners, however, with downing three North Vietnamese MiGs. The first fell to a Talos missile fired from the USS *Long Beach* in November 1968, the second to a Terrier fired by the USS *Sterett* on 19 April 1972, and the third to a Talos fired by the USS *Chicago* on 9 May 1972. See History, Seventh Fleet, 1972, enclosures 1, 20, 25, NHC; and McCrea, "Fixed-Wing Aircraft Losses and Damages," 2–30.

Chapter 4

Operations between Vietnam and the Persian Gulf

There have been several instances since the Vietnam War where ground-based air defense systems made significant contributions to the conduct of a conflict. This chapter discusses the Arab-Israeli Wars, American air strikes in the Middle East, Indo-Pakistani Wars, the Falkland War, and other recent and ongoing conflicts. During this period, air war shifted from dominance by the defense to dominance by the offense.

Arab-Israeli Wars: 1948, 1956, 1967–1973

Of the numerous non-American conflicts since World War II, none have stirred more military interest than those between Arabs and Jews. Their number, Israeli successes against great odds, and the employment of modern equipment on a large scale have helped to generate this interest. Israeli predominance in the air attracts particular attention. All of these wars illustrate the swings in dominance between offense and defense.

Although Arabs and Jews have been fighting each other for a long time, the Airmen's interest focuses on their conflicts since 1967, in which air power has played a significant role. Both sides employed aircraft in the 1948 and 1956 wars, but these forces consisted of small numbers of obsolete, or obsolescent, aircraft. In 1956, the Israelis lost 10 to 18 aircraft out of a total inventory of 136–55 and claimed eight aerial victories. In this war, the Egyptians lost 12, and the Anglo-Franco forces lost 10 aircraft. While the bulk of the Arab aircraft may have fallen in air-to-air combat, we would expect that ground fire downed most of the Israeli aircraft.[1] In the 1967 and 1973 conflicts, however, the combatants used modern equipment, and air power became critical, if not predominant.

It can be argued that air power won one of its most striking victories of all time in the June 1967 war. Preemptive strikes by the Israeli air force (IAF) on the first day destroyed the bulk of the numerically superior Arab air forces on the ground, permitting Israeli armor and close air support (CAS) aircraft to decisively crush the numerically superior Arab ground forces. On that first day, the IAF destroyed 85 percent of the Egyptian air force and 410 Arab aircraft in exchange for 19 aircraft lost (all but two or three to ground fire). This short, sharp war cost the Israelis 40 to 50 aircraft (all but three to 12 to ground fire). In contrast, the Arab air forces lost about 450 aircraft, mostly on the ground, with 60 to 79 to Israeli aircraft and about 50 to Israeli ground-based air defenses.[2]

Although the Egyptians had 18 to 25 batteries of SA-2s, these SAMs had no direct effect on the battle. Their operators fired perhaps a dozen missiles but claimed only one possible hit. While the unclassified sources do not mention a breakdown of Israeli credits for their surface-based air defense systems, apparently an Israeli Hawk downed an IAF A-4 on 5 June. The damaged fighter bomber apparently penetrated a restricted area around an Israeli nuclear facility.[3]

The Israelis gained a phenomenal military victory and new territories in the 1967 war, but they did not win peace. Soviet resupply of Arab clients led to a drawn-out land and air war of attrition along the Suez Canal, the new border between Egypt and Israel. Between July 1967 and January 1970, the IAF lost 15 aircraft (13 to ground fire), while it claimed 74 Egyptian and Syrian aircraft. In September–October 1969, the IAF took out the Egyptian SAMs along the canal. In January 1970, the Israelis received US ECM pods and, within three months, neutralized the Egyptian air defense system by destroying three-fourths of its early warning radar. The offensive was again triumphant.

The Soviets countered in early 1970 by sending more missiles, including the SA-3, to Egypt. Although the SA-3's range was about one-third to one-half that of the SA-2 (slant range of 13–17 miles compared to the SA-2's slant range of 25–30 miles), the former could operate against lower-flying aircraft. The missiles became operational in April 1970, and by the end of June, the Egyptians had 55 SAM batteries. Soviet technicians and operators bolstered the Egyptian air defenses, which, in essence, they took over. The air war heated up in late June when SAMs downed three IAF aircraft in one week. In response, the IAF attacked and destroyed five Egyptian SAM batteries. On 8 July 1970, the two opponents agreed to a cease-fire; and, although the battle subsided, tensions remained, and the lull permitted the Egyptians to rebuild their defenses along the canal. In the War of Attrition (July 1967 to May 1973), the Israelis lost 27 aircraft (25 to ground fire), and the Arabs lost 162 aircraft, most in air-to-air conflict, but at least 13 to Hawks and 24 to 37 mm and 40 mm guns.[4]

The 1973 War

The joint Egyptian-Syrian attack on Israel on 6 October 1973 took the world and the Israelis by surprise. Because of the overwhelming superiority of the IAF, no one expected the Arab armies to win; therefore, no one expected them to attack. In addition, conventional wisdom held that air superiority was vital to victory. After all, aviation had ruled the battlefield since 1939, or, put another way, victory was possible only under friendly or at least neutral skies. This view conveniently over-looked the various guerrilla wars and, most especially, the Vietnam War. During the first days of the conflict, the two Arab states used their air forces sparingly. They relied primarily on ground-based air defense systems and were modest in their air plans, attempting only to gain local and limited air superiority. On day one, the Egyptians flew 200–240 sorties while their armies advanced under a protective umbrella of surface-based air defense weapons.

This air defense umbrella was massive, mixed, and mobile. The Egyptians emphasized their surface-based air defense force (formed as a separate service in 1968) that had three times as many personnel as did their air force and made up one-fourth of their total armed forces. The Syrian air defense was smaller but denser because of the smaller battlefield. The Syrians manned nearly 47 SAM batteries (32–35 SA-6s and the rest SA-2s and SA-3s), while the Egyptians operated 150 batteries, of which 46 were SA-6s.[5]

The Arabs fielded not only a large number but also a great assortment of Soviet equipment. The vast number of guns was imposing and included a small number of the new four-barrel

23 mm ZSU-23-4. The missile arsenal included the SA-2 and the SA-7 employed in Vietnam, the SA-3 employed in the War of Attrition, and a new missile, the SA-6. The Arab air defense system was more than just large and varied, for, unlike the immobile North Vietnamese defenses (except for light AAA and SA-7s), the Arab air defenses could move, as both the ZSU-23-4 and SA-6 were vehicle-mounted, and the SA-7 was man-portable. What must be emphasized is that the impact of the Arab air defenses came from the combination of numbers, mixture, mobility, and modernity, as the IAF soon found out.[6]

The SA-6, the most modern of these weapons, had been observed in 1967 but had not been seen in action. It was a relatively small missile, weighing about 1,200 pounds and permitting three to be mounted on a (PT-76) tank chassis (fig. 67). Its size, speed, and smokeless sustainer engine made it difficult to spot visually. The missile was faster (Mach 2.5–2.8) and much more sophisticated than the other Soviet SAMs, as it used

Figure 67. SA-6. The mobile SA-6 did not see service over Vietnam, but was effective against the Israeli air force in the 1973 war. (Reprinted from US Army Air Defense Museum.)

radar to guide its initial flight and rapidly changed frequencies and then homed in on its prey using heat-seeking sensors. Perhaps more important, it employed radar frequencies outside of the range covered by Israeli ECM. (The SA-6 used a filter, as did the SA-7, to counter the use of flares intended to decoy its infrared sensor.) Its slant range of 17–25 miles is comparable to the SA-2's and the SA-3's; additionally, the SA-6 can kill aircraft flying at low altitudes. Therefore, the combination of newness, mobility, high speed, sophisticated guidance, and low-altitude capability gave the SA-6 great potential. While it did not produce the 97-percent kill rate promised by the Soviets, it downed many aircraft and forced IAF aircraft into Arab AAA, especially the ZSU-23.[7]

The ZSU-23-4 was a very effective AAA piece (fig. 68). Mounted on a PT-76 tank chassis, its four 23 mm barrels could fire at a maximum rate of 4,000 shots per minute, although gunners never just held the trigger down but instead were trained to fire in short bursts of 75 or so rounds. Radar with a 12-mile

Figure 68. ZSU-23. The ZSU-23-4 proved an unpleasant surprise for Israeli aircraft in the 1973 Middle East War. It mounted four 23 mm cannons guided by radar on a tracked vehicle. (Reprinted from US Army Air Defense Museum.)

range directed the guns, which could reach an effective range of about 4,000 feet. There were also optical sights. Similar to the SA-6, the weapon's chief assets were its low-altitude capability, mobility, and the absence of previous observation in action by the West.[8]

Following the initial Arab assault, as expected, the Israelis quickly launched tank and aircraft counterattacks to blunt the advance of the invading Arab armies, to succor the outnumbered and outgunned forward defenders, and to shield its own mobilization. However, Israel's tankers, airmen, equipment, and tactics failed against Arab missiles and guns. On the Suez front, the IAF lost four aircraft in their first strike; and, on the Golan Heights front, they lost four out of four aircraft on the first wave and two of four aircraft on the second wave. Some claim that Arab gunners downed as many as 30 to 40 Israeli aircraft on the first day of the war.

During the first three days, the IAF lost dozens of aircraft, perhaps as many as 50, at the Suez front. These heavy losses (twice the rate of the 1967 war) shocked the Israelis, who, for the moment, stopped flying within 10–15 miles of the Suez Canal. However, the grave military situation required the IAF to continue its efforts, especially on the critical Syrian front. During the first week, the IAF lost a total of 78–90 aircraft, a sizable percentage of its force.[9]

The SA-7 had little direct impact on the battle and probably served most as a nuisance to the Israelis and a morale booster to the Arabs. The shoulder-fired SAM downed only two fixed-wing aircraft and damaged 30 others. Aircraft could outrun and outmaneuver the missile, as US Airmen had proved the year before. In addition, the SA-7 lacked killing power; it hit aircraft in their tail, where its small warhead usually did not inflict catastrophic damage. A vehicle-mounted arrangement, the SA-8, fitted with eight SA-7s, was no more effective.[10]

On the other hand, the SA-6 proved especially effective by destroying a sizable proportion of IAF aircraft and indirectly by forcing Israeli aircraft into Arab AAA fire. The SAM's rapid speed and its new and changing frequencies were difficult to counter. The overconfidence of the Israelis, their neglect of ECM (at one point, the IAF stripped ECM from their aircraft for greater economy, speed, and maneuverability), and US restrictions on ECM sales left the IAF in a serious bind. The result was that "The IAF could go anywhere except near the Golan Heights and the Suez fronts, where it was needed most. As they had begun to do three years earlier, the Soviet missiles successfully redefined the nature of modern war."[11] In response, Israeli improvisation was speedy and effective, yet costly.

The IAF used a variety of means to deal with the SAM threat. To defeat heat-seeking missiles, it employed violent maneuvers, turning toward the missile to present the IR seeker a "cold side," and maneuvering aircraft to cross in the sky creating a "hot spot." In addition, Israeli airmen dropped flares, even jettisoned fuel, and then ignited it to decoy the heat-seeking missiles. Spotters in helicopters warned pilots of missile launches. The IAF also used chaff, first carried in speed brakes, later in a more conventional manner; improved American ECM pods; and standoff jammers operating from the ground, helicopters, and transports.

In addition, the Israelis directly assaulted the SA-6s. The SA-6's low initial trajectory encouraged the IAF to dive-bomb the SAMs from very steep angles—desperate measures improvised for a desperate situation. The IAF also fired Shrike anti-radiation missiles.[12]

The Israelis turned around the air war and to a degree the ground action by taking out the Arab SAMs. Concentrating first on the Syrians, the IAF destroyed half of their SAMs in four days. Another factor that aided the IAF was that the Syrians ran out of SA-6s. One source claims that the Israelis knocked out a Syrian control center that seriously hampered the Syrian missile defenses. The Syrians were defeated, and only political restraints prevented a much greater Israeli victory.[13]

The solution to the IAF's problem on the Egyptian front came from an unexpected source, the Israeli army. The Egyptians made one major thrust from their formidable position along the canal, venturing outside of their protective antiaircraft cover, and suffering a decisive defeat on 14 October in the largest tank battle since World War II. The Israelis quickly followed up their tactical victory. In the early morning of 16 October, Israeli forces crossed the canal and in short order created havoc in the Egyptian army. By midday, the Israelis had destroyed four SAM sites, and by the next morning, the IAF was operating in full support of the ground forces. In reverse of the accepted practice, the army made it possible for the air force to operate. According to one account, an Israeli armored division destroyed 34 missile batteries, about one-half of the Egyptian SAMs defending the canal. The Israelis now had the initiative and easily could have inflicted an overwhelming defeat on the Egyptians. But, the major powers intervened, which led to a cease-fire on 22 October. The Israelis won the war and in the process destroyed approximately 40 of the 55–60 SAM batteries that the Egyptians had in action. This destruction was inflicted by the IAF, as well as by Israeli ground forces.[14]

Nevertheless, the ground-based air defenses took a substantial toll. Secondary sources state that the Arabs lost 40 to 75 aircraft (one or two dozen to Hawks) and the Israelis perhaps 82 to 100 to SAMs and flak.[15] A US Army study put the total number of Israeli losses at 109, 81 to ground-based air defenses. The study credits AAA with 31 aircraft, SAMs (other than SA-7) 40, SA-7s 4, and a combination of SAMs and AAA 6. Of the 516 Arab aircraft losses, the study attributed 36 to ground weapons, 42 to 20 mm guns, and 23 to Hawks.[16]

The ground defenses also claimed a number of friendly aircraft. Israeli gunners apparently downed two of their own aircraft, which probably were Mirages mistaken for the same type aircraft the Egyptians received from the Libyans. The Arabs destroyed 45 to 60 of their own aircraft. On 8 October, for example, Syrian SAMs destroyed 20 Iraqi MiGs, while Egyptian SA-6s may have downed 40 Egyptian aircraft. Thus, Arab SAMs destroyed more Arab aircraft (45–58) than Israeli aircraft (39–44). This "friendly fire" accounted for about 10 to 12 percent of total Arab losses.[17]

Helicopters again proved vulnerable. Israeli air and ground defenses devastated an Egyptian commando strike on the first day of the war, downing 20–35 of approximately 50 Mi-8 helicopters. An Egyptian attack on the critical Israeli canal bridge on 18 October ended with all five helicopters downed. On the Arab side, SA-7s claimed six IAF rotary-wing aircraft.[18]

The IAF clearly won the air war, destroying about 450 Arab aircraft, while losing about 107 aircraft in combat, 115 overall. Compared to the 1967 war, the Arabs lost about the same number of aircraft—although many more in the air—while the Israelis lost twice as many. On a sortie basis, however, IAF losses actually declined from 4 percent in 1967 to just over 1 percent in 1973. Arab losses in 1973 were just under 5 percent.[19]

Although the IAF defeated the Arab air forces in the air, it failed to use air power as it had in the 1967 war. CAS proved limited and disappointing, especially in the first three critical days of the war. One study concluded that aircraft did not unequivocally damage or destroy one tank. Even if this decline in CAS effectiveness is overdrawn, air power clearly influenced the war less in 1973 than it had in 1967. A dense, mobile, mixed, surface-based air defense system thwarted arguably the best-trained and highest motivated air force in the world and inflicted severe losses on it. Just as American Airmen underestimated North Vietnamese air defenses, so had the Israeli airmen underestimated Arab air defenses. Both paid the price. The 1973 war seemed to indicate that the balance between the offense and defense (specifically aircraft versus ground defenses) had swung in favor of the latter. Aircraft appeared to have lost its battlefield dominance.[20] The IAF action in Lebanon in the summer of 1982 altered this view.

Combat since 1973: Bekaa Valley

Lebanon existed in a state of chaos from the occupation by militias of right and left, Palestinian guerrillas, the Syrian army, and from fighting among these groups and between them and the Israelis. The Syrians rebuilt their military forces from the defeat of the 1973 war and, in so doing, almost tripled their ground-based air defenses, increasing them from 30 to 80 batteries and manning them with their best personnel. In late April 1981, the Syrians moved 19 missile batteries, including SA-6s, into Lebanon's Bekaa Valley. Here, the Syrians established a dense and, what appeared from the record of the 1973 war, to be a formidable air defense system.[21]

In early June 1982, the Israelis invaded Lebanon, primarily fighting the Palestinian guerrillas but also engaging the Syrians. The Israelis battered the latter, despite their large arsenal of modern Soviet equipment and the "lessons" of the 1973 war. In this brief but intense action, the Israelis won a lopsided victory, destroying 80 to 90 Syrian aircraft and 19 to 36 batteries of missiles, for the destruction of three to six Israeli aircraft. In addition, Israeli ground fire downed at least one Syrian jet (a Vulcan gun got an Su-7) and two helicopters.[22]

On 9 June, the IAF took on the Syrian air defenses in the Bekaa Valley with a complex, carefully planned, well-coordinated, and effectively executed attack. The Israelis used air- and ground-launched drones as decoys to activate Syrian radar. This allowed the Israeli EC-135s to obtain the location and frequency of the Syrian radars, information they rapidly relayed to strike elements. The Israelis thereby coupled real-time intelligence with rapid response to give their pilots precise locations of the SAMs and accurate tuning information for their jamming equipment. In the electronics war, the IAF used ECM pods, chaff rockets, possibly chaff from drones, and standoff jammers in CH-53, Boeing 707, and Arava transports. The Israeli airmen employed diversionary tactics, precise timing, sharply executed low-level tactics, and weapons such as ARMs, standoff munitions, iron bombs, and cluster bombs. In addition, the Israelis used a new surface-to-surface ARM, the Wolf missile. Ground forces fired artillery, launched ground assaults along the front, and just before the air attack, took out a control center with a commando raid. The Syrians did not help their own cause, as they failed to dig in, sited their radar poorly, and ignited smoke screens that guided, rather than confused, the IAF. On the first day, the IAF destroyed 17 missile batteries and severely damaged two others. The Syrians pushed more SAM units into the Bekaa Valley, but to no avail. On the second day of the action, the IAF destroyed 11 more missile batteries. On 24 July, the Israelis knocked out three batteries of SA-8s. A few days later, they destroyed some SA-9s. Reportedly, the IAF destroyed four SA-9 batteries in September (fig. 69).[23]

Figure 69. SA-9. The Soviet SA-9 mounts eight SA-7 missiles on a mobile platform. (Reprinted from USAF.)

American Air Strikes in the Middle East, 1983–1986

American strikes in the Middle East a little more than a year later were much less successful. The United States intervened in Lebanon in 1983, and that December the US Navy responded to Syrian firing on American reconnaissance aircraft with an air strike consisting of 12 A-7Es and 16 A-6Es. The naval aviators used tactics proven in Vietnam: they penetrated at 20,000 feet, then descended to 3,000 feet for their attacks. To counter Syrian heat-seeking missiles, they dropped numerous decoy flares—but to little effect. The American flyers encountered intense defenses, more than expected, and Soviet SA-7 and SA-9 missiles modified to counter the decoy flares. The Syrians launched 40–50 SAMs, which downed one A-7 and one A-6 and damaged another A-7. While the Navy blamed the losses on changes in Soviet missile sensors, the Israelis criticized American planning, tactics, and experience. Later Syrian fire against US aircraft was met by ship bombardment.[24]

This less-than-satisfactory experience jarred the Americans and probably influenced the next US air operation, the April 1986 raid on Libya. One factor driving American planning was to avoid the SA-7s, which meant operating at night. There were, of course, other reasons for night operations, such as achieving maximum surprise, avoiding a major engagement with Libyan air defenses, avoiding casualties to both Soviet advisers and Libyan civilians, and revealing as little American ECM as possible. However, night operations also meant that only two American aircraft could be effectively used: the Air Force's FB-111 and the Navy's A-6. While the A-6s were aboard carriers cruising in the Mediterranean, the FB-111 bombers were stationed in Britain, a round-trip of 5,600 miles (a 14-hour flight). The FB-111s would require numerous aerial refueling because of the distance and air space overflight restrictions.[25]

US Airmen launched a large strike force of 32 bombers (18 FB-111s and 14 A-6s) supported by almost 70 aircraft. The mammoth supporting force was required because Libyan air defenses were both large and sophisticated for a third world country. Besides MiGs, the defenses consisted of 100 batteries of SA-2s, SA-3s, and SA-6s (about 30 to 60 batteries were operational), as well as SA-5, SA-8, SA-9, and French Crotale missiles, and perhaps 450 AAA guns.[26]

American aircraft successfully penetrated Libyan defenses, suppressing and evading fire from Libyan SAMs and AAA and encountering no aerial opposition. Airmen used low-level and high-speed tactics—the FB-111s at 400 feet and 500 knots, the A-6s as low as 200 feet and 450 knots—to deliver both laser-guided and iron bombs. One FB-111 went down, the cause was not publicly known. Although the Libyans received 30 to 45 minutes' notice from Maltese air controllers that unidentified aircraft were heading for North Africa, apparently Libyan radar did not activate until about four minutes before the 0200 attack. Standoff jamming by EF-111s and EA-6Bs, on-board ECM, and about 50 antiradiation missiles almost completely nullified Libyan radar. The mission was both a technical and political success: the Airmen got their bombs on target (mostly), losses were light (one FB-111 downed), and since the air attack, there has been a lack of terrorist activity openly and directly associated with the Libyans. Thus, the 12-minute raid demonstrated that the American military could hit difficult targets despite distance and other natural obstacles as well as penetrate numerous and sophisticated defenses with light losses.[27]

Indo–Pakistani War

In September 1965, war erupted on the Asian subcontinent between India and Pakistan and lasted 23 days. Both sides fielded small air forces equipped with a few modern aircraft (Indian MiG-21s and Pakistani F-104s), but most aircraft were at least a decade beyond their prime (Indian Hunters and Vampires and Pakistani F-86s).

Just as the ground war ended in a stalemate, so did the air war. But even at this writing (2005), it is difficult from the conflicting claims to sort out exactly what happened. The Pakistanis claim to have destroyed 110 Indian aircraft, 35 in air-to-air combat, 32 by antiaircraft guns, and the remainder in attacks on airfields. They admit to losing 19 aircraft, eight in air combat, two to their own AAA, and nine to other causes. The Pakistanis admit that Indian guns downed a few aircraft but claim that none of the F-86s engaged in almost 500 CAS sorties were lost, although 58 were damaged. The Indians claim 73 Pakistani aircraft were destroyed and admitted losing 35. The Indians fired a few SA-2 missiles and claimed one C-130. The Pakistanis dispute this claim, stating that they did not lose a C-130 to the SAMs, and counter that the SA-2 got an Indian An-12 transport. The Pakistanis do admit that an SA-2 damaged an RB-57F at 52,000 feet.[28]

In December 1971, the two countries fought another brief (two-week) war. By this time, both sides had upgraded their air forces in quality and quantity but still fielded forces that were relatively small and of mixed vintage. Pakistan lost the war and its eastern territory—what is now Bangladesh. Again, the combatants' claims markedly conflict, and these differences remain along with the political problems. Indians claimed to have destroyed 94 Pakistani aircraft for the loss of 54 and stated that one aircraft fell to an SA-2 missile. The Pakistanis claimed the destruction of 104 Indian aircraft at the cost of 26 planes. They admit losing three to four aircraft to flak as well as two aircraft to friendly fire. The Pakistanis assert that AAA registered 49 of their 104 kills. Another source states that one-half of the lost Pakistani aircraft fell to ground defenses.[29]

The Falkland Islands/Malvinas War, 1982

Early in the 1980s, another brief campaign in a remote part of the world captured the public's attention. The Falkland campaign surprised the civilians and military alike on a number of counts: that Argentina and Britain went to war, Britain successfully liberated the islands over such a great distance, and Argentina inflicted startling losses on the more modern British forces. The conflict pitted a small, well-trained, and well-equipped modern force of a European nation operating 7,000 miles from home against a larger, less well-trained conscript force armed with a mixture of old and modern equipment of a developing nation.

From the standpoint of the air war, the Argentines fielded an air force of mixed capabilities equipped with old Canberras and A-4s, counterinsurgency Pucaris, and the more modern Mirages and Super Etendards. For ground-based defenses, the Argentines had, in addition to automatic weapons, British (Sea Dart, Seacat, and Blowpipe) and Franco-German (Roland) surface-to-air missiles (fig. 70).

Although the British used the old Vulcan bomber, their primary combat aircraft was the vertical-takeoff-and-landing Harrier. The Royal Navy ships operated a mixture of gun defenses and SAMs (Seacat, Seawolf, Sea Dart, and Seaslug) (fig. 71). British troops ashore used three SAM systems: Blowpipe, Stinger, and Rapier.[30]

Figure 70. Blowpipe. The British Blowpipe was another shoulder-fired SAM. It was used by both sides in the Falklands War, and both sides claimed it downed aircraft. (Reprinted from Imperial War Museum.)

The Argentine air defense proved minimal against the British Harriers and helicopters. However, it should be quickly noted that, in contrast to the Argentine air force, which flew and fought without ECM, the British employed both airborne ECM jammers aboard Vulcan bombers, chaff dispensers on Sea Harriers, shipborne ECM jammers, and Corvus chaff rockets. The British used antiradiation missiles (Shrikes) against the

Figure 71. Sea Dart launch. The Sea Dart, shown here in a peacetime launch, equipped both Argentine and British forces. It downed five to eight Argentine aircraft. (Reprinted from Imperial War Museum.)

main Falkland-based Argentine radar without success, but the missile did destroy one other radar set.[31] The Argentine air arms lacked similar weapons. Argentine fire destroyed 22 British aircraft, 13 of which were helicopters destroyed aboard ships sunk or damaged by air attack. Argentine ground fire destroyed all but one of the remaining nine, a Scout helicopter downed by a Pucari. The British flew 2,000 sorties but state that they lost only five Harriers in combat: one to a Roland missile, one to small arms, and three to 35 mm antiaircraft fire (fig. 72). Small arms or Blowpipe missiles accounted for three Gazelle helicopters. One source claims that the Argentines engaged two of their own helicopters—not unlikely, as both sides flew the same kind of machines.[32]

The effectiveness of the Argentine air force provided one of the big surprises of the war, especially considering its limita-

Figure 72. Roland launch. The Roland was developed by the French, who claimed it destroyed four British aircraft in the Falklands War, a claim denied by the British. (Reprinted from Redstone Arsenal.)

tions. The Argentine airmen flew mostly outdated aircraft during daytime, in clear weather, without ECM, and at the limits of their range. In addition, with the exception of five French-made Exocet missiles, they dropped gravity bombs on targets (mainly ships) that they had not been trained to engage. Nevertheless, they sank seven ships and damaged another dozen. British losses could have been far worse, but at least one-fifth (perhaps three-quarters) of the Argentine bombs failed to explode due to faulty fuze settings, defective fuzes or bombs, and most of all, to extremely low-level and short bomb releases. (One-half of the dozen ships damaged were hit by dud bombs.) The Argentine pilots demonstrated their courage and dedication by their repeated attacks, despite the formidable odds and high losses. For example, between 21 and 25 May, they lost 19 aircraft on 117 sorties.[33]

The British also operated under a number of severe handicaps in the campaign. The British supply line stretched 7,000 miles between the Falkland Islands and Britain, relieved only by the spare, American-operated base on Ascension Island. The British had only two small carriers available to support the campaign. (The British planned to reduce even this small force. Thus, had the Argentines delayed their action, British difficulties would have multiplied.) Their small decks forced the British to rely for air superiority on a handful of Harriers, an aircraft neither designed nor equipped for such a role. British ship designs also proved flawed in that damage-control systems were inadequate, and some of the ships lacked armored cables. Initially, only two ships in the invasion fleet carried modern missiles (Seawolf) for defense against low-level attacks.

Combat revealed the biggest British problem to be the lack of early warning aircraft. Although the British brilliantly and rapidly improvised to make good other serious deficiencies (such as adapting the land-based Harrier GR3 to operate off aircraft carriers, expanding air-to-air refueling capabilities, mating the Sidewinder to the Harrier, and installing ECM aboard the Vulcan), this one glaring gap remained. In addition, the inadequacy of early warning proved costly to the British. In short, the British entered the conflict ill prepared.[34]

British authorities claimed the destruction of 72 aircraft in the air, not an unreasonable number when compared with the Argentine admission of 36 pilots killed in the campaign on 505 sorties. They believe that the Harriers downed 20 aircraft; small arms, as many as six; and naval 4.5-inch guns, one. Forty-five aircraft fell to various surface-to-air missiles.[35]

As usual, these numbers are probably overstated. Secondary accounts based on Argentine documents and interviews put total Argentine air losses between 44 and 55. The most detailed account, based upon Argentine sources, puts the losses to the Harriers at 21; to SAMs, 18; AAA, 3 (fig. 73); and friendly fire, to at least two.[36]

The official British account credits the Blowpipe with destroying nine Argentine aircraft, while other authors say the true number is from two to four. The troops who carried the 47-pound Blowpipe across the difficult Falklands' terrain criticized its weight. This is understandable under the circumstances, but the missile did give the troops some protection against Argentine

Figure 73. Bofors 40 mm shipboard. In addition to numerous SAMs, the Royal Navy retained guns to protect against air strikes. This Bofors 40 mm L/60 and crew are aboard either the HMS *Fearless* or HMS *Intrepid* during the Falklands War. (Reprinted from Imperial War Museum.)

aircraft. The Blowpipe, like the SA-7 and the American Redeye and Stinger, is operated by one man; but, unlike the heat-seeking Soviet and American devices, Blowpipe is optically guided. It proved it could do the job, both ashore and afloat. One detachment aboard a Royal Fleet auxiliary fired six missiles and claimed three aircraft destroyed. The Argentines also used the Blowpipe and claimed hits on one Harrier and two helicopters. In addition, the British used the lighter-weight Stinger but fired only four missiles for one kill. (However, there is some controversy about that particular claim.)[37]

The British initially credited the Rapier, their other ground-based SAM, with 13 kills, later raised to 20 (fig. 74). Just as the Roland kills are hotly disputed by the British, so are the Rapier kills by those who have seen Argentine documents and talked to Argentine pilots. (Perhaps this argument has more to do with future sales of these weapons than with history.) Authors using Argentine sources put the Rapier credits at one to three. While the British stated that the campaign validates the

Figure 74. Rapier. Another British SAM employed in the Falklands campaign was the Rapier. (Reprinted from USAF.)

weapon, the question of the actual kills casts some doubt on these assertions. The army unit (T Battery) fired only with optical tracking and achieved 40 percent of its kills in the tail-chase mode. The missile's kinetic (direct hit) system coupled with contact (not proximity) fuzes worked well, as British gunners often had to fire over their own men and ships. Firing over friendly forces also highlighted the manual-control feature (it is not a fire-and-forget weapon), which proved useful because the operator could pull the missile off a target if it flew behind friendly forces.[38]

The British naval air defense concept consisted of Harriers as air cover, destroyers armed with Sea Dart missiles as long-range defenses, and a close-in air defense of ships armed with guns and other missiles. The British claim that Royal Navy SAMs downed 21 aircraft. The large Seaslug missile, which entered service in 1962, received no credits. The two-stage Sea Dart destroyed five to eight aircraft, but more importantly, forced Argentine aircraft into low-level tactics. However, it could handle only one target at a time, as was dramatically demonstrated when four A-4s attacked the HMS *Coventry* (fig. 75). The destroyer's Sea Darts destroyed the first two Argentine aircraft,

Figure 75. HMS *Coventry*. Argentine airmen suffered high losses in the Falklands War but pressed home attacks that nearly repelled the British counter invasion. They sank a number of ships, one of which was the HMS *Coventry*. (Reprinted from http://www.jove.prohosting.com-sinking/falklands/shtml.)

but the third scored a direct hit, which sank the ship. According to the manufacturer, obsolescent radar and computers hampered the missile. In addition, seas rougher than anticipated in its design degraded the system's performance against low-flying aircraft.[39]

The small, short-range Seacat began development in 1958 and is in service with a number of countries (fig. 76). Although British sources credit it with eight kills, other sources put this figure at one. The other short-range missile system was the more advanced Seawolf. Although clearly a better system than the Seacat, which it was designed to replace, Seawolf was only fitted on two ships. (Argentine duds hit both.) Nevertheless, this SAM received credit for downing three to five aircraft and at least one air-to-surface missile.[40]

Regardless of the actual number of kills and the dispute over claims, the fact is the Royal Navy's defenses proved barely adequate; the Argentine air force came close to driving off the

Figure 76. Seacat. The short-range British Seacat was an older SAM used by the Royal Navy, as well as by the Argentines. There is some dispute as to its effectiveness in the Falklands War. This picture is of a training exercise before that war. (Reprinted from Imperial War Museum.)

British fleet. The Argentine air force sank seven ships and hit another dozen.[41] Clearly, the Argentines came off better in the air-sea battle in terms of resources expended. Each British ship cost tens if not hundreds of millions of dollars; the HMS *Sheffield*, for example, cost $225 million. Argentine Exocets and aircraft cost far less, approximately $200,000 for the missiles and perhaps $5 million for a modern jet fighter.[42] But, the British did win the war and did achieve their national objective.

Other Actions in the 1980s

There were no major air operations by developed powers in the 1980s. Three other actions deserve mention, however, before moving on to the next major conflict. Ground-based air defenses played varying roles in the Iran-Iraq War, the invasion of Grenada, and the Afghan-Soviet War.

The war between Iran and Iraq was the bloodiest conflict since the Korean War. Both countries had considerable quantities of relatively modern aircraft and air defense equipment: the Iranians using American aircraft and British and American missiles (Hawk, Rapier, and Tigercat); and the Iraqis relying on Soviet equipment, including 70 SAM batteries (SA-2s, SA-3s, and a few SA-6s). Reportedly, both sides lost about 150 aircraft by the end of 1981, with most of the combat losses to ground weapons. Neither side made effective use of SAMs, but man-portable SAMs did have a major impact on the air war. While registering few hits, perhaps one for every 20 to 30 fired, the missiles forced attacking aircraft higher and thus degraded their effectiveness. The inability of either side to make good use of modern technology stems from problems with parts, maintenance, and training. In addition, the main objective of both air forces apparently was to avoid attrition and defeat and to deter attacks. The lessons of this conflict therefore may be that modern equipment does not automatically make modern forces and that air forces without access to secure support and resupply may adopt a defensive strategy to preserve their forces.[43]

In contrast to the long and costly Iran-Iraq War, US action in Grenada was short and cheap. The 1984 invasion will probably best be remembered for its nonmilitary aspects; nevertheless, air power played a significant role in the short, one-sided operation. The United States faced neither hostile aircraft nor any heavy antiaircraft weapons (greater than 23 mm), only small arms and 24 ZSU-23 guns, lacking radar guidance. Despite this imbalance, the defenders downed four helicopters (a fifth was destroyed after colliding with a damaged helicopter) and severely damaged at least four others (fig. 77). The loss of so many machines against such minor resistance here and in the 1975 *Mayaguez* incident, during which eight of nine helicopters employed were disabled, again raised the question of helicopter survival in combat operations.[44]

Finally, in recent years guerrilla groups have claimed success against aircraft. Although it is difficult to separate insurgents'

Figure 77. Helicopter kill in Grenada. The 1983 American invasion of Grenada was not much of a war due to the overwhelming US military superiority. Nevertheless, antiaircraft guns shot down four Army helicopters, again demonstrating their vulnerability to ground fire. (Reprinted from http://www.2arts.net/.../grenada_thumbs_downed_helicoper.htm.)

claims from their propaganda, a number of aircraft have gone down in anti-guerrilla operations in Angola, Chad, Nicaragua, and the Sudan. Whether they were victims of SAMs, small arms, operational problems, or propaganda remains to be determined. In any case, the acquisition of shoulder-launched SAMs gives the guerrillas a potent antiaircraft weapon.[45]

The man-portable SAM has had an impact on air warfare. Airmen—Americans in Vietnam and Soviets in Afghanistan— quickly found countermeasures to the first-generation SA-7 and Redeye missiles. Both missiles are limited by lack of electronic identification capability and three performance factors: they are strictly tail-chase (revenge) weapons, susceptible to decoy flares, and are restricted in maneuverability. The second-generation Stinger is a different story. It is a foot longer than the four-foot Redeye and weighs an additional 16 pounds. More importantly, the Stinger has improved its performance in four areas. In addition to having an electronic IFF capability, the Stinger has a forward-firing capability, more resistance to decoy flares, greater speed, and outranges the two-mile Redeye by a mile. General Dynamics began development of the Stinger in 1971, and it became operational in 1981. The missile's biggest success has been in Afghanistan. In fact, its influence in that conflict prompted one reporter to write, "What the long-bow was to English yeomen . . . the Stinger antiaircraft missile is to today's American-backed guerrilla fighters."[46]

The war in Afghanistan clearly shows how missile technology has given the guerrillas a valuable weapon. Initially, the Soviets, while bogged down on the ground and largely confined to the cities and fortified positions, made effective and growing use of both fixed-wing and rotary-wing aircraft against sparse rebel antiaircraft defenses (the United States sent 40 20 mm guns in 1985), including SA-7 missiles. Soviet successes prompted the United States to increase its support. In 1985, Blowpipes were ordered, and reportedly, the rebels received 225 missiles. Then, after an intra-governmental battle that pitted the US State Department against the Central Intelligence Agency, in which the former prevailed, the United States in late 1985 decided to send Stingers to the insurgents.

The American Stingers were initially criticized for their weight and complexity, but after a month in which 11 were fired without a miss, they clearly demonstrated their effectiveness. One secondary account asserts that the rebels scored their first confirmed Stinger kills in late September 1986, downing three Hind helicopters. Other accounts claim that the guerrillas downed two helicopters and one fighter in October and 11 helicopters and one MiG-23 in November (fig. 78). These losses forced the Soviets to fly higher, to operate at farther distances from their targets, and to restrict, if not abandon, their gunship strikes, markedly reducing the military effectiveness of air power and the Soviet military in general. In February 1987, Air Force chief of staff Larry Welch testified that "somewhere between 150 and 300 Stingers have absolutely driven the Russian air force out of the skies in Afghanistan."[47] The rebels claimed to have downed as many as 15 to 20 Soviet helicopters a month and by the summer of 1987 may have downed one aircraft a

Figure 78. Helicopter kill in Afghanistan. Afghan forces downed this Soviet helicopter in 1979. The later introduction of shoulder-fired SAMs, particularly the Stinger, shifted the balance of the air war and played a major role in the Soviet withdrawal. (Reprinted from USAF.)

day. During the fall 1987 offensive, the Afghan government reportedly lost 17 helicopters, an An-22 transport, and four MiG-21s to the Stingers. A US Army study estimated that the Afghans achieved 269 hits from the 340 Stingers they fired.

The Stinger's impact goes beyond the aircraft losses and less effective offensive tactics. A Western journal reports that 20 Afghanistan pilots refused to fly against rebel positions defended by the American-built missiles. The leader of the Afghanistan Communist Party acknowledged the weapon's effectiveness and how it changed the conflict, noting that in the siege of Khost, a city about 100 miles south of Kabul, US and British SAMs halted Communist daytime air supply of the city. Thus, the Communists were forced to concede the countryside to the rebels and concentrate their forces in Kabul and other major cities. The Stinger tipped the air balance, and it is not far-fetched to assert that it overturned the military balance as well. The Soviets began their withdrawal from the conflict in February 1989. Defeat in Afghanistan surely was a factor in the demise of the Soviet Union only a short time later.[48]

Summary

Any war is difficult to evaluate, but small wars are especially tricky. Because the amount of equipment used is usually small and for the most part less than the most modern, it is difficult to extrapolate the findings into more general and future uses. When wars are fought between other countries, problems of analysis increase. Nevertheless, war is the only laboratory the soldier has, and he or she must make the most of it.

The 1973 Arab-Israeli War presented many surprises, from its origin to the way it was fought. The Arabs defied the conventional wisdom in two respects: by attacking a country having a superior military and attacking without air superiority. Initially, the Arabs used their air forces sparingly and advanced under a dense and lethal umbrella of SAMs and guns. This air defense proved effective and inflicted heavy losses on the Israeli air force. Arab missiles and guns sorely tested the IAF; but, the Israelis changed their tactics, adopted new equipment, persisted, and won. However, Arab air defenses did not permit the Israelis to fight the air and ground war as they had in 1967 and as they would have liked. Because of this war, some commentators spoke of the demise of the tank and aircraft, victims of the modern missile. The defense seemed to be supreme.

However, the wars of 1982 seemingly offered different lessons. The IAF won a striking victory against Syrian aircraft and SAMs. This came about with coordinated efforts of all arms and especially with high-technology equipment such as ARMs, remotely piloted vehicles (RPV), and electronics aircraft.

The implications of the war in the Falklands appear less clear. It might be thought of as the converse of Vietnam; that is, a relatively sophisticated but small British force pitted against a larger but less-modern Argentine one. The Argentines used mostly old aircraft and old bombs, without ECM protection and at the limits of their range. Not surprisingly, the British,

173

even with small numbers of aircraft and SAMs, imposed heavy losses on these aircraft and aircrews. But the Argentines did penetrate the defenses, did inflict much damage on the more costly British fleet, and came close to repulsing the British counterinvasion. Nevertheless, the British won the war.

Immediately after the invasion of Afghanistan, the Soviets made good use of air power in support of ground operations against the guerrillas. Initially, limited rebel antiaircraft protection could not disrupt this air support; but, the introduction of more modern and lethal man-portable SAMs did. These missiles not only inflicted substantial losses on Soviet aircraft, they forced the Airmen to use less-effective tactics and eroded the morale of the Afghan pilots. In brief, these weapons neutralized air power, which, in turn, turned the tide on the ground. In short order, the Soviets withdrew in defeat.

If these wars demonstrated anything, they showed the potential of high technology. At the same time, they indicated that numbers and weapons handling are extremely important to the final outcome. High-technology weapons demand high-quality personnel.

Notes

1. Victor Flintham, *Air Wars and Aircraft: A Detailed Record of Air Combat, 1945 to the Present* (New York: Facts on File Yearbook, Inc., 1990), 46; Moshe Dayan, *Diary of the Sinai Campaign* (New York: Schocken Books, Inc., 1965), 177–78, 221; Chaim Herzog, *The Arab-Israeli Wars: War and Peace in the Middle East* (New York: Random House, 1982), 145; Trevor Dupuy, *Elusive Victory: The Arab-Israeli Wars, 1947–1974* (New York: Harper and Row, 1978), 212; and Stephen Peltz, "Israeli Air Power," *Flying Review International*, December 1967, 1019.

2. Edward N. Luttwak and Daniel Horowitz, *The Israeli Army* (New York: Harper and Row, 1975), 229–30; Nadav Safran, *From War to War—The Arab-Israeli Confrontation, 1948–1967* (Indianapolis, Ind.: Bobbs-Merrill Co., Inc., 1969), 324–25; Murray Rubenstein and Richard Goldman, *Shield of David* (Englewood Cliffs, N.J.: Prentice Hall, Inc., 1978), 100; Robert Jackson, *The Israeli Air Force Story* (London: Stacey, 1970), 218; Warren Wetmore, "Israeli Air Punch Major Factor in War," *Aviation Week*, 3 July 1967, 22; and Edgar O' Ballance, *The Third Arab-Israeli War* (Hamden, Conn.: Archon Books, 1972), 67, 75, 82.

3. Jackson, *The Israeli Air Force*, 153, 248; Wetmore, "Israeli Air Punch," 2; James Hansen, "The Development of Soviet Tactical Air Defense," *Inter-

national Defense Review, May 1981, 532; and "Off the Record," *Journal of Defense and Diplomacy*, January 1988, 63.

4. Soviet pilots also were involved, but that is another subject for another study. See Jackson, *Israeli Air Force*, 233; Luttwak and Horowitz, *The Israeli Army*, 302, 321–23; Chaim Herzog, *The War of Atonement, October 1973* (Boston, Mass.: Little, Brown and Co., 1975), 8, 9, 232, 235–37, 253; Insight Team of the *Sunday Times* (London), *The Yom Kippur War* (Garden City, N.Y.: Doubleday and Co., 1974), 33, 36; and Lon Nordeen, *Air Warfare in the Missile Age* (Washington, D.C.: Smithsonian Institution Press, 1985), 134.

5. Hansen, "The Development of Soviet Tactical Air Defense," 533; Nordeen, *Air Warfare*, 149–50; Herzog, *War of Atonement*, 256; and Ronald Bergquist, *The Role of Airpower in the Iran-Iraq War* (Maxwell AFB, Ala.: Air Power Research Institute, 1988).

6. Herzog, *War of Atonement*, 256; Hansen, "The Development of Soviet Tactical Air Defense," 533; C. N. Barclay, "Lessons from the October War," *Army*, March 1974, 28; Charles Corddry, "The Yom Kippur War, 1973—Lessons New and Old," *National Defense*, May–June 1974, 508; Robert Ropelewski, "Setbacks Spur System to Counter Israel," *Aviation Week*, 7 July 1975, 15; Amnon Sella, "The Struggle for Air Supremacy: October 1973–December 1975," *RUSI Journal for Defense Studies*, December 1976, 33; and Insight Team, *The Yom Kippur War*, 189.

7. Brereton Greenhouse, "The Israeli Experience," in *Case Studies in the Achievement of Air Superiority*, ed. Benjamin Cooling (Washington, D.C.: Center for Air Force History, 1994), 590; Nordeen, *Air Warfare*, 149; Luttwak and Horowitz, *The Israeli Army*, 348; Herbert Coleman, "Israeli Air Force Decisive in War," *Aviation Week*, 3 December 1973, 19; "US Finds SA-6 to be Simple, Effective," *Aviation Week*, 3 December 1973, 22; Robert Ropelewski, "Egypt Assesses Lessons of October War," *Aviation Week*, 17 December 1973, 16; "SA-6–Arab Ace in the 20-Day War," *International Defense Review*, December 1973, 779–80; and Robert Hotz, "The Shock of Technical Surprise," *Aviation Week*, 24 March 1975, 9.

8. Nordeen, *Air Warfare*, 149; Ropelewski, "Egypt Assesses," 16; and "Soviet Antiaircraft Gun Takes Toll," *Aviation Week*, 22 October 1973, 19.

9. Insight Team, *The Yom Kippur War*, 161, 184–85; Herzog, *The Arab-Israeli Wars*, 281, 346; Herzog, *The War of Atonement*, 87, 256; J. Viksne, "The Yom Kippur War in Retrospect," *Army Journal*, April 1976, pt. 1:41; "Israeli Aircraft, Arab SAMs in Key Battle," *Aviation Week*, 22 October 1973, 14; Historical Evaluation and Research Organization, "The Middle East War of October 1973 in Historical Perspective," study, February 1976, 145, AUL; Dupuy, *Elusive Victory*, 551; Bryce Walker, *Fighting Jets* (Alexandria, Va.: Time-Life Books, 1983), 149; and Peter Borgart, "The Vulnerability of the Manned Airborne Weapon System, pt. 3: Influence on Tactics and Strategy," *International Defense Review*, December 1977, 1066.

10. Nordeen, *Air Warfare*, 165; Luttwak and Horowitz, *The Israeli Army*, 349; Coleman, "Israeli Air Force Decisive," 19; "SA-7 Avoids Homing on Flares," *Aviation Week*, 5 November 1973, 17; Robert R. Rodwell, "The Mid-East War:

A Damned Close-Run Thing," *Air Force Magazine,* February 1974, 39; and Hotz, "The Shock," 9.

11. Ehud Yonay, *No Margin for Error: The Making of the Israeli Air Force* (New York: Pantheon, 1993), 321; Nordeen, *Air Warfare,* 349, 351; and Jeffrey Greenhunt, "Air War: Middle East," *Aerospace Historian,* March 1976, 22.

12. Rodwell, "The Mid-East War," 39; Dupuy, *Elusive Victory,* 552; Nordeen, *Air Warfare,* 156; Luttwak and Horowitz, *The Israeli Army,* 349; Insight Team, *The Yom Kippur War,* 187–88, 370; Coleman, "The Israeli Air Force," 19; Bill Gunston et al., *War Planes: 1945–1976* (London: Salamander, 1976), 58; Walker, *Fighting Jets,* 149; and Borgart, "The Vulnerability," pt. 3, 1064.

13. Insight Team, *The Yom Kippur War,* 204; Walker, *Fighting Jets,* 150; Coleman, "The Israeli Air Force," 18; and Yonay, *No Margin for Error,* 353.

14. Yonay, *No Margin for Error,* 313. Another author states that the IAF destroyed 28 SAM sites and the Israeli army 12 others. See Herzog, *War of Atonement,* 242, 259; Insight Team, *The Yom Kippur War,* 338; Herzog, *Arab-Israeli Wars,* 285, 341; and Rubenstein and Goldman, *Shield,* 127, 129.

15. Greenhouse, "The Israeli Experience," 597–98; Herzog, *Arab-Israeli Wars,* 346–47; Herzog, *War of Atonement,* 257; Luttwak and Horowitz, *The Israeli Army,* 347; Nordeen, *Air Warfare,* 163–66; M. J. Armitage and R. A. Mason, *Air Power in the Nuclear Age,* 2d ed. (Urbana, Ill.: University of Illinois, 1985), 134; Roy Braybrook, "Is It Goodbye to Ground Attack?" *Air International,* May 1976, 234–44; Charles Wakebridge, "The Technological Gap in the Middle East," *National Defense* (May–June 1975): 461; and "SA-6–Arab Ace," 779.

16. John Kreis, *Air Warfare and Air Base Air Defense, 1914–1973* (Washington, D.C.: Office of Air Force History, 1988), 336.

17. "Bekaa Valley Combat," *Flight International,* 16 October 1982, 1110; Herzog, *The War of Atonement,* 260; Insight Team, *The Yom Kippur War,* 315; Kreis, *Air Warfare and Air Base,* 336; Thomas Walczyk, "October War," *Strategy and Tactics* (March–April 1977): 10; Martin van Creveld, *The Washington Papers, Military Lessons of the Yom Kippur War—Historical Perspectives,* no. 24 (Beverly Hills/London: Sage Publications, 1975): 31; Borgart, "The Vulnerability," 1064, 1066; Rubenstein and Goldman, *Shield,* 128; Herzog, *Arab-Israeli Wars,* 347; and Ropelewski, "Egypt Assesses," 16.

18. Rubenstein and Goldman, *Shield,* 13; Dupuy, *Elusive Victory,* 592; Nordeen, *Air Warfare,* 151; Herzog, *Arab-Israeli Wars,* 266; Herzog, *War of Atonement,* 258; and Lawrence Whetten and Michael Johnson, "Military Lessons of the Yom Kippur War," *World Today,* March 1974, 109.

19. Herzog, *The War of Atonement,* 260–61; Corddry, "The Yom Kippur War–1973," 508; Historical Evaluation and Research Organization, appendix; Walczyk, "October War," 10; William Staudenmaier, "Learning from the Middle East War," *Air Defense Trends,* April–June 1975, 18; "Israeli Aircraft, Arab SAMs in Key Battle," 14; Rubenstein and Goldman, *Shield,* 128; and Borgart, "The Vulnerability," 1066. A number of factors contribute to the discrepancy in losses. Besides the differences in the training, leadership, motivation, and doctrine of the opposing forces, two other factors stand out: Soviet versus Western hardware and the Arab lack of ECM equipment and

Israel's use of it. See Dupuy, *Elusive Victory*, 549; Coleman, "The Israeli Air Force," 18; and Nordeen, *Air Warfare*, 162–63.

20. Van Creveld, *The Washington Papers*, 31–32; Luttwak and Horowitz, *The Israeli War*, 350–51; Hansen, "The Development of Soviet Air Defense," 533; Historical Evaluation and Research Organization, "The Middle East War," 148, 177; and Drew Middleton, "Missiles Blunt Thrust of Traditional Tank-Plane Team," *New York Times*, 2 November 1973, 19.

21. "Bekaa Valley Combat," 1110; William Haddad, "Divided Lebanon," *Current History*, January 1982, 35.

22. "Antiaircraft Defence Force: The PLO in Lebanon," *Born in Battle*, no. 27, 7, 32; R. D. M. Furlong, "Israel Lashes Out," *Interavia*, August 1982, 1002–3; Clarence Robinson Jr., "Surveillance Integration Pivotal in Israeli Successes," *Aviation Week*, 5 July 1982, 17; Edgar Ulsamer, "In Focus: TAC Air Feels the Squeeze," *Air Force Magazine*, October 1982, 23; and Anthony Cordesman, "The Sixth Arab-Israeli Conflict," *Armed Forces Journal International*, August 1982, 30. The IAF may have destroyed as many as 108 Syrian aircraft. See "Syrian Resupply," *Aerospace Daily*, 15 November 1982, 74.

23. Furlong, "Israel," 1002–3; Robinson, "Surveillance,"17; Ulsamer, "In Focus," 23; Cordesman, "Sixth Arab-Israeli Conflict," 30; "Bekaa Valley Combat," 1110; Drew Middleton, "Soviet Arms Come in Second in Lebanon," *New York Times*, 19 September 1982, 2E; "Israeli Defense Forces in the Lebanon War," *Born in Battle*, no. 30, 22, 45–47; "The Syrians in Lebanon," no. 27, 12, 28, 31–33; and "SA-9 Firings Seen Part of Attempt to Probe Israeli Capabilities," *Aerospace Daily*, 8 November 1982, 45.

24. Eugene Kozicharow, "Navy Blames Aircraft Loss on Soviet Sensor Change," *Aviation Week*, 12 December 1983, 25–26; Richard Halloran, "Navy, Stung by Criticism, Defends Cost of Bombing Raid in Lebanon," *New York Times*, 7 December 1983, 1, 19; and Thomas Friedman, "US Ships Attack Syrian Positions in Beirut Region," *New York Times*, 14 December 1983, 1.

25. "US Demonstrates Advanced Weapons Technology in Libya," *Aviation Week*, 21 April 1986, 19; Fred Hiatt, "Jet Believed Lost, 5 Sites Damaged in Raid on Libya," *Washington Post*, 16 April 1986, A25; and Anthony Cordesman, "After the Raid," *Armed Forces*, August 1986, 359.

26. Cordesman, "After the Raid," 358, 360.

27. Ibid., 355–60; "US Air Power Hits Back," *Defence Update/73*, 1986, 27–32; Hiatt, "Jet Believed Lost," A25; "US Demonstrates Advanced Weapons Technology in Libya," 20, 21; David North, "Air Force, Navy Brief Congress on Lessons from Libya Strikes," *Aviation Week*, 2 June 1986, 63; and Judith Miller, "Malta Says Libya Got Tip on Raid," *New York Times*, 6 August 1983, 1, 8.

28. Flintham, *Air Wars and Aircraft*, 195; John Fricker, *Battle for Pakistan: The Air War of 1965* (London: Allan, 1979), 122, 124, 183–84. Slightly different claims can be found in Nordeen, *Air Warfare*, 113.

29. Flintham, *Air Wars and Aircraft*, 200–202; John Fricker, "Post-Mortem of an Air War," *Air Enthusiast*, May 1972, 230, 232; Nordeen, *Air*

177

Warfare, 103–4; Borgart, "The Vulnerability," 1066; and Pushpindar Chopra, "Journal of an Air War," *Air Enthusiast*, April 1972, 177–83, 206.

30. Great Britain, Ministry of Defence, *The Falklands Campaign: The Lessons* (London: Her Majesty's Stationery Office, 1982), annex B, AUL; and Dov Zakheim, "The South Atlantic: Evaluating the Lessons" (paper presented at Southern Methodist University Conference on The Three Wars of 1982: Lessons to be Learned, Dallas, Tex., 15 April 1983), 29.

31. Jeffrey Ethell and Alfred Price, *Air War South Atlantic* (New York: Macmillan Publishing Co., Inc., 1983), 146.

32. Ibid., 180–81; David Brown, "Countermeasures Aided British Fleet," *Aviation Week*, 19 July 1982, 18; "British Government on Performance of Roland, Rapier in Falklands," *Aerospace Daily*, 27 October 1982, 309; "British SAMs Credited with Most Kills in Falklands Conflict," *Aerospace Daily*, 9 August 1982, 211; Insight Team of the *Sunday Times* (London), *War in the Falklands* (Cambridge, Mass.: Harper and Row Publishers, 1982), 201; Ministry of Defence, *Falklands Campaign*, 19, annex C; Derek Wood and Mark Hewish, "The Falklands Conflict, pt. 1: The Air War," *International Defense Review* 8 (1982): 978, 980; Brian Moore, "The Falklands War: The Air Defense Role," *Air Defense Artillery* (Winter 1983): 19; "Blowpipe Draws Commendation for Falklands Performance," *Aerospace Daily*, 12 August 1982, 239; and David Griffiths, "Layered Air Defense Keyed British Falklands Victory," *Defense Week*, 30 August 1982, 13. The French claimed that nine Roland missiles downed four Harriers and damaged another, a claim fiercely disputed by the British. Interestingly, the British had attempted to sell their Rapier missile to the Argentines. See "Euromissile on Performance of Roland in Falklands, Middle East," *Aerospace Daily*, 23 September 1982, 126; "Exocet, Roland Combat Performance Rated High," *Aviation Week*, 1 November 1982, 26; and Anthony Cordesman, "The Falklands: The Air War and Missile Conflict," *Armed Forces Journal International*, September 1982, 40.

33. Anthony Cordesman and Abraham Wagner, *The Lessons of Modern War*, vol. 3, *The Afghan and Falklands Conflicts* (Boulder: Westview, 1990), 337–38; Brad Roberts, "The Military Implications of the Falklands/Malvinas Island Conflict," report no. 82-140F, Congressional Research Service, Library of Congress, August 1982, 15, AUL; Cordesman, "The Falklands," 33, 35; Steward Menaul, "The Falklands Campaign: A War of Yesterday?" *Strategic Review* (Fall 1982): 87–88; Wood and Hewish, "The Falklands Conflict, pt. 1," 978; Ezio Bonsignore, "Hard Lessons from the South Atlantic," *Military Technology*, June 1982, 32; John Guilmartin, "The South Atlantic War: Lessons and Analytical Guideposts, A Military Historian's Perspective," 17, Southern Methodist University Conference, April 1983; Ethell and Price, *Air War South Atlantic*, 120–21, 183, 217–18; and Jesus Briasco and Salvador Huertas, *Falklands: Witness of Battles* (Valencia, Spain: Domenech, 1985), 172.

34. Guilmartin, "The South Atlantic," 12; and Ethell and Price, *Air War South Atlantic*, 179.

35. I have relied primarily on the official British reports for the statistics. See Ministry of Defence, *Falklands Campaign*, annex B. See also the figures,

which vary at times from these numbers, in Wood and Hewish, "The Falklands Conflict, pt.1," 980; Moore, "The Falklands War," 21; Cordesman, "The Falklands," 32; and Guilmartin, "The South Atlantic," 17.

36. Briasco and Huertas, *Falklands*, 165–68, 173; Ethell and Price, *Air War South Atlantic*, 207; and Rodney Burden et al., *Falklands: The Air War* (London: Arms and Armour, 1986), 33–147.

37. Derek Wood and Mark Hewish, "The Falklands Conflict, pt. 2: Missile Operations," *International Defense Review*, September 1982, 1151, 1154; Moore, "The Falklands War," 20; Christopher Foss, "European Tactical Missile Systems," *Armor*, July–August 1975, 24; Ethell and Price, *Air War South Atlantic*, 196–209; Briasco and Huertas, *Falklands*, 165–69; and Terry Gander, "Maintaining the Effectiveness of Blowpipe SAM," *Jane's Defence Review*, 4, no. 2 (1983): 159.

38. Some accounts claim that Rapier's radar interfered with the Royal Navy's radar. After all, the British army did not expect to fight alongside destroyers on the plains of central Europe! Others state that the British sent the army unit to the Falklands without radar, in contrast to the Royal Air Force regiment that arrived later with Rapier and radar. Whatever the case, the initial unit that went ashore in the campaign, and the only one that saw action, fired optically guided missiles. See "UK Planned to Use Shrike Missiles against Argentine Radars," *Aerospace Daily*, 30 August 1982, 334; "Air Defense Missiles Limited Tactics of Argentine Aircraft," *Aviation Week*, 19 July 1982, 21; Great Britain, Ministry of Defence, *Falklands Campaign*, 22; Wood and Hewish, "The Falklands Conflict, pt. 2," 1153; Moore, "The Falklands War," 19; and Price, *Air War South Atlantic*, 196–208; Briasco and Huertas, *Falklands*, 165–69; and Jacques du Boucher, "Missiles in the Falklands," *African Defence*, October 1983, 60.

39. John Laffin, *Fight for the Falklands* (New York: St. Martin's Press, 1982), 92–93; Ministry of Defence, *Falklands Campaign*, 9, annex B; Wood and Hewish, "The Falklands Conflict, pt. 2," 1151, 1154; Ethell and Price, *Air War South Atlantic*, 196–208; and Briasco and Huertas, *Falklands*, 165–69.

40. Cordesman, "The Falklands," 38; Ministry of Defence, *Falklands Campaign*, annex B; Insight Team, *War in the Falklands*, 216; Ethell and Price, *Air War South Atlantic*, 196–208; Briasco and Huertas, *Falklands*, 165–69; Roger Villar, "The Sea Wolf Story-GW S25 to VM40," *Jane's Defence Review* 2, no. 1 (1981): 75.

41. Cordesman and Wagner, *Afghan and Falklands Conflicts*, 337–38, 351.

42. Cordesman, "The Falklands," 34; Alistair Horne, "A British Historian's Meditations: Lessons of the Falklands," *National Review*, 23 July 1982, 888.

43. Anthony Cordesman and Abraham Wagner, *The Lessons of Modern War*, vol. 2, *The Iran-Iraq War* (Boulder: Westview, 1990), 460–62; Anthony Cordesman, "Lessons of the Iran-Iraq War: pt. II, Tactics, Technology, and Training," *Armed Forces Journal International*, June 1982, 70, 78–79; "The Iranian Air Force at War," *Born in Battle*, no. 24, 13; "The Iraq-Iran War," *Defence Update*, no. 44 (1984): 43–44; and Nordeen, *Air Warfare*, 185–88.

44. Stephen Harding, *Air War Grenada* (Missoula, Mont.: Pictorial Histories, 1984), 9, 33, 36, 51; and Thomas D. Des Brisay, "The *Mayaguez* Incident," in *Air War–Vietnam* (Indianapolis, Ind.: Bobbs-Merrill Co., Inc., 1978), 326.

45. Jean de Galard, "French Jaguar Shot Down in Chad," *Jane's Defence Weekly* 1, no. 4 (4 February 1984): 142; Charles Mohr, "Contras Say They Fear a Long War," *New York Times*, 16 June 1986, 8; Pico Iyer, "Sudan: Stranded Amid the Gunfire," *Time*, 1 September 1986, 34; and William Claiborne, "S. African Military Says Intervention in Angola Staved Off Rebel Defeat," *Washington Post*, 13 November 1987, A28.

46. John Cushman, "The Stinger Missile: Helping to Change the Course of a War," *New York Times*, 17 January 1988, E2; Ray Barnes, ed., *The U.S. War Machine* (New York: Crown Publishers, 1978), 234–35; Maurice Robertson, "Stinger: Proven Plane Killer," *International Combat Arms*, July 1985; and General Dynamics, *The World's Missile Systems* (Pomona, Calif.: General Dynamics, 1982).

47. Cordesman and Wagner, *Afghan and Falklands Conflicts*, 170, 174; Bill Gertz, "Stinger Bite Feared in CIA," *Washington Times*, 9 October 2000; "Soviets Press Countermeasures to Stinger Missile," *Aerospace Daily*, 6 August 1987, 205; "Disjointed Rebels Join Forces as They Oust Their Enemy," *Insight*, 25 January 1988, 21; and Anthony Cordesman, "The Afghan Chronology: Another Brutal Year of Conflict," *Armed Forces*, April 1987, 156–60.

48. Cordesman and Wagner, *Afghan and Falklands Conflicts*, 177; Cordesman, "Afghan Chronology," 158–60; Cushman, "The Stinger Missile," E2; Rone Tempest, "Afghan Rebel Rockets Jar Government Assembly," *Washington Post*, 30 November 1987, A24; John Kifner, "Moscow Is Seen at Turning Point in Its Intervention in Afghanistan," *New York Times*, 29 November 1987, 1; Peter Youngsband, "Grappling for the Advantage When Talk Replaces Gunfire," *Insight*, 7 December 1987, 43; Robert Schultheis, "The *Mujahedin* Press Hard," *Time*, 18 May 1987, 51; and Steven R. Weisman, "US in Crossfire of Border War," *New York Times*, 17 May 1987, E3.

Chapter 5

Ballistic Missile Defense:
The Early Years to 1991

In contrast to the eventual successful defense against the German V-1 flying bomb, Allied efforts against the V-2 ballistic missile proved futile.[1] The Allies bombed German missile test sites, manufacturing, launching, and storage faculties but had no impact on the V-2s (fig. 79). Despite total air dominance, the Allied air forces never successfully attacked a single German launch unit. Although a large device, it proved mobile and elusive. Technical difficulties delayed the V-2s, not the bombing.[2]

Figure 79. V-2 launch. V-2s at the German Peenemünde test site during World War II. The World War II V-2 campaign was the first, largest, and deadliest missile campaign yet seen. (Reprinted from US Army Aviation and Missile Command.)

Downing ballistic missiles after launch was essentially impossible. One secondary source claims there were two such instances, but, alas, neither can be confirmed.[3] There is documentation, however, of British investigations of the concept of firing an artillery barrage into the missile's path after the defenders were alerted by radar. Although the British estimated that they could down 3 to 10 percent of the V-2s they engaged, the scheme would have required 20,000 shells to destroy one V-1. Of greater consequence, the British expected that about 2 percent of the shells would not detonate and that these duds and the debris from the exploding shells would cause more casualties than the V-2s that might be intercepted.[4]

Meanwhile, the US military was looking into ballistic missile defense (BMD). In March 1946, the Army Air Forces (AAF) began two missile defense projects: General Electric's Project Thumper (MX-795) that lasted only until March 1948, while the other, the University of Michigan's Project Wizard (MX-794), survived somewhat longer. It was designed to defend the continental United States but was pitted against the Army's Nike project that was intended for theater operations. In 1958, the Air Force conceded it was too costly, and thus the Department of Defense (DOD) merged it with the Nike-Zeus project.[5]

Army Development

The Army was making progress on the issue of ballistic missile defense. In January 1949, the Army established a formal requirement for ballistic missile defense that early in 1951 spawned the PLATO Project that was to provide antiballistic missile (ABM) protection for the field army. The Army increased the requirement in 1954 to defend against intercontinental ballistic missiles (ICBM) in the 1960–70 time frame. A number of studies emerged, with one in 1956 suggesting a Nike-Zeus variant. PLATO was shut down in 1959, not for technical reasons, but because of funding problems.[6]

The follow-on to PLATO was the Field Army Ballistic Missile Defense System (FABMDS) program that began in 1959. However, as this had a long lead time, with an expected operational date of 1967, the Army sought other equipment. Early on, the

Army considered using Hawk in this role, and before this concept was discarded in 1960, a Hawk intercepted a short-range HONEST JOHN ballistic missile. The Army wanted more but settled for the Nike-Hercules as an interim system. An improved Hercules intercepted a higher-performing Corporal missile in June 1960 and then another Hercules. The Army deployed the Nike-Hercules as an antitactical ballistic missile to Germany in the early 1960s. Meanwhile, DOD cancelled FABMDS in late 1962. In October, the Army renamed the project AAADS-70, which became known as SAM-D.[7]

In March 1955, the Army gave Bell Labs a contract to study future (1960–70) threats presented by air-breathing vehicles and ballistic missiles. In short order, the Army began to focus on the latter problem, which led to a proposal for a new defensive missile, the Nike II. The missile was to have interchangeable noses, one with an active sensor for use against air breathers and the other a jet-control device (thrust vector motor) that would permit maneuver above 120,000 feet to enable interception of ballistic missiles outside the atmosphere. The system would use two sets of radars: one considerably distant from the missile site and the other more closely located.[8]

The Army and Air Force dueled for the BMD role. In November 1956, Secretary of Defense Charles Wilson directed the Army to develop, procure, and man the land-based surface-to-air missile (SAM) for terminal defense, and the Air Force was to handle area defense—long-range acquisition radars and the communications network that tied this system to the terminal defenses. In January 1958, the secretary assigned responsibility for development of all antiballistic missiles to the Army and assigned the Air Force the development of the system's long-distance radar acquisition system, the ballistic missile early warning system (BMEWS).[9]

Challenges to the BMD system were powerful, enunciated early, and have persisted over the decades. Most of these objections have been technical. The opponents have doubted that the ABM could sort out warheads, especially of small radar cross sections, from decoys or debris. There has also been a question regarding the system's effectiveness against a massive saturation attack. A further difficulty has been the system's vulnerability to direct attack and to radar blackout caused by nuclear explosions. Another issue was that the system could not be tested against a surprise mass attack. In addition, of course, there have been concerns involving cost.[10] Perhaps this is best summarized by one critical study that bluntly states that "BMD proposed against an exaggerated threat, incapable of being effectively deployed, destructive of arms control agreements, and likely to provoke a new arms race, destroys the national security it is designed to enhance."[11]

The services had contrasting views on supporting the ABM. Both the Air Force and Navy opposed production. While critics and cynics might see the US Air Force as being a "poor sport" after losing the ABM mission, this position is closer to the traditional Air Force offensive view reaching back to the Air Corps Tactical School in the 1930s. It is also consistent with bomber exploits over both Germany and Japan in World War II. Offensive Air Force weapons bolstered deterrence, the strategic paradigm of the Cold War.[12] For its part, the Army sought a larger piece of the military budget. At this point, nuclear weapons seemed to be the way to gain access to these funds, and ballistic missile defense seemed the surest path to that end.[13] The Executive Branch of government had other ideas.

The military buildup that had begun during the Korean War tapered off in the late 1950s under the frugal hand of Pres. Dwight D. "Ike" Eisenhower. Despite the shock of the sputnik launch in October 1957, the next year Ike rejected the ABM proposal as he slashed military spending in a massive economy effort. But industry countered with an effective campaign that forced the administration to continue ABM research efforts.[14]

Meanwhile, in February 1957 the Army pressed forward by awarding Western Electric a contract to become the prime contractor for an anti-ICBM missile now called Nike-Zeus (fig. 80). The next January, the National Security Council assigned the project the highest national priority.[15] Nike-Zeus was subjected to a thorough testing program, with the Army firing the first of 69 missiles in August 1959. In December 1961, the ABM intercepted a ballistic missile over the White Sands range. Overall, the Army considered nine of the 13 tests against the ICBMs successful.[16]

Figure 80. Nike family. America's first ABM family. From right to left (and in the order of their deployment), the Nike Ajax, Nike Hercules, and Nike Zeus. (Reprinted from US Army Aviation and Missile Command.)

As with most missiles, the Zeus encountered problems. But using the experience gained in other missile programs, these problems were largely overcome. Throughout, the missile encountered difficulties involving the radar detecting the incoming target and discriminating the warhead from the decoys and debris (and with the electronics to properly guide the interceptor).[17]

The Kennedy Administration

In 1961, the outgoing Eisenhower administration passed the ABM program on to the new president, John F. Kennedy, who was caught between the desire to expand nonnuclear military capabilities and the growing Soviet ICBM threat (not to mention Kennedy's campaign issue of the "missile gap"). The new secretary of defense, Robert S. McNamara, studied the ABM program and in April concluded that the system could not handle a massive attack or decoys and that the program would only prompt the Soviets to build more ballistic missiles. Despite these misgivings, and probably for political purposes, McNamara allowed about $250 million for ABM research and development.[18]

A few months later in 1961, the secretary requested estimates of an ABM production program. In September, he approved the first of a three-phase program that would protect six cities with 12 batteries with just fewer than 1,200 missiles for about $3 billion. McNamara briefed Kennedy on the proposal in November, and the president gave it his tentative approval. But budget talks in December 1961 convinced the president to forego this interim deployment.[19]

By this time, American engineers developed two technologies that promised to overcome two of the difficulties (penetration aids and sheer numbers) that doomed Nike-Zeus: the phased array radar and a new high-acceleration missile.[20] McNamara directed development of the newer missile system in January 1963, which was named Nike X in February 1964. The system would employ the Zeus missile, renamed Spartan in January 1967, to intercept incoming missiles at ranges of about 300 nautical miles (nm) and altitudes of 100 nm (fig. 81).[21] A new close-in defense missile, the Sprint, would use the atmosphere to sort out the warhead from decoys and debris, as these would decelerate at different speeds due to atmospheric friction. It would then intercept these surviving warheads between 5,000 and 100,000 feet at a maximum range of 100 nm (fig. 82). The missile first flew in November 1965 and then underwent flight-testing in 1965–70, during which time 42 Sprints were flight-tested with results significantly better than the requirements.[22]

Phased array radar was the system's other innovation and a major improvement. In contrast to the Nike-Zeus radars that could only track one target and one interceptor missile at a time, the new radar could handle many more objects and serve more than one function simultaneously. Another advantage of this radar was that it operated in the UHF spectrum that was

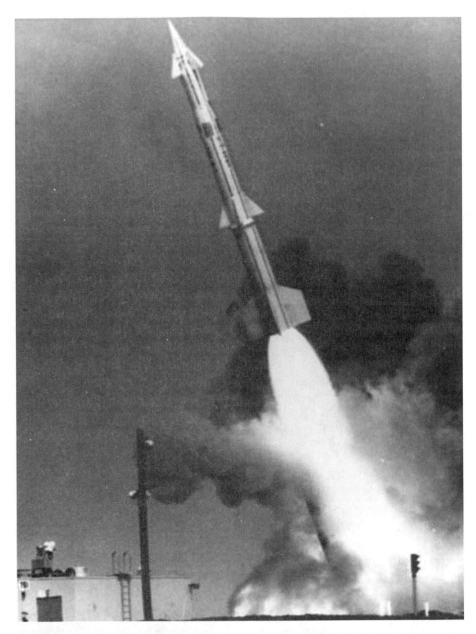

Figure 81. Spartan launch. The Spartan missile was the long-range component of the first American ABM system. It was designed to hit incoming ballistic missiles before their reentry. (Reprinted from US Army Aviation and Missile Command.)

Figure 82. Sprint. The Sprint missile was the short-range component of the American ABM system. It was a high-acceleration missile designed to destroy incoming warheads that eluded the Spartan. (Reprinted from http://www.brook.educ/FP/projects/nucwcost/sprint.htm.)

more resistant to nuclear blackout than the existing radar that operated in the VHF spectrum. This system also had greater power and thus greater range. The Army awarded the radar contract to Raytheon in December 1963.[23]

In the early and mid-1960s, the rationale for the ABM system expanded in two different directions. The first was to provide protection for US strategic forces. The military began to study this issue in 1963–64 and in November 1965 concentrated on the defense of hardened ICBM sites.[24] The other effort that began in February 1965 was to look at the problem of Nth country threats, that is, nuclear-armed missiles possessed by countries other than the Soviet Union. (The decision makers recognized that defending against a massive Soviet missile attack would be extremely difficult, if not impossible, whereas a defense against a limited attack, although difficult, was perhaps possible.) At this point, the major country of interest was the People's Republic of China, which had detonated a nuclear device in October 1964 and test-fired an ICBM in October 1966. These two objectives merged in the December 1966 Plan I-67 that identified the Chinese as a potential nuclear missile threat and also focused on ABM defense of US land-based missiles.

The Soviets' ABM efforts also prodded the US system. In July 1962, for example, Nikita Khruschev boasted that the Soviets could hit a fly in space. The first missile to attract Western attention with the possibility of ABM capability was code-named Griffon (fig. 83). It resembled a large-sized SA-2 (the surface-to-air missile type that had downed American U-2s over Russia and Cuba and was used by the communists in the Vietnam War). The Soviets began flight tests in 1957, deployed the missile outside Leningrad in 1960, and built 30 firing sites within two

Figure 83. Griffon. The first Soviet ABM known to the West was the Griffon. Flight tests in 1957 led to the construction of 30 firing sites in the early 1960s. But the Soviets stopped construction in 1963 and abandoned the sites the next year. (Reprinted from Federation of Atomic Scientists.)

years. Then, in 1963, the Soviets stopped work around Leningrad and by the end of 1964 abandoned these sites.[25]

The Soviets began work on a successor to the Griffon in the mid-1950s. Code-named Galosh (ABM-1) by NATO, it was a much larger missile than the Griffon and larger than the ICBMs it was intended to intercept outside the atmosphere (fig. 84). Western intelligence first detected it in early 1964 and two years later noted 64 deployed in four sites in a ring about 40–50 miles from the center of Moscow. The United States believed it had limitations similar to the Nike-Zeus: it could only engage a limited number of ICBMs and was vulnerable to nuclear blackout. It achieved initial operational capability (IOC) in 1968 and was fully operational in 1970.[26]

US intelligence detected the construction in northwestern Russia of another potential ABM site called Tallinn in 1963–64. The Defense Intelligence Agency thought this system had ABM capabilities, although there were those in both military intelligence and the Central Intelligence Agency who believed it was an antibomber defense system. If it did have ABM capabilities,

Figure 84. Galosh 1. The Soviets deployed the Galosh in four sites in a ring around Moscow. It was fully operational in 1970. (Reprinted from Department of Defense.)

these were marginal and only capable against earlier missiles. The SA-5 (Gammon) was first flight-tested in 1962 but did not become operational until 1968. In the early 1980s, the Soviets deployed more than 2,000 launchers at 120 sites.[27]

The Soviets clearly were making a much greater effort in the ABM field than was the United States. In a benign view, this could be explained by the traditional defensive mind-set of the Russians or attributed to their horrific experience in World War II. A more ominous view was that the Soviets were trying to obtain strategic nuclear superiority. In any case, it was believed that the Soviets had invested $4 to $5 billion in ABM programs by 1967 as compared to about $2 billion by the United States. In 1967, Secretary McNamara estimated the Soviets were spending 2.5 times as much as the United States on air defense, while two years later, Secretary Melvin Laird put that figure at 3.5 to 4 times.[28]

In the early 1960s, ABM opponents focused on three major aspects of the system. They raised the issue of the adverse impact of a successful ABM system on the system of deterrence, mutually assured destruction (MAD). Their fear was that ABM defense would lead to an arms race (of both defensive and offensive weapons) that would destabilize the international balance of power. Cost was always a factor. While some used figures as "low" as $4 to $5 billion, others saw much higher costs, ranging between $4 billion for a thin ABM system to perhaps $40 billion over 10 years for a more complete one. Some believed that since fielding the ABM would only lead to the deployment of more ICBMs that would nullify the defense, both sides would only spend a lot of money for nothing. In the end, however, the major objection to the deployment of an ABM system was technical: would the system work against a mass attack, work the first time it was needed, and work against sophisticated threats that included decoys and jammers?[29]

There was a wide range of opponents to the system, both inside and outside the government. Perhaps the most prominent within the administration was the secretary of defense. His objections centered on the ABM cost and what it might encourage (or force) the Soviets to do. He was consistent in his position and tied the ABM to a nationwide shelter program that was ex-

191

pensive and unpopular with both the public and politicians.[30] McNamara instead supported a deterrent strategy.[31]

There were, of course, supporters of the system. Systems analysts opposed a growth in offensive systems and instead supported ABM defense for silo-based Minuteman ICBM missiles. And, while both the Advanced Research Projects Agency and the director of Defense Research and Engineering opposed deploying a Nike-X system, they both were "quite enthusiastic" about an ABM system oriented against a smaller ICBM threat. The military at the highest level, the Joint Chiefs of Staff (JCS), put aside its interservice bickering to unite behind the Army's ABM, one of a number of core programs. Within the administration, there were conflicting voices. The secretary of the Air Force (Harold Brown) and secretary of the Navy (Paul Nitze) favored some sort of deployment. There were also political pressures from Congress and not only from Republicans. Pres. Lyndon B. Johnson feared that failure to deploy the system could generate a potential ABM gap that would be used by the Republicans in the upcoming election, just as the Democrats had effectively used the proported missile gap in the 1960 election. Johnson also feared that the military (specifically the JCS), unhappy about the conduct of the Vietnam War, would cause political woes. At this point, the public, as is so often the case, was uninformed and uninterested in the issue. In fact, a 1965 public opinion poll in Chicago revealed that 80 percent of the respondents thought the United States already had an ABM system in place![32] As a side note, this misperception continues to this day.

In late 1966, McNamara sold the president on a dual-track strategy to deal with the issue. The Johnson administration would attempt to fend off ABM proponents by continuing development and procuring long-lead items, while trying to placate opponents and negate a need for ABM by negotiating an arms control treaty with the Soviets. President Johnson favored arms control, as he preferred spending on his beloved Great Society domestic programs rather than on an unproductive, if not provocative, arms race. But the Soviets were not interested. In June 1967, President Johnson met with Soviet Premier Alexi Kosygin at Glassboro, New Jersey, and discussed an arrangement to curtail ABM deployment. McNamara told the Russians that limitations on defensive weapons were necessary to avoid an arms race. In response, the Soviet leader pounded the table and angrily replied: "Defense is moral, offense is immoral!"[33] Pressure on the administration mounted shortly thereafter when the Chinese announced they had detonated a hydrogen bomb. A few days after the Glassboro meeting, Johnson told McNamara that he would approve deployment.[34]

In September 1967, McNamara delivered a key speech in San Francisco. Although he made clear that an ABM defense against a Soviet ICBM attack was both futile and expensive, the secretary of defense announced that the United States would deploy a "light" ABM system to protect the United States from a Chinese attack.[35] Another purpose of the US ABM system was to protect US (Minuteman) ICBMs and the United States against an accidental ICBM launch. The system would consist of the Spartan area defense and Sprint terminal defense of 25 major cities. The system would be known as Sentinel and cost an estimated $4–$5 billion.[36]

ABM supporters had won a significant victory and thought the way was now clear. But if politics played an important role in bringing this about, the politics of the times played a role in derailing, or at least deflecting, ABM deployment. Citizen groups rose to oppose siting of the missiles in and around the major cities in which they lived. This was unexpected, as public opinion polls indicated that the public (the 40 percent of the public who expressed an opinion) supported ABM deployment by a margin of almost two to one. The problem was the classic one of "not in my backyard." Stimulated by the activism and anti-establishment wave of the late 1960s and supported by the leadership and advice of numerous articulate, activist, and passionate scientists and academics, a protest movement upset the administration's and proponent's plans. Another, albeit less pervasive factor, was that intelligence agencies downgraded the threat of Chinese ICBMs to the United States.[37]

Meanwhile, diplomatic efforts continued. In July 1968, President Johnson announced that talks with the Soviets would begin in September, but the Soviet invasion of Czechoslovakia derailed this effort.[38] This was the situation when a new administration came into office.

Proponents of ABM expected the incoming Republicans to press forward with the ABM deployment. But Pres. Richard M. Nixon, the stereotypical cold warrior, was also a shrewd politician. Reacting to the popular discontent over the path Sentinel was taking, he changed the direction of the project within weeks. In March 1969, Nixon announced that the ABM system was being renamed (Safeguard), scaled down (from 17 Sprint sites to 12), relocated (from the cities), and reoriented (to defend the United States ICBMs). This was not only a compromise between the extremes of increase or cancellation; it also was a different path from the one trod by the previous Democratic administration. The fact of the matter was that Nixon saw the system as a bargaining chip in the ongoing arms negotiations.[39]

The public and political battle continued. Early 1969 saw one of the hottest discussions of defense policy of post–World War II America. The public remained relatively uninformed or confused about the issue, but those who expressed an opinion continued to support ABM by a margin of nearly two to one. The Senate was a different matter. After a record 29-day debate, on 6 August 1969 the Senate voted and divided evenly, allowing Vice Pres. Spiro T. Agnew to cast the deciding vote to preserve the system.[40]

Then, to the surprise of some and relief of many, America and the Soviet Union reached an agreement after difficult negotiations. In May 1972, the two superpowers signed the Strategic Arms Limitation Treaty (SALT) agreement that limited the number of strategic weapons.[41] As important as that treaty was, more important to this story was the agreement to limit ABMs.

The ABM treaty was also concluded in May 1972. It permitted each country to have two ABM sites, one within 150 kilometers (km) of its national capital and another at least 1,300 km from the first and within 150 km of ICBM sites. Each site was limited to a maximum of 100 launchers and 100 interceptor missiles. The treaty prohibited developing, testing, and deploying systems (or their air-, mobile-, sea-, or space-based components) and upgrading existing systems to ABM capabilities. It further forbade developing, testing, and deploying rapid reload launchers and multiple, independently guided warheads and testing of ABMs against strategic missiles. The treaty could be revoked by giving six months' notice. In 1974, the two countries amended the treaty by reducing the permitted sites for each country from two to one. The Soviets chose to defend Moscow, the United States to continue to work on its Grand Forks, North Dakota, site.[42]

The life of the US system was brief. The Air Force declared the installation at Grand Forks operational in September 1975 (fig. 85). By this time, the military decided that the system was expensive and of dubious value. Therefore, the next February, the JCS ordered the site deactivated, leaving the United States without an active ABM system. Safeguard cost the United States about $6 billion. Meanwhile, the Soviets continued to operate their one system in the Moscow area.[43]

Figure 85. US ABM site at Grand Forks, North Dakota. The 16 round objects in the foreground are Sprint silos, the longish objects behind them are the Spartan silos, and the pyramid-shaped structure to the rear is the missile site radar. (Reprinted from http://www.paineless.id.au/missile/Hsafeguard.html.)

The American ABM appeared dead. It would not come back to life for another decade.

Ballistic Missile Defense: Rebirth

Ballistic missile defense continued after the demise of Safeguard, albeit on a much-reduced scale. Funding dropped from about $1 billion a year in the late 1960s to about a tenth of that by 1980. It would take major events to reverse this trend.

Meanwhile, one effort attempted to connect the BMD with the defense of Minuteman sites. It began in 1971 as Hardsite Defense, a prototype program built around a modified Sprint and hardened silos. From this, the Army proposed a system it called LoAD (low altitude defense) that featured a high-acceleration missile armed with a nuclear warhead like the Sprint but considerably smaller (fig. 86).[44] It came into view linked to the siting of the MX (missile experimental) ICBM that followed the Minuteman series in a basing proposal, known as Multiple Protective Shelter (MPS).[45] The defenders would bury a mobile BMD system in a tunnel, one defensive unit per ICBM complex, which they believed would effectively double the number of missiles the attacker would have to use to ensure destruction of the ICBMs. There were major obstacles to this arrangement. First, this scheme could require modification or abrogation of the ABM treaty because of LoAD's mobility. Second, an October 1980 Army study estimated its cost at $8.6 billion over 10 years. Third, MPS required a massive land area, sparking resistance by the residents and congressmen of the affected areas.[46]

Pres. Ronald Reagan created a commission, chaired by retired US Air Force lieutenant general Brent Scowcroft, to study the issues of ICBM basing and updating of strategic forces. The report in April 1983 concluded that no current BMD technology appeared to combine "practicability, survivability, low cost and technical effectiveness sufficient to justify proceeding beyond the stage of technology development."[47] Partially because of this report, the government cancelled the BMD system for MPS in 1984 and decided to put the new missiles into silos that had housed Minuteman III missiles.[48] Reagan ended this one BMD scheme and went on to start another more far-reaching one.

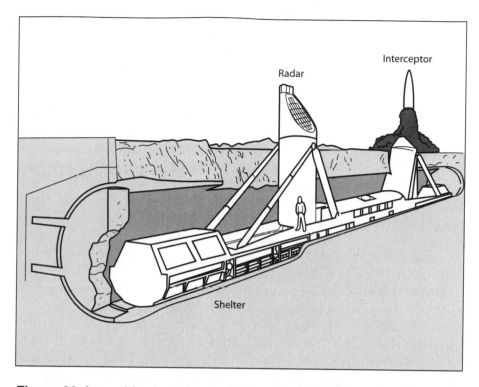

Figure 86. Low altitude defense system (LoADS). The low altitude defense system was a mobile underground ABM system designed to protect American missile fields. Neither the missile field (Multiple Protective Shelter) nor LoADS was built. (Reprinted from Office of Technology Assessment.)

The Strategic Defense Initiative: Star Wars

On 23 March 1983, President Reagan delivered probably his most memorable speech and one of the country's more significant presidential speeches, certainly in defense matters, in a number of decades.[49] The president called for new strategic defense thinking and a shift from a policy of nuclear deterrence to one of defense. Unlike those who pushed for a diplomatic solution to the problems of nuclear weapons and superpower rivalry, Reagan sought a technical solution. In his words, "Wouldn't it be better to save lives than to avenge them?" He put forward a new vision based on American technical and industrial capabilities to render offensive nuclear weapons "impotent and obsolete."[50]

The space-based Strategic Defense Initiative (SDI) promised a way out of the "balance of terror," the system of nuclear deterrence that had been American policy for decades.[51] Those who distrusted the movement toward arms control and feared that these treaties and the unrelenting arms buildup gave the Soviets parity, if not superiority, in strategic weapons cheered the proposal.[52] SDI would give the United States more options, play to American technical and industrial strengths, serve as a counter to Soviet BMD and heavy ICBMs, defend against both an accidental (or unauthorized) attack, and add uncertainty to an attacker's considerations. Finally, an American BMD would provide insurance against the possibility of the Soviets cheating or breaking out of the ABM treaty.[53]

Opponents of BMD quickly responded. They attempted to ridicule the system by naming it Star Wars for the popular, futuristic movie of the day, a tag quickly picked up and circulated by the media. There was substantial opposition from both the Air Force and Navy—both feared that SDI would take money from other programs. Of course, the arms-control community along with many in academia rose against the project. Close to 7,000 scientists pledged not to accept SDI money, including 15 Nobel Laureates and the majority in the physics departments at the nation's top 20 colleges. The criticisms were perhaps best summarized by former president Jimmy Carter who called SDI "infeasible, extremely costly, misleading and an obstacle to nuclear arms control."[54]

The problems were as grand as the scheme. The technical obstacles were daunting, as this project was well beyond the state of the art, as were the costs, which were estimated in the range of hundreds of billions, with some going as high as one trillion, dollars.[55] A third major criticism of SDI was that it would unravel the various arms-control agreements (specifically violate the ABM treaty) and lead to an arms race. Opinion polls indicated that the public opposed SDI, especially when informed of its price.[56]

The system made technical progress in the 1980s. One new development was a nonnuclear warhead, forced on the project when the proponents were unable to convince the public that exploding defensive nuclear warheads overhead would defend them against nuclear annihilation. There were test successes. Perhaps most impressive was the Homing Overlay Experiment (HOE) that in June 1984 successfully intercepted a Minuteman over 100 miles in altitude and traveling at upwards of 15,000 miles per hour. Although some critics charged that the tests were rigged, this certainly appeared to be an outstanding success.[57] The SDI deployment plan also evolved. The original concept called for 300 satellites, each carrying about 100 interceptors, sometimes called "battle stations" or "smart rocks." This plan changed to one of smaller interceptors that would independently engage targets, so-called brilliant pebbles.[58]

Before the end of the decade, the world was turned upside down when the Soviet Union collapsed. A major factor in this momentous event was the US arms buildup in the 1980s that bolstered and highlighted the significant and growing technological gap between America and the Soviet Union. SDI was the most prominent of these technologies.

But the demise of the Soviet system didn't end the BMD story. In fact, it brought a new ballistic missile threat, not from a superpower that was deterred by offensive nuclear weapons, but by third world countries that might not be. The end of the bipolar superpower system also meant the end of the control that each nation had over its alliance members and client states. This threat from countries other than the Soviet Union became clearly visible for decision makers and the public alike in the 1990–91 Gulf War.

The Gulf War: Patriot versus Scud

The Gulf War was an overwhelming coalition, military, and technological success, with one notable exception. What looked to be a mismatch between the coalition's overwhelming technical superiority and the Iraqis' outdated missiles turned out far differently in the campaign against Iraqi tactical ballistic missiles. The Iraqis effectively used their Scuds to frustrate the coalition, seize the initiative, and apply great political and psychological pressure that had the potential to unravel the alliance.

199

Scud is the NATO code name for a Soviet surface-to-surface ballistic missile that evolved from the German V-2. Compared to the German missile, it has a longer range, greater accuracy, but a lighter payload (fig. 87).[59] The Iraqis modified the Scud B to extend its range to 650 km. This conversion also increased missile speed 40 to 50 percent but reduced both warhead weight and accuracy. Because of shoddy manufacturing, the modified missile also had a tendency to break up during its terminal phase.[60] Unintentionally, the corkscrewing, disintegrating missile became in effect a maneuvering reentry vehicle with decoys—a much more difficult target to intercept than the designed Scud warhead.[61]

Before the war, there were fears that fatalities from missile attacks might be on average as high as 10 per Scud fired, an estimate in line with the five killed by each V-2 during World War II. However, this did not take into account the impact of chemical warheads, which would have inflicted even greater

Figure 87. Scud missile. The Iraqis modified the Soviet Scud missile which extended its range but lessened its accuracy. Iraqi Scud attacks put political pressure on the coalition and, as a result, diverted resources. (Reprinted from http://www.acq.osd.mil.)

casualties. During the war, the Iraqis launched about 91 Scuds: three at Bahrain, 40 at Israel, and 48 at Saudi Arabia.[62] Despite considerable coalition and Israeli concerns, the Iraqis did not employ chemical warheads, and casualties were far lower than estimated. The Israelis suffered only two direct deaths from the Scuds and another 11 indirectly. In addition, probably 12 Saudis were killed and 121 were wounded.[63]

There were also American casualties. On 26 February, a Scud hit a Dhahran warehouse being used as a billet by about 127 American troops, killing 28 and wounding 97 others (fig. 88). This one Scud accounted for 21 percent of the US personnel killed during the war and 40 percent of those wounded.[64] A number of factors explain this incident. Apparently, one Patriot battery was shut down for maintenance, and another had cumulative computer timing problems. Another factor was just plain bad luck. This Scud not only hit the warehouse, but unlike so many other Iraqi missiles, this one remained intact, and the

Figure 88. Scud hit on barracks. The coalition suffered amazingly low casualties in the first Gulf War. The worst single incident was a Scud hit on an American barracks in Dhahran, Saudi Arabia, that killed 28 Americans and wounded another 97. (Reprinted from Defense Visual Information Center.)

warhead detonated.[65] Nevertheless, the overall death rate was less than one killed for each missile fired.[66]

The political power of the Scud far exceeded its military impact. The Israelis were not about to stand by as Iraqi missiles showered their cities with death and destruction. If they intervened, however, the carefully constructed coalition would quickly unravel, which, of course, was what the Iraqis desired.[67]

Although the Israelis rejected American aid before the shooting started, they changed everything after the firing of the first Scud. The Israelis quickly requested both American Patriot missiles and identification friend or foe codes to allow their aircraft to strike Iraqi targets without tangling with coalition aircraft. The United States quickly agreed to the first request but refused the second. However, American decision makers understood that the Scud menace had to be contained to keep the Israelis out of the conflict.[68] One important element in this effort was the Army's Patriot.

The Patriot

The Army had been concerned about defense against tactical ballistic missiles since the V-2s appeared in World War II. As already related, the ground service had conducted a number of various projects to accomplish this goal. In August 1965, DOD established a project office at the Redstone Arsenal for the system that was renamed SAM-D (surface-to-air missile development). The Army wanted a system that was mobile, included an antimissile capability, and could replace its Hawk and Nike-Hercules missiles. To be clear, the missile was designed mainly as a point defense weapon (meaning it had limited range) against relatively lower-flying and lower-speed aircraft rather than against much higher- and faster-flying ballistic missiles.

There were various efforts to cancel the program. The Army responded by simplifying the technology and cutting costs. More to the point, in 1974 DOD dropped the BMD requirement to save money. Now SAM-D was to be strictly a mobile SAM to counter aircraft. In May 1976, the program was renamed Patriot (phased-array tracking to intercept of target), which was a rather strained acronym. However, some say this was intended to please influential Speaker of the House of Representatives Tip O'Neil of Massachusetts, while others believed that no program named Patriot would be cancelled in the nation's bicentennial year.[69]

The Patriot first flew in February 1970. Two features distinguished it. First, it carried a conventional warhead that made its task of intercepting missiles much more difficult. This led to a new guidance-system approach called track-via-missile (TVM). A single ground-based phased-array radar guided the interceptor missile toward the incoming missile. As the two missiles approached one another, the interceptor's seeker attempted to detect radar energy emanated by the ground radar that had bounced off the incoming missile. The system relayed this information to the ground computer to guide the interceptor toward interception. In theory, this makes the system more accurate and more difficult to jam. TVM was so critical to the Patriot that in February 1974, DOD stopped the project for two years until the concept was successfully demonstrated.[70]

In 1980, the Army decided to modify the Patriot to enable it to defend against a Soviet ballistic missile threat. The first version (PAC-1, Patriot ATM Capability) was only a minor change to the system's software and was completed by December 1988. The second upgrade, PAC-2, was somewhat more involved. It included changes in the software, a better warhead, a different fuze, and improved radar that gave it some capability against ballistic missiles, increasing its radius of defense from 3 to 12 miles.[71]

Patriot was flying high. DOD granted full production authority in April 1982. In 63 flight tests in April through June 1982, the missile scored 52 successes. Therefore, the Army scheduled first production deliveries for June 1982 and IOC for June 1983. Operational testing in May and June 1983, however, revealed serious reliability and maintainability problems that threatened Patriot with cancellation. Raytheon recovered from this crisis and exceeded expectations in the retest, scoring 17 hits on 17 tests between 1986 and January 1991. Most impressive was what the Patriot promised against ballistic missiles. In September 1986, Patriot intercepted a Lance ballistic missile and then in November 1987 intercepted another Patriot acting as a surrogate for an incoming ballistic missile.[72]

The 2,200-pound missile (at launch) carries a 200-pound conventional warhead up to almost 79,000 feet and out to a distance of 37 nm. The Patriot's electronics can simultaneously track up to 50 targets and handle five engagements at the same time. It is able to defend an area 20 km forward of its position and 5 km to both right and left. Four missiles are mounted on a trailer pulled by a tractor or a truck.[73]

Patriot in Action

The Patriot was the only US weapon used against an incoming ballistic missile, and it formed the last line of active defense against the Scuds (fig. 89). The United States airlifted 32 Patriot

Figure 89. Patriot missile in Desert Storm. The Patriot missile was the American counter to the Iraqi Scud during the first Gulf War. Its performance was controversial, but it did ease political and psychological pressures. (Reprinted from Redstone Arsenal.)

missiles to Israel within 17 hours and got them operational within three days. Patriot deployment in the Gulf War eventually consisted of seven batteries to Israel, 21 to Saudi Arabia, and four to Turkey.[74]

Crucial to the active BMD was early warning provided by strategic satellites. Although American Defense Support Program satellites were designed to give warning of ICBM launches, they had the ability to track the lower-flying, cooler, shorter-range, tactical ballistic missiles, as demonstrated against hundreds of tactical ballistic missiles during their tests and in two Mid-Eastern wars.[75] Before the shooting started in the Gulf War, Strategic Air Command (SAC) worked out a system that coordinated information from the satellites, routed it through three widely separated headquarters (SAC, Space Command, and Central Command), and passed it to the user in the field. While the satellite did not precisely indicate either the location of launch or anticipated point of impact, it did give general information. The bottleneck was the communications; nevertheless, the jury-rigged system gave a few minutes' warning to both the defending Patriot crews and people in the target area. During the war, the satellites detected all 88 Scud launches.[76]

One of the main controversies of the war centered on how many Patriots hit Scuds. The Patriots engaged most of the 53 Scuds that flew within their area of coverage, 46 to 52 according to secondary accounts, with 158 SAMs (fig. 90). Gen Norman Schwarzkopf initially claimed 100 percent Patriot success. After the war, the manufacturer boasted of 89 percent success over Saudi Arabia and 44 percent over Israel. Then, in December 1991, the Army asserted 80 percent and 50 percent successes, respectively. The following April, they were further reduced to 70 and 40 percent, respectively.[77]

Outside experts criticized these figures. Congressional researchers noted that the Army had little evidence on which to base its high claims. The General Accounting Office (GAO) stated that while the Army was highly confident that 25 percent of the engagements resulted in kills of the Scud warhead, it had the strongest supporting evidence in only one-third of these cases. The most visible critic, Theodore Postal of the Massachusetts Institute of Technology, was much sharper in his attack on the

Figure 90. Scud. Scud debris, first Gulf War. The coalition's inability to throttle the Scud attacks was an embarrassment, but otherwise the missile was not an effective military weapon. (Reprinted from Defense Visual Information Center.)

Army's claims. He wrote that his studies "indicate[d] that Patriot was a near total failure in terms of its ability to destroy, damage, or divert Scud warheads."[78] Postal went on to state that there was only one clear example of a hit but that it was uncertain whether this impacted on a Scud warhead or fuel tank. He approvingly quoted Yitzhak Rabin: "The biggest disappointment of the war is reserved for the Patriot. It was excellent public relations, but its intercept rate was rather poor."[79] Postal claimed that not only was the Patriot unsuccessful in neutering the Scud, it may have caused more ground damage than did the Scuds. The defenders fired three Patriots at each of the incoming Scuds, and each interceptor missile weighed more than did the Scud's warhead.[80]

Whatever the facts of the matter, this line of argument misses the main point. Just as the Scuds were primarily a psychological weapon, so too were the Patriots. They provided great theater, with live videos of fiery launches, smoke trails, and aerial fireworks made more vivid with a dark, night background that had a positive impact on civilians and decision makers in the United States, Saudi Arabia, and Israel. (There is no indication that any Iraqis saw this very visible performance, and, if so, what impact it had on them.) The situation was manageable for the defenders as long as the Scud attacks were limited in number, accuracy, and lethality. Missile warning protected civilians from death and injury, while active missile defenses bolstered morale. The Patriots were an important factor in keeping Israel out of the war.

Another factor in deterring Israel's intervention was the intense direct offensive campaign waged against the Scuds. The Airmen flew almost 4,000 sorties, about 3.5 percent of the total scheduled by the coalition and three times the planned effort.[81] The Army joined the Air Force in the anti-Scud campaign with both surface-to-surface rockets ATACMS (Army Tactical Missile System) and American and British Special Forces. According to secondary sources, they claimed between 10 and 20 Scud launchers destroyed. But to be clear, despite this massive coalition air and ground effort, similar to the World War II experience against the V-2, there is no confirmation of the destruction of a single mobile Scud launcher.[82]

In short, the Scuds were the greatest difficulty encountered by US forces in the Gulf War. Although not a military threat and inflicting few casualties, they certainly presented a valid challenge to the coalition's unity and diverted considerable resources. While the Airmen did not perform as they would have liked against the Scuds, they did enough to help keep the Israelis out of the war. The Airmen also can take some credit for reducing the Iraqi launch rates from a one-third to one-half that seen in the Iran-Iraq War, even though the Iraqis had more missiles in 1991. Suppressing the launch rate meant the Iraqis could not fire in salvos that had the potential to swamp the Patriots.[83] The Scuds were much less deadly than the German V-2s. In brief, although the Iraqis beat the coalition tactically with the Scuds, as coalition forces could not find and thus destroy the dated tactical ballistic missiles, the coalition was able to manage

207

the political aspects by using the Patriot. However questionable BMD was in fact, it appeared successful to the press and public, and this political and psychological impression was most important.[84]

The Patriot-Scud duel had implications well beyond the Persian Gulf War. The Iraqi Scud indicated the threat that faced the United States and its friends. The war showed how this crude weapon could create great political problems and force a significant diversion of military resources. Especially grave were the implications of ballistic missiles armed with nuclear, biological, or chemical warheads. At the same time, the apparent success of the Patriot against the Scud gave impetus to BMD programs.

Notes

1. A fuller version of the ballistic missile defense story can be found in this author's "Hitting a Bullet with a Bullet: A History of Ballistic Missile Defense," CADRE Research Paper 2000–02 (Maxwell AFB, Ala.: College of Aerospace Doctrine, Research and Education, 2000).

2. *United States Strategic Bombing Survey, Overall Report* (Washington, D.C.: Government Printing Office [GPO], 1945), 88–89; Adam Gruen, *Preemptive Defense: Allied Air Power versus Hitler's V-Weapons, 1943–1945* (Washington, D.C.: Air Force History and Museums Program, 1998), 15; Robert Allen, "Counterforce in World War II," in *Theater Missile Defense: Systems and Issues—1993* (Washington, D.C.: American Institute of Aeronautics and Astronautics, 1993), 109; and Military Intelligence Division, *Handbook on Guided Missiles of Germany and Japan*, February 1946, R.

3. David Johnson, *V-1, V-2: Hitler's Vengeance on London* (New York: Stein and Day, 1981), 168–69.

4. Donald Baucom, *The Origins of SDI, 1944–1983* (Lawrence, Kans.: University Press of Kansas, 1992), 4; and Frederick Pile, *Ack-Ack: Britain's Defence against Air Attack during the Second World War* (London: Harrap, 1949), 388.

5. Army Ordnance Missile Command, *Surface-to-Air Missiles Reference Book*, V-1, 2, R; Stephen Blanchette, "The Air Force and Ballistic Missile Defense" (thesis, Air Command and Staff College, February 1987), 10–11, 15–16, AUL; Baucom, *The Origins of SDI*, 4, 6, 12–13; Georgia Institute of Technology, "Missile Catalog: A Compendium of Guided Missile and Seeker Information," April 1956, 101, 128, 130, R; "History of Air Research and Development Command: July–December 1954," vol.1, 225–27, Historical Research Agency, Maxwell AFB, Ala.; and James Walker, Frances Martin, and Sharon Watkins, *Strategic Defense: Four Decades of Progress* (n.p.: Historical Office, US Army Space and Strategic Defense Command, 1995), 4.

6. Army Ordnance Missile Command, "SAM Reference Book," IV-16, V-1, 2–3, 6, R; John Bullard, "History of the Field Army Ballistic Missile Defense System Project, 1959–1962," December 1963, 5, R; Mary Cagle, "History of Nike Hercules Weapon System," April 1973, 191, R; and Woodrow Sigley, "Department of the Army Presentation to the Department of Defense Antiballistic Missile Committee: Scheduling and Costs for the Army Antiballistic Missile Program," October 1956, 4, R.

7. Bullard, *History*, 2, 4, 9, 12–13, 80; Cagle, "Nike Hercules," 173, 191, 192n; and Tony Cullen and Christopher Foss, eds., *Jane's Land-Based Air Defence, 1996–97*, 9th ed. (Coulsdon, Surrey, U.K.: Jane's, 1996), 290.

8. "ABM Research and Development at Bell Laboratories: Project History," I-1, I-2, I-3, I-5, I-6, I-10, I-15, R; and Walker, Martin, and Watkins, *Strategic Defense*, 10.

9. "ABM Project History," I-15; Space and Missile Defense Command (SMDC), "A Discussion of Nike Zeus Decisions," 5, HRA; and Ralph Taylor, "Space Counter Weapon Program: Air Defense Panel Presentation," February 1961, HRA.

10. "ABM Project History," I-5, I-32; and K. Scott McMahon, *Pursuit of the Shield: The US Quest for Limited Ballistic Missile Defense* (Lanham, Md.: University Press of America, 1997), 15; SMDC, "Discussion of Nike Zeus Decisions," 5–7; and Walker, Martin, and Watkins, *Strategic Defense*, 18.

11. Craig Eisendrath, Melvin Goodman, and Gerard Marsh, *The Phantom Defense: America's Pursuit of the Star Wars Illusion* (Westport, Conn.: Praeger, 2001), xix.

12. A clarification on terminology may be in order. In the early years, ballistic missile defense was oriented primarily, if not exclusively, against strategic missiles and was usually referred to as ABM. Later, defensive efforts were aimed at both strategic and tactical weapons, and the term *ballistic missile defense* was used. To keep matters simple, I have used ABM and BMD interchangeably to indicate ballistic missile defense in general against either strategic or tactical weapons. See Daniel Papp, "From Project Thumper to SDI: The Role of Ballistic Missile Defense in US Security Policy," *Air Power Journal*, April 1987, 41.

13. Army Ordnance Command, "SAM Reference Book," IV-4; North American Air Defense Command (NORAD), "Quest for Nike Zeus and a Long-Range Interceptor," historical reference paper no. 6, 7–13, HRA; B. Bruce Briggs, *The Shield of Faith: A Chronicle of Strategic Defense from Zeppelins to Star Wars* (N.Y.: Simon and Schuster, 1988), 141; Edward Jayne, "The ABM Debate: Strategic Defense and National Security" (PhD diss., Political Science, Massachusetts Institute of Technology, 1969), 24; NORAD, "Quest for Nike Zeus," 2; and Walker, Martin, and Watkins, *Strategic Defense*, 18.

14. For example, the Eisenhower administration cut the planned interceptor fighter buy from 4,500 aircraft to 1,000, and the planned buy of 8,300 Nike Hercules to 2,400. See Briggs, *The Shield of Faith*, 137, 141; and Edward Reiss, *The Strategic Defense Initiative* (New York: Cambridge University, 1992), 22.

209

15. "ABM Project History," I-15; and NORAD, "Quest for Nike Zeus," 1.

16. "ABM Project History," I-24, I-26; History of the 1st Strategic Aerospace Division: The Nike–Zeus Program, August 1959–April 1963, 17–18, 29, HRA; and Walker, Martin, and Watkins, Strategic Defense, 19.

17. "ABM Project History," I-22, I-23.

18. Walker, Martin, and Watkins, Strategic Defense, 19.

19. SMDC, "Discussion of Nike-Zeus Decisions," 10; and NORAD, "Quest for Nike Zeus," 16–17.

20. SMDC, "Discussion of Nike-Zeus Decisions," 8–9.

21. SMDC, "ABM Project History," 2–9, X-1, I-36, I-37; and Walker, Martin, and Watkins, Strategic Defense, 23.

22. Army Ordnance Missile Command, reference book, IV-14; "ABM Project History," I-37, 2–9, 9-1, IX-4, IX-21, IX-23; and Briggs, The Shield of Faith, 246–47.

23. "ABM Project History," I-37, I-44, II-1; Baucom, The Origins of SDI, 19; and Walker, Martin, and Watkins, Strategic Defense, 23, 26.

24. Other methods to enhance survivability of offensive forces were to launch on warning, disperse, proliferate, and increase the number of weapons on alert.

25. Steven Zaloga, Soviet Air Defence Missiles: Design, Development and Tactics (Coulsdon, Surrey, U.K.: Jane's, 1989), 121–22.

26. Galosh was a three-stage liquid-fuel rocket that carried a nuclear warhead of 2–3 megaton yield out to a maximum range of 300 km and to a maximum altitude of 300 km. See David Yost, Soviet Ballistic Missiles and the Western Alliance (Cambridge, Mass.: Harvard University, 1988), 28; and Zaloga, Soviet Air Defence Missiles, 128, 133, 135, 137.

27. According to a highly placed official and creditable academic, the majority of the intelligence community believed Tallinn was an air defense system. See Morton Halperin, The Decision to Deploy the ABM: Bureaucratic and Domestic Politics in the Johnson Administration (Washington, D.C.: Brookings Institution, 1973), 82; "ABM Project History," I-41, I-43, I-44, 2–4; Briggs, The Shield of Faith, 277; David Grogan, "Power Play: Theater Ballistic Missile Defense, National Ballistic Missile Defense and the ABM Treaty" (Master of Laws, George Washington University Law School, May 1998), 9; Jayne, "The ABM Debate," 307, 318; Benjamin Lambeth, "Soviet Perspectives on the SDI," in Samuel Wells and Robert Litwak, eds., Strategic Defenses and Soviet-American Relations (Cambridge, Mass.: Ballinger, 1987), 50; Kerry Stryker, "A Bureaucratic Politics Examination of US Strategic Policy Making: A Case Study of the ABM" (MA thesis, San Diego State University, 1979), 107, 156; Walker, Martin, and Watkins, Strategic Defense, 29–30; and Zaloga, Soviet Air Defence Missiles, 15, 100, 102.

28. Douglas Johnston, "Ballistic Missile Defense: Panacea or Pandora?" (PhD diss., Harvard, 1982), 195; and Yost, Soviet Ballistic Missiles, 26.

29. Interview with Lt Gen Austin Betts, 12 March 1971, 8, HRA; Briggs, The Shield of Faith, 259; Donald Bussey, "Deployment of Antiballistic Missile (ABM): The Pros and Cons," Library of Congress Legislative Reference Service,

April 1967, 17, 24; Halperin, *The Decision to Deploy*, 63; and Walker, Martin, and Watkins, *Strategic Defense*, 26. See also "The ABM Debate," 129–31, for example.

30. McNamara's predecessor, Thomas Gates, was also against deployment because he believed the public would not support the required shelter program. See Jayne, "The ABM Debate," 90; and Howard Stoffer, "Congressional Defense Policy-Making and the Arms Control Community: The Case of the Antiballistic Missile" (PhD diss., Columbia University, 1980), 117. McNamara's position on the limits of the ABM system remained constant. The Kennedy administration had pushed through a shelter request in August 1961 but had difficulties with follow-up programs the next year. One DOD study in the early 1960s concluded that shelters could save a life for $20 versus $700 per person for the Nike-X. See Briggs, *The Shield of Faith*, 252; and Jayne, "The ABM Debate," 182, 230.

31. The arguments for and against the ABM during this period are most clearly set out in Halperin, *The Decision to Deploy*, 79–81. See also Baucom, *Origins of SDI*, 23; Betts interview, 4; Stryker, "A Bureaucratic Politics Examination," 104; Briggs, *The Shield of Faith*, 285; and Walker, Martin, and Watkins, *Strategic Defense*, 29–30.

32. Betts interview, 8; Halperin, *The Decision to Deploy*, 78, 83; Jayne, "The ABM Debate," 309, 359; Stryker, "A Bureaucratic Politics Examination," 171, 181–82, 208, 227; and Senate Committee on Foreign Affairs, "Staff Memorandum on Current Status of the Antiballistic Missile (ABM) Program," 90th Cong., 1st sess., March 1967, 2.

33. Baucom, *Origins of SDI*, 33, 34; Halperin, *The Decision to Deploy*, 84–86; and Jayne, "The ABM Debate," 360.

34. Baucom, *Origins of SDI*, 34; and Jayne, "The ABM Debate," 372.

35. Casualty estimates for a small Chinese attack against the United States were about 6 to 12 million without defenses, 3 to 6 million with terminal defenses, and zero to 2 million with terminal and area defenses. See Jayne, "The ABM Debate," 302; and Halperin, *The Decision to Deploy*, 89n.

36. Baucom, *Origins of SDI*, 35–37; Briggs, *The Shield of Faith*, 286, 327; Jayne, "The ABM Debate," 249n38, 374n2; and Walker, Martin, and Watkins, *Strategic Defense*, 33.

37. James Bowman, "The 1969 ABM Debate" (PhD diss., University of Nebraska, 1973), 127–32, 170; McMahon, *Pursuit of the Shield*, 45, 47; Stoffer, "Congressional Defense Policy Making," 149; Walker, Martin, and Watkins, *Strategic Defense*, 33.

38. Jayne, "The ABM Debate," 413–14; Thomas Longstreth and John Pike, *A Report on the Impact of US and Soviet Ballistic Missile Defense Programs on the ABM Treaty* (n.p.: National Campaign to Save the ABM Treaty, 1984), 4; and McMahon, *Pursuit of the Shield*, 45.

39. Baucom, *Origins of SDI*, 38; Bowman, "The 1969 ABM Debate," 178; Briggs, *The Shield of Faith*, 299; Erik Pratt, "Weapons Sponsorship: Promoting Strategic Defense in the Nuclear Era" (PhD diss., University of California,

Riverside, 1989), 148; Stryker, "A Bureaucratic Politics Examination," 229; and Walker, Martin, and Watkins, *Strategic Defense*, 33, 38.

40. Baucom, *Origins of SDI*, 43; and Bowman, "The 1969 ABM Debate," 173, 177.

41. The SALT I agreement gave the Soviets a numerical edge with both ICBMs (1,618 to 1,054) and submarine-launched strategic missiles (62 boats and 950 missiles to 44 boats and 710 missiles). See Baucom, *Origins of SDI*, 51–71; and Longstreth and Pike, *A Report on the Impact*, 4.

42. Baucom, *Origins of SDI*, 70; Grogan, "Power Play" (May 1998), 11; and L. Maust, G. W. Goodman, and C. E. McLain, "History of Strategic Defense," System Planning Corporation (SPC) final report, SPC 742, September 1981, 16–17.

43. Walker, Martin, and Watkins, *Strategic Defense*, 38; Bradley Graham, *Hit to Kill: The New Battle over Shielding America from Missile Attack* (N.Y.: Public Affairs, 2001), 12; and Eisendrath, Goodman, and Marsh, *The Phantom Defense*, 7.

44. The radar was about one-tenth the size of the SAFEGUARD system and the missile one-fourth the size of the Sprint.

45. It consisted of randomly moving the ICBMs and decoys between the shelters so that an attacker would have to target all 4,600 shelters to take out the 200 strategic missiles. The Air Force opposed such a system, but in the interest of maintaining military solidarity, muted its views. See Desmond Ball, "US Strategic Concepts and Programs: The Historical Context," in Wells and Litwak, eds., *Strategic Defenses*, 25; Baucom, *Origins of SDI*, 95, 172–73; and Douglas Johnston, "Ballistic Missile Defense: Panacea or Pandora?" (PhD diss., Harvard University, 1982), 54.

46. *Air Force Magazine*, May 1999, 150; and Office of Technology Assessment, *MX Missile Basing* (Washington, D.C.: GPO, 1981), 5–6, 17, 125.

47. Reiss, *The Strategic Defense Initiative*, 56.

48. The BMD system was renamed SENTRY in 1982. See Reiss, *The Strategic Defense Initiative*, 57; and Walker, Martin, and Watkins, *Strategic Defense*, 43.

49. The key source on SDI is Baucom, *Origins of SDI*.

50. Kerry Hunter, "The Reign of Fantasy: A Better Explanation for the Reagan Strategic Defense Initiative" (PhD diss., University of Washington, 1989), 182–84.

51. Ibid., 91–95, 142.

52. The major US concern was that the Soviets could convert their advantage of heavier missile throw weight into many more maneuvering warheads and move toward strategic superiority. See Baucom, *Origins of SDI*, 77–85.

53. David Dennon, *Ballistic Missile Defense in the Post-Cold War Era* (Boulder: Westview Press, 1995), 97; William Kincade, "The SDI and Arms Control," in Wells and Litwak, *Strategic Defenses*, 102; and Roberto Zuazua, "The Strategic Defense Initiative: An Examination on the Impact of Constructing a Defensive System to Protect the United States from Nuclear Ballistic Missiles" (MA thesis, Southwest Texas State University, 1988), 28.

54. Reiss, *The Strategic Defense Initiative*, 2, 89; Dennon, *Ballistic Missile Defense*, 90; Paul Uhlir, "The Reagan Administration's Proposal to Build a Ballistic Missile Defense System in Space: Strategic, Political and Legal Implications" (MA thesis in International Relations, University of San Diego, 1984), 101.

55. Hugh Funderburg, "The Strategic Defense Initiative and ABM Efforts: An Analysis" (MA thesis, Political Science, Western Illinois University, 1985), 17; Longstreth and Pike, *A Report on the Impact of US and Soviet Ballistic Missile Defense Programs*, 10; Reiss, *The Strategic Defense Initiative*, 60; and Zuazua, "A Strategic Defense Initiative," 38.

56. Hunter, "The Reign of Fantasy," 154–69; Kincade, "The SDI and Arms Control," 103; Zuazua, "A Strategic Defense Initiative," 38.

57. Dennon, *Ballistic Missile Defense*, 13, 105n53; Aengus Dowley, "A Review of the Strategic Defense Initiative and Ballistic Missile Defenses" (MS thesis, Southwest Missouri State University, 1995), 69, 124; Funderburg, "Strategic Defense Initiative," 17; Papp, "From Project Thumper to SDI"; and Zuazua, "A Strategic Defense Initiative," 28.

58. Dennon, *Ballistic Missile Defense*, 111; and McMahon, *Pursuit of the Shield*, 7.

59. Norman Freidman, *Desert Victory: The War for Kuwait* (Annapolis: Naval Institute, 1992), 340.

60. Rick Atkinson, *Crusade: The Untold Story of the Persian Gulf War* (New York: Houghton Mifflin, 1993), 79; Freidman, *Desert Victory*, 340; McMahon, *Pursuit of the Shield*, 298; David Snodgrass, "Attacking the Theater Mobile Ballistic Missile Threat," School of Advanced Airpower Studies, n.d., 89, AUL; Roy Braybrook, *Air Power: The Coalition and Iraqi Air Forces* (London: Osprey, 1991), 9; James Coyne, *Airpower in the Gulf* (Alexandria, Va.: Aerospace Education Foundation, 1992), 55; Warren Lenhart and Todd Masse, "Persian Gulf War: Iraqi Ballistic Missile Systems," CTS, February 1991, 1–2, AUL; and R. A. Mason, "The Air Power in the Gulf," *Survival*, May/June 1991, 216.

61. Friedman, *Desert Victory*, 340.

62. Anthony Cordesman and Abraham Wagner, *The Lessons of Modern War*, vol. 4, *The Gulf War* (Boulder: Westview Press, 1996), 856; Coyne, *Airpower in the Gulf*, 55, 122; Richard P. Hallion, *Storm over Iraq: Air Power and the Gulf War* (Washington, D.C.: Smithsonian Institution, 1992), 186; George Lewis, Steve Fetter, and Lisbeth Gronlund, "Casualties and Damage from Scud Attacks in the 1991 Gulf War" (DSCS working paper, March 1993), 5; and, Atkinson, *Crusade*, 90.

63. *Gulf War Air Power Survey (GWAPS)*, vol. 4, *Weapons, Tactics, and Training* (Washington, D.C.: GPO, 1993), 332; and Hallion, *Storm over Iraq*, 185–86.

64. Atkinson, *Crusade*, 418, 420; *GWAPS*, vol. 5, *Statistical Compendium* (Washington, D.C.: GPO, 1993), 657–58; and Hallion, *Storm over Iraq*, 185.

65. Atkinson, *Crusade*, 416–17, 419; Hallion, *Storm over Iraq*, 185; Michael Hockett, "Air Interdiction of Scud Missiles: A Need for Alarm," Air War College paper, April 1995, 40, AUL; and McMahon, *Pursuit of the Shield*, 299–300.

66. *GWAPS*, vol. 2, *Operations and Effects and Effectiveness*, 191; Michael Gordon and Bernard Trainor, *The Generals' War* (Boston: Little, Brown and Company, 1995), 239; and Edward Marolda and Robert Schneller, *Shield and Sword: The United States Navy and the Persian Gulf War* (Washington, D.C.: The Naval Historical Center, 1998), 197.

67. There certainly was a reluctance on the part of many of the Arab countries to do battle with the Iraqis. Some, if not most, would much rather have fought Israel. Reportedly, Egyptian and Syrian soldiers cheered when they learned that Iraq had launched Scuds against Israel. See *GWAPS*, vol. 4, *Weapons, Tactics, and Training*, 35; and Gordon and Trainor, *The Generals' War*, 235.

68. Gordon and Trainor, *The Generals' War*, 231; Hallion, *Storm over Iraq*, 180; and Robert Scales, *Certain Victory* (Washington, D.C.: Brassey's, 1994), 183.

69. Richard Barbera, "The Patriot Missile System: A Review and Analysis of Its Acquisition Process," Naval Postgraduate School, March 1994, 9, AUL; Donald Baucom, "Providing High Technology Systems for the Modern Battlefield: The Case of Patriot's Antitactical Ballistic Missile Capability," *Air Power History* (Spring 1992): 4–6, 8; Tony Cullen and Christopher Foss, eds., *Jane's Battlefield Air Defence 1988–89*, 9th ed. (Coulsdon, Surrey, U.K.: Jane's, 1988), 206; William Gregory, "How Patriot Survived: Its Project Managers," *Interavia Space Review*, March 1991, 66; and Steven Hildreth and Paul Zinsmeistser, "The Patriot Air Defense System and the Search for an Antitactical Ballistic Missile Defense," Congressional Research Service, June 1991, 9, AUL.

70. Barbera, "The Patriot Missile System," 11, 48; Baucom, "Providing High Technology," 7; Cullen and Foss, *Jane's Battlefield Air Defence 1988–89*, 206; Theodore Postal, "Lessons of the Gulf War Experience with Patriot," *International Security* (Winter 1991/92): 129–33; Frank Schubert and Theresa Kraus, *The Whirlwind War: The United States Army in Operations Desert Shield and Desert Storm* (Washington, D.C.: Center of Military History, 1995), 241.

71. Barbera, "The Patriot Missile System," 13–14, 23–24; Baucom, "Providing High Technology," 7, 9; and Cordesman and Wagner, *The Lessons of Modern War*, 869.

72. Barbera, "The Patriot Missile System," 13–17; Baucom, "Providing High Technology," 9; Cullen and Foss, *Jane's Battlefield Air Defence 1988–89*, 206; Hans Fenstermacher, "The Patriot Crisis" (Cambridge, Mass.: Harvard University, Kennedy School of Government Case Program, 1990), 3, 5, 7–9, 13; Gregory, "How Patriot Survived," 67; and Hildreth and Zinsmeistser, "The Patriot Air Defense System," 11.

73. Jorg Bahneman and Thomas Enders, "Reconsidering Ballistic Missile Defence," *Military Technology*, April 1991, 50; Barbera, "The Patriot Missile System," 22, 37, 65; Cullen and Foss, *Jane's Battlefield Air Defence 1988–89*, 209; and Schubert and Kraus, *The Whirlwind War*, 264.

74. *GWAPS*, vol. 2, *Operations and Effects and Effectiveness*, 118; Hallion, *Storm over Iraq*, 180; and Snodgrass, "Attacking the Theater Mobile Ballistic Missile," 87.

75. The Scuds emitted one-third the heat signature of an ICBM. See Cordesman and Wagner, *The Lessons of Modern War*, 862; and Donald Kutyna, "Space Systems in the Gulf War," draft, 138.

76. *Gulf War Air Power Survey, Command and Control* (Washington, D.C.: GPO, 1993), 248–50; *GWAPS*, vol. 4, *Weapons, Tactics, and Training*, 280–81. This warning was an important factor in the relatively low casualty rate. One reason the V-2 ballistic missile was so much more deadly (five killed per missile) than the V-1 flying bomb (0.6 kills per missile) during World War II was that the former gave no warning as it arrived at supersonic speeds, while the latter flew at subsonic speeds with a very distinctive sound that stopped before its last plunge. See Hallion, *Storm over Iraq*, 186; and Kenneth P. Werrell, *The Evolution of the Cruise Missile* (Maxwell Air Force Base, Ala.: Air University Press, 1985), 60–61. For slightly different figures but the same conclusion, see Lewis, "Casualties and Damage," 4–5. The satellites were not infallible. For example, on one occasion, they mistook a B-52 strike for a Scud launch. See Tom Clancy with Chuck Horner, *Every Man a Tiger* (New York: Putnam, 1999), 385, 464; and Gary Waters, *Gulf Lesson One—The Value of Air Power: Doctrinal Lessons for Australia* (Canberra, Australia: Air Power Studies Centre, 1992), 217.

77. Part of the reason for the disparity in the rate of success in the two areas came from different crews, doctrine, and conditions. See Cordesman and Wagner, *The Lessons of Modern War*, 871–74; Coyne, *Airpower in the Gulf*, 122; *GWAPS*, vol. 2, *Operations and Effects and Effectiveness*, 118n; *GWAPS*, vol. 4, *Weapons, Tactics, and Training*, 280n; Hallion, *Storm over Iraq*, 185; Stewart Powell, "Scud War, Round Three," *Air Force Magazine*, October 1992, 35; and Snodgrass, "Attacking the Theater Mobile Ballistic Missile," 88–90.

78. Ted Postal, letter to the editor, *International Security* (Summer 1992), 226; General Accounting Office, *Operation Desert Storm: Data Does Not Exist to Conclusively Say How Well Patriot Performed*, September 1992, 3–4; and Steven Hildreth, "Evaluation of US Army Assessment of Patriot Antitactical Missile Effectiveness in the War Against Iraq," Congressional Research Service, April 1992, 7, 16.

79. Postal letter, 235n, 237–39.

80. Postal, "Lessons of the Gulf War Experience with Patriot," 146; and Theodore Postal, "Lessons for SDI from the Gulf War Patriot Experience: A Technical Perspective," testimony before the House Armed Services Committee, 16 April 1991, 4, AUL. For a defense of the Patriot, see Robert Stein, "Patriot ATBM Experience in the Gulf War," *International Security* (Summer 1992): 199–225. The participants in this fight had a specific agenda—they were contesting the facts for the impact of the Patriot's Gulf War performance on SDI and National Ballistic Missile Defense. For a more balanced

view, see Alexander Simon, "The Patriot Missile: Performance in the Gulf War Reviewed," July 1996, http://www.cdi.org/issues/bmd/Patriot.html.

81. Atkinson, *Crusade*, 147–48, 175; Clancy, *Every Man a Tiger*, 321, 379; *GWAPS*, vol. 2, *Operations and Effects and Effectiveness*, 182; 330, 335; *GWAPS*, vol. 5, *Statistical Compendium*, 418; Gordon and Trainor, *The Generals' War*, 237–38; Thomas Keaney and Eliot Cohen, *Revolution in Warfare?* (Annapolis: Naval Institute, 1995), 73n; Mason, "The Air Power," 217; and Snodgrass, "Attacking the Theater Mobile Ballistic Missile," 3.

82. Atkinson, *Crusade*, 177–81; *GWAPS*, vol. 2, *Operations and Effects and Effectiveness*, 330–31; Gordon and Trainor, *The Generals' War*, 241, 245–46; Hallion, *Storm over Iraq*, 181; Keaney and Cohen, *Revolution*, 73; and Scales, *Certain Victory*, 186.

83. Cordesman and Wagner, *The Lessons of Modern War*, 331–32; *GWAPS*, vol. 4, *Weapons, Tactics, and Training*, 292–93; and Gordon and Trainor, *The Generals' War*, 240. The Scud problem could have been much worse. If the missile had been more modern, it could have been maneuvering and more accurate. It also could have been used in greater numbers, armed with chemical warheads, or with a more dependable warhead. (Of 39 warheads that impacted in Israel, only a third detonated. See Lewis, "Casualties and Damage," 1.)

84. James Winnefeld, Preston Niblack, and Dana Johnson, *League of Airmen* (Santa Monica, Calif.: RAND, 1994), 132, 134.

Chapter 6

Ground-Based Air Defense since 1990: The Gulf, the Balkans, and Afghanistan

In the half century since World War II, the US military has been designed to battle masses of communist ground and air forces on and over the plains of Central Europe. Many believed the military could operate as well in other locales against lesser threats; and since it could fight and win a large war against a major foe, surely it could fight and win a small one against a lesser one. But the conflicts in both Korea (1950–53) and Vietnam (1965–72) demolished this assumption, as air units there had at best mixed results. Some would even insist the Airmen's efforts in Vietnam were both expensive and counterproductive. The American military's next major combat test would come within months of the fall of the communist empire and the end of the Cold War. Like the previous two wars, this one would also be thousands of miles from Europe, against a foe mainly equipped with Soviet materiel, and fought with a force configured for the NATO defense of Western Europe. However, unlike the conflicts in Northeast and Southeast Asia, after more than 40 years, the US military would finally fight its kind of fight.[1]

War in the Persian Gulf

The Iraqis had just fought a long, bitter war against the Iranians (1980–88). They survived that costly war, and arguably won it, or at least did not lose it. During that conflict, air operations were secondary, with both sides preserving rather than employing their air forces. Apparently, the Iraqis intended to repeat that strategy in the Gulf War, that is, to preserve their air force and rely on ground-based air defenses to protect them from coalition air power. As one commentator so well put it: the Iraqis were "prepared to refight their last war while the coalition prepared to fight the next [one]."[2] The Iraqis failed to recognize that the coalition was a far different foe than the Iranians.

217

Iraqi air defenses were certainly impressive in numbers and did include some very modern elements. The Iraqi air force was perhaps the sixth largest air force in the world, consisting of about 915 aircraft. These included almost 180 high-quality fighters (Mirages, MiG-25s, MiG-29s, and Su-24s) and more than 300 moderate-quality aircraft (MiG-23s, Su-7s, Su-25s, Tu-16s, and Tu-22s), with the remainder a mixed bag of older Soviet equipment, including MiG-17s and MiG-21s. Iraqi aircraft lacked air-to-air refueling capabilities; so, their aircraft had limited range compared with coalition aircraft. The difference between the Iraqi airmen and their coalition foes in terms of training and experience was even greater than the equipment gap.[3]

The Iraqi ground-based air defenses were imposing. This arsenal consisted of hundreds of surface-to-air missiles and thousands of antiaircraft guns and included a whole range of Soviet weapons (130–80 SA–2s, 100–125 SA–3s, 100–125 SA–6s, 20–35 SA–8s, 30–45 SA–9s, 3 SA–13s, and SA–14 launchers) as well as 55 to 65 French Crotale-Roland units. While most of the SAMs were older Russian systems (SA-2s and SA-3s), others were more modern and lethal.[4] In addition, the Iraqis had 20 to 25 American-built Improved Hawk launchers captured from the Kuwaitis that were of some, but not a serious, concern to the coalition.[5]

The Iraqi flak assets were both large and impressive. Their self-propelled inventory consisted of 167 ZSU-23/4, 425 30 mm, and 60 57 mm guns. The number of towed guns was a staggering 3,185 14.5 mm, 450 20–23 mm, 2,075 35–40 mm, and 363 100 mm and larger.[6] Iraqi defenses were particularly numerous around the capital and major city of Baghdad. The most detailed (unclassified) source states that there were 58 SAM launchers with 552 missiles and almost 1,300 guns defending the city. While other sources give other numbers, in any case, there was a lot of firepower. Baghdad was protected by more SAMs and guns than any eastern European city during the height of the Cold War, with seven times the number of SAMs as there were around Hanoi at the peak of the Vietnam War. Gen Charles A. "Chuck" Horner, the air commander in the Gulf War, later told a Senate committee that Iraqi defenses were twice as thick as those in eastern Europe "from the air standpoint, we looked at about as tough a threat as you are going to find anywhere."[7]

These air- and ground-based defenses were highly centralized. The key to the system was a computerized control system called KARI (Iraq spelled backwards in French in honor of its developers and installers). It consisted of 1970s technology that became operational in 1987. KARI was oriented against a threat from the west (Israel) and the east (Iran) consisting of a number of radars and more than two dozen operations centers. Built to handle attacks of 20 to 40 aircraft, KARI showed the capability of handling up to 120 tracks at one time during the Iran-Iraq War. It was highly automated and "user friendly," demanding little of lower-level operators. In fact, it was designed to be operated by personnel with the equivalent of a sixth grade education. KARI was both extensive and redundant, covering all of Iraq and, after the August invasion, Kuwait as well.[8]

As with their other systems, the Iraqis had a great number and variety of radars, about 500 located at 100 sites. American intelligence considered six Chinese (Nanjing) low-frequency radars the most dangerous, as they were least susceptible to jamming and, in theory, could detect the stealth aircraft.[9]

Thus, the Iraqis fielded a potent air force and air defenses. However, they faced the strongest, largest, and most modern air force in the world, bolstered by allies. Clearly, the coalition had air power superiority across the board in terms of numbers, aircraft quality, communications, and doctrine. Coalition airmen had other major advantages as well.

The coalition airmen greatly benefited from the maturation of two recent technologies that tilted the balance in favor of the offensive: stealth and precision-guided munitions (PGM) (fig. 91). Stealth greatly reduced the ability of radar to detect aircraft and, combined with carefully planned flight routing, made night and bad weather attacks essentially invisible. Thus, radar, which had been the air defender's chief asset from the early 1940s, was nullified, leaving the defenders dependent on blind luck and eyeballs for detection of attacks and guidance of guns and missiles. (Infrared homing was somewhat lessened but not to the same degree as radar.) The impact of this technology was enhanced by the development of PGMs. PGMs permitted almost

Figure 91. F-117 Stealth aircraft. The F-117 Stealth, an aircraft with extremely low detectability, introduced a new element into air warfare. Some believe it has revolutionized air warfare. If not, clearly it has radically changed air combat. (Reprinted from Defense Visual Information Center.)

"one shot, one hit" accuracy, which meant that a few aircraft could exact significant damage on the defender. Great fleets of attack and support aircraft were no longer needed to inflict critical damage on an opponent.[10]

The coalition had significant intelligence advantages. Certainly, the American fleet of sophisticated photographic, infrared, and electronic surveillance satellites was crucial. Airborne platforms added to this capability. In addition, the coalition contacted and received information from the companies that had built and installed equipment in potential targets. The Airmen also utilized agents on the ground.[11] On the other side, the Iraqis had a good idea of US reconnaissance capabilities because of US intelligence assistance to the Iraqis during the Iran-Iraq War. Therefore, they employed various methods to deny US overhead capabilities. In the end, however, seldom has one force so well informed fought another so ill informed.

Perhaps the greatest advantage the coalition forces had over the Iraqis was in the quality of personnel. The allied airmen were competent and highly trained. Not only did they have more flying experience than their opponents, but also many (certainly from the NATO forces) had trained in the highly realistic flag exercises. Even had the two combatants exchanged equipment, the coalition would have won—albeit at a greater cost.

The coalition planned to use its overwhelming air power to simultaneously attack both air defense and strategic targets.[12] The initial plan called for the F-117s to attack key air defense centers, cruise missiles to hit the electric power grid, along with attacks on command and communications facilities. These assaults would be followed by flights of American F-14 and F-15 fighters to counter any Iraqi interceptors. Later, massive coalition air attacks supported by drones, jammers, and aircraft equipped with radar-homing missiles would overload, neutralize, and destroy the Iraqi air defense system.[13]

The strategic plan called for a four-phase operation to achieve the coalition's military and political goals. The Airmen's target list grew from 84 in August 1990 (Instant Thunder) to 481 by the start of the shooting on 15 January 1991. At the same time, the number of targets in the target set "Strategic Air Defense" grew from 10 to 56, and those in "Airfields" grew from 7 to 31.[14]

The coalition shooting war began with an effort to blind the Iraqi air defense system. Task Force Normandy, nine Army AH-64 Apache helicopters led by three Air Force helicopters, attacked two early warning radars 21 minutes before the main assault (H-hour). (This, in fact, may have alerted the defenders.) Shortly after the initial assault, cruise missiles launched from B-52s and Navy ships and laser-guided bombs dropped from F-117s slammed into crucial targets. The stealth bombers and cruise missiles and the suddenness, accuracy, and fury of the assault caught the Iraqis by surprise. The coalition had lulled the Iraqi defenders during the prewar buildup by repeatedly flying a standard set of flights along the border. Forty minutes after H-hour, massive numbers of coalition aircraft supported by drones and defense suppression aircraft hit the Iraqis.[15] Within hours, the coalition had achieved air superiority, if not air supremacy. Or, to put it a bit more elegantly, "The initial strike delivered a paralyzing blow from which Iraq never recovered."[16] Now the Airmen could pick the helpless Iraqis apart at their leisure.

The Airmen used a variety of technologies and considerable resources to combat the Iraqi air defenses. These were successful well beyond their most optimistic hopes. In hindsight, it is easy to forget that while there was no doubt as to the ultimate outcome of a war with Iraq, there were questions and concerns about its cost. As one observer wrote after the war: "It was a war that could not be lost. The only question was the price to be paid in winning it."[17] Gen H. Norman Schwarzkopf writes that some feared that as many as 75 aircraft would be lost on the first night. Gen Buster C. Glosson, who would run the air campaign, thought that 10 to 18 aircraft might go down, while Col John A. Warden III, a major planner, estimated that number might be 10 to 15. The estimates for total losses were also varied and considerable. At the high end, one Central Command (CENTCOM) official opined that as many as 10 to 15 percent of the attackers would be lost. Another estimate out of that headquarters was that the coalition's aircraft losses could be as high as 114 to 141 in the first three phases of the war, with additional losses in the ground phase. Gen Merrill M. McPeak, Air Force chief of staff, would not accept one estimate of 0.5

percent losses and instead expected losses of about 150 aircraft in a 30-day campaign. Warden thought that probably no more than 40 would be lost over a six-day campaign. At his dramatic and crucial briefing of General Horner, Warden used the figures of 3 percent losses on the first day and then a 0.5 percent attrition rate. He believed that about 150 aircraft would be lost. Retired Air Force general Charles Donnelly told a House committee that 100 aircraft would be lost in a 10-day campaign of 20,000 sorties. Horner writes in his postwar memoirs that he expected to lose 42 US Air Force aircraft, while Glosson thought no more than 80 aircraft would be lost. A computer study that did not employ stealth aircraft (it is unclear why, but it apparently also did not include cruise missiles) indicated losses of one-half of the Air Force F-111Fs and Navy A-6s. This led to the decision to only use the F-117 and cruise missile against targets in Baghdad. A postwar account notes that in contrast to the predictions of an attrition rate of 0.5 percent of sorties, combat losses amounted to 0.05 percent.[18]

The coalition employed three principal means to neuter Iraqi ground-based air defenses: deception, jamming, and destruction. The Airmen used drones to spoof Iraqi radar, not only to confuse the operators but also to encourage them to disclose their position and thus make them vulnerable to direct countermeasures. The Navy was out in front with this concept, learning from the successful Israeli use of spoofing drones in the 1982 Bekaa Valley operation. The Navy bought versions of the Israeli Sampson drone, which they named TALD (Tactical Air Launched Decoy) (fig. 92). Marine and Navy aircraft could carry up to eight of the small (less than eight feet long and fewer than 400 pounds), cheap ($18,000) drones on a standard bomb rack. It was equipped with various means to simulate American aircraft and in addition, could drop chaff. The major disadvantage of the unpowered device was its limited range, which was dependent on launch altitude.[19]

The Air Force, at the initiative of one of Warden's subordinates, Maj Mark "Buck" Rogers, proposed using some Navy BQM-74 target drones for the same purpose (fig. 93). Although the deputy chief of staff for planning, Gen Jimmie Adams, rejected the plan, a request from CENTCOM led to its adoption.

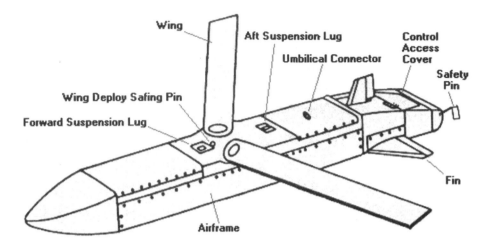

Figure 92. TALD decoy. The TALD is an unpowered, short-range decoy used to confuse and pinpoint enemy radars. (Reprinted from http://www. topedge.com/.../aircraft/sites/mats/f14-detail-tald.htm.)

The Air Force fitted reflectors to the drone and formed crews to operate them with men who had manned the US Air Force's discarded ground-launched cruise missile. They were to fly "figure eight" patterns over targets in the Baghdad and Basra areas until they ran out of fuel (they could fly about an hour) or were shot down.[20]

The drones worked wonderfully well for the coalition. The Air Force launched 38 of the devices from two different sites against their targets, while the Marines and Navy used 137 TALDs during the first three days. Intelligence noted an increase of 25 percent in SAM and AAA radar activity during the first wave. The Airmen estimated that the decoy use doubled or tripled the kills achieved by the antiradiation missiles. General Glosson noted that the Iraqis fired an average of 10 SAMs at each of the decoy drones.[21]

The Airmen found themselves short of jamming platforms. The Air Force used 36 EF-111Fs and 18 EC-130Hs, while the Marine and Navy employed 39 EA-6Bs. There were no allied jammers. Therefore, while the coalition had jamming aircraft, it realized the density of the defenses and the number of aircraft and strikes demanded more. Nevertheless, the jamming

Figure 93. BQM-74 drone. The Airmen used the BQM-74 drone to deceive enemy radars as well as force them to reveal their positions to more active defensive measures. (Reprinted from http://www.multipull.com/twascasefile/bqm74e.gif.)

worked well, with the EA-6B and EF-111 receiving praise as "highly effective."[22]

The coalition also employed 60 F-4G Wild Weasels whose airframes and basic mission had first seen action in the Vietnam War. They carried electronic equipment that enabled them to detect, identify, and locate radar signals and then attack the radars with homing air-to-ground missiles. According to the Air Force's *Gulf War Air Power Survey*, the F-4G was the weapon of choice for combating the Iraqi radars. One reason was that it was the only US Air Force aircraft that could program the HARM (high-speed antiradiation missile) in flight as to what targets not to hit, making them "smart weapons." The Weasels flew both autonomous and support missions, in all 2,700 sorties during the war with one combat loss.[23]

The Marines and Navy fielded 39 EA-6B Prowlers. These aircraft also dated back to the Vietnam War and used both jammers and missiles to counter enemy radars. They flew 1,630 combat sorties while firing more than 150 HARMs without a combat loss. The Navy claimed it flew 60 percent of the suppression of enemy air defenses (SEAD) missions.[24]

The Air Force also used two dozen EF-111A Ravens. The aircraft had a speed and range advantage over the Prowler, while the latter had jammers that were more effective. The EF-111's airframe also dated back to the Vietnam War era when they were used as bombers. (The US Air Force converted 42 to the electronic warfare role.) The Raven carried equipment to detect and jam enemy radars in both a standoff role and along with the penetrating attackers. The EF-111s flew 1,105 combat missions with one noncombat loss.[25]

Another Air Force jamming platform was the EC-130H Compass Call, a modified C-130 four-engine turboprop transport. Its mission was to intercept and jam enemy radio communications to confuse and disrupt the Iraqis. Although automated, the crew included nine Airmen who operated the electronic equipment. The US Air Force had 18 of these aircraft that flew 450 sorties during Desert Storm.[26]

The coalition used direct attack as well and employed a variety of air-to-surface missiles that homed in on the Iraqi radars. Shrike was the oldest of these missiles, having first seen service in Vietnam in 1965. Carrying a 149-pound warhead against Iraqi radars, the missile was limited by its range. American forces fired 78 of these during the campaign, more than half by the US Air Force.[27]

The most used antiradiation missile, however, was the HARM. This missile first flew in 1979 and achieved IOC in 1984. It could carry its 145-pound warhead more than 10 miles (dependent on launch altitude).[28] Because of the HARMs, after the first three hours of the war, the Iraqis seldom used their radars to guide their SAMs. The Air Force concluded that 45 percent of the HARMs fired by the Wild Weasels caused Iraqi radars to stop operating. Instead, the Iraqis fired their radar-guided SAMs ballistically, scary—but ineffective. On the first night, the coalition forces fired 200 HARMs and during the first week used most of the 2,000 expended in the war.[29]

Another antiradiation missile was the ALARM (air-launched antiradar missile). The British completed its trials in October 1990 and rushed it to the theater. The two-stage missile climbed to about 40,000 feet, where after rocket burnout, a parachute deployed and allowed the missile to slowly float earthward. During this 10-minute period, the missile searched for radars entered into its electronic library and, if detected, discarded the parachute and sought them out. In all, the Royal Air Force flew two dozen missions and fired 113 ALARMs.[30]

The Airmen were especially effective against Iraqi electronic equipment. Iraqi radar activity on day seven of the war was only 10 percent of that on day one. Reportedly, 85 percent of the radar-guided SAMs launched by the Iraqis were unguided, and these missiles accounted for only 10 percent of the coalition aircraft losses.[31]

In addition to the intimidation and destruction caused by the antiradiation missiles, the coalition airmen made tactical changes that degraded the Iraqi ground-based air defenses. Specifically, after suffering losses in the first three days of combat employing low-level tactics with which they had trained before the war, the airmen shifted their operations to medium altitudes of around 15,000 feet.[32] Higher-altitude operations decreased the effectiveness of both AAA and infrared-guided SAMs. However, operations from higher altitudes also decreased bombing accuracy with "dumb" bombs, increased the interference of weather to precision-guided munitions delivery, and reduced the effectiveness of the A-10's potent 30 mm cannon. For example, the F-16s achieved peacetime accuracy of 30 feet with unguided bombs, but during the war, this rose to 200 feet.[33] One postwar study notes that this change in altitude "was one of the most significant changes in allied strike planning, since peacetime training for most of the contributors for air power (including the most important, the United States and the United Kingdom) had emphasized low-level delivery of weapons."[34] The Gulf War demonstrated that the better way to combat dense air defenses was to use SEAD operations (US Air Force tactics) rather than the low-level tactics of NATO.[35]

227

Coalition efforts against Iraqi ground defenses were effective. The combination of destructive measures, the antiradiation missiles along with attacks on the KARI system, and jamming overwhelmed the Iraqi air defenders. Offensive air power was effective because the defenses could not enact a serious cost on the attackers. Both aggregate aircraft losses and rate of losses were dramatically below those seen in previous wars and those anticipated and, perhaps most remarkably, at a lower rate than Air Force training.

The coalition lost 38 aircraft along with another 48 due to damage suffered in combat. The coalition attributed 71 percent of these incidents to infrared SAMs and AAA, 16 percent to radar-guided SAMs, and 13 percent to MiGs (one) and unknown causes (fig. 94). On just over 4,800 combat sorties, the non-American forces lost 11 aircraft: two to antiaircraft artillery,

Figure 94. Damaged A-10. Of the 38 coalition air forces lost in combat, only one fell to enemy aircraft. AAA also damaged 24, IR SAMs 15, and radar-guided SAMs four aircraft, including this A-10, one of 13 Warthogs damaged. (Reprinted from Defense Visual Information Center.)

one to infrared-guided SAMs, five to radar-guided missiles, and three to unknown agents. Of the 27 US aircraft lost on over 60,200 combat sorties, seven were credited to AAA, 12 to infrared-guided SAMs, five to radar-guided SAMs, one to MiGs, and two to other or unknown causes. Only one of the five American aircraft downed by Iraqi radar-guided SAMs was flying under the protection of Air Force Wild Weasels.[36]

Coalition forces had won a great success. While some would later debate its political dimensions, it was clearly a great and overwhelming military victory. Air power played a major role in this achievement. In sharp contrast to the heavy losses the Airmen had suffered in previous wars and contrary to expectations, the cost in the Gulf conflict was relatively low. The Airmen had clearly beaten the ground defenders. For the moment, the offensive and Airmen had the advantage over the defensive and the ground defenders.

Air Defense since 1991:
Iraq, Balkans, and Afghanistan

US dominance continued after the great military success in the Gulf War. While there were no direct challenges to US supremacy, there were smaller probes. These actions pitted the numerically and technically superior American Airmen against smaller and technically inferior third world (developing world) air defenses.

Political success failed to follow the glorious 1991 military victory in the Persian Gulf. To protect rebellious Iraqis in the northern and southern portions of the country, the coalition flew aerial patrols to prevent Iraqi use of fixed-winged aircraft. Operations out of Incirlik Air Base, Turkey, covered the country north of 36 degrees under the code name Northern Watch, while operations south of 32 degrees (extended in September 1996 to the area south of 33 degrees) were initially called Provide Comfort, and in 1997, Southern Watch. Both saw spasmodic action as the Iraqis played cat-and-mouse games. The Iraqis sent their aircraft through the two zones to test and taunt the coalition airmen, turned on their radar, and fired both AAA and SAMs. The airmen responded. Up through May 1998, the coalition flew more than 175,000 sorties in the south and a comparable number in the north without combat loss. It also shot down a few Iraqi aircraft, fired rockets, and dropped bombs.[37]

In December 1998, the Airmen took the initiative in response to Iraqi obstructionism regarding weapons' inspectors. They flew 650 sorties in a four-day attack of 93 targets in Iraq. The Iraqis did not launch aircraft or medium-range SAMs against the coalition forces but did respond with short-range SAMs and AAA. Operation Desert Fox claimed to have destroyed 14 targets and severely damaged another 26 without loss or damage to Anglo-American aircraft. The two Watch operations were still in effect in 2002.[38]

The breakup of Yugoslavia led to a conflict that drew NATO into the Balkans. In April 1993, the United Nations requested that NATO enforce a no-fly zone in the area. As in Iraq, the Airmen faced a large, partially modern, but certainly dangerous air defense system. The Air Force history of the engagement noted that the "planners recognized that the Serbian integrated air defenses were a fairly sophisticated system, but consisted principally of older equipment with limited numbers of potentially modified or third-generation weapons systems."[39] It consisted of almost the full spectrum of Soviet air defense equipment: SA-2 (three launchers), SA-3 (16), SA-7/14/16 (more than 10,000), SA-6 (80), and SA-9 (130). The Serbs also fielded 54 ZSU-57-2 (57 mm) and 350 M53/59 (30 mm) AAA guns.

The Serbs fired at the Airmen and were able to down a British Sea Harrier in April 1994 with a SAM and a US Air Force F-16 in June 1995 with an SA-6. In August of that year, Serb mortar attacks on Sarajevo ignited Operation Deliberate Force, an air campaign that continued from 30 August until 14 September 1995. Airmen from eight NATO countries flew 3,500 sorties on 11 days of attacks on 48 targets. There was one combat loss, a French Mirage claimed by a man-portable missile.[40]

In mid-1999, the NATO alliance engaged in an air campaign to force the Serbian army out of Kosovo. Beginning with strikes on 24 March, Operation Allied Force lasted 78 days during which time the Airmen flew about 10,500 combat sorties (38,000 aircraft sorties in all) and almost 500 unmanned aerial vehicle (UAV) sorties. The Serbs fired nearly 850 SAMs and untold

AAA at the airmen but were able to down only one F-117 and one F-16. However, the loss of the F-117 was shocking, as none had been hit, much less lost, in the Gulf War. The cause of loss was not made public, but it was probably due to an SA-3. Nevertheless, the aircraft loss rate was less than that of the Gulf War. However, the loss of 15 UAVs by one account (25 UAVs by another) and three to five percent of the sorties indicates both their vulnerability and, in fact, why they were employed.[41]

The Serbs learned from the Iraqi experience. On only a few occasions did they directly confront allied forces; instead, they attempted to preserve their air defense system as a force in being. They were successful, as Serbs were firing as many SAMs at allied aircraft on the last days of the operation as on the first. Thus, the Airmen had to maintain high levels of support aircraft and operate from higher altitudes (above 15,000 feet) throughout the campaign, unlike the action in Iraq where both altitude and support sorties declined later in the operation after the air defenses had been suppressed.[42]

The United States responded to the 11 September 2001 attacks on the World Trade Center and the Pentagon with an assault on the terrorist sanctuary in Afghanistan as well as the government of Afghanistan that protected them. On 7 October, US air strikes hit command and control, air defense, and airfields in Afghanistan. Compared to the operations against Iraq and Serbia, the opposition was weaker and American capabilities greater. The American Airmen used not only the equipment that proved so successful against Iraq but such new equipment as the B-1 and B-2 bombers, UAVs, and munitions: wind-corrected munitions dispenser, joint direct attack munition, and GPS-guided bombs. Neither the terrorists nor the Afghans had much of an air defense. In the one-sided conflict, American Airmen lost three aircraft in accidents and two of three UAVs to icing but none to enemy causes. Against this minimal resistance, the principal problem was that of distinguishing the correct target.[43]

A year and a half later, Iraq was the site of another swift war. On 21 March 2003, coalition air forces began air strikes on Iraq. Iraqi air defenses were significantly weaker than they were in the first Gulf War, consisting of 325 combat aircraft and 210 large SAMs. Coalition air forces were also smaller in number than in the earlier war: 1,800 aircraft compared with 2,400. However, this force was much more capable because more aircraft were able to deliver precision-guided munitions, some of the technology used in small numbers in the Gulf War were more widely used (such as unmanned aerial vehicles [UAV]), and new technology was introduced (some new guided munitions). As a consequence, the Airmen dropped more than twice as many guided weapons as they did in the first war, although they flew fewer sorties. Whereas in the first war 8 percent of the total munitions delivered were guided weapons, in the second war, 68 percent were guided. There was no air-to-air combat; in fact, the Iraqi air force buried its best fighters in the sand rather than risk them in combat or in shelters.[44]

Therefore, it is not surprising that Iraqi air defenses were even less effective than they had been a decade earlier. The coalition air forces logged 1,224 incidents of antiaircraft fire and 1,660 SAM launches, mostly fired without radar assistance. Enemy fire downed only seven aircraft, six helicopters, and one A-10.[45] The coalition air forces effectively neutralized Iraqi air defenses, gained air superiority, and applied air power as they wished. Nevertheless, some old problems remained. With such an ineffective enemy opposition, the instances of friendly fire stand out. Patriots downed both an RAF Tornado and a Navy F/A-18 Hornet. In addition, an F-16 fired a HARM (AGM-88) that took out a radar sited with a Patriot battery.[46] Helicopters again faired far worse than fixed-winged aircraft, accounting for six of the seven US losses. Another indication is that on one raid, Iraqi ground fire hit 27 of 35 Army helicopters and downed one.[47] While the conflict itself was a walkover, the end of major combat did not end the war, only changed its character from a conventional campaign into a guerrilla clash. As this is written (November 2003), five US helicopters have been destroyed mostly by rocket-propelled grenades (RPGs) or shoulder-launched SAMs since the end of the conventional war.[48]

Notes

1. A further irony is that the US military trained (for practical reasons) in the western American desert on terrain perhaps as close to the actual battlefield in the Persian Gulf War as could be expected.

2. Anthony Cordesman and Abraham Wagner, *The Lessons of Modern War*, vol. 4, *The Gulf War* (Boulder: Westview, 1996), 396.

3. The numbers were pulled from Cordesman and Wagner, *The Gulf War*, 127. Apparently, the Iraqis did convert some transports to tankers in Libya between the invasion of Kuwait and the onset of the Gulf War. See Michael Gordon and Bernard Trainor, *The Generals' War* (Boston: Little, Brown and Company, 1995), 104; and *Gulf War Air Power Survey (GWAPS)*, vol. 4, *Weapons, Tactics, and Training* (Washington, D.C.: Government Printing Office [GPO], 1993), 22.

4. These numbers are primarily from Cordesman and Wagner, *The Gulf War*, 431, supplemented by *GWAPS*, vol. 4, *Weapons, Tactics, and Training*, 10, which are somewhat different from the less-detailed figures in *GWAPS*, vol. 2, *Operations and Effects and Effectiveness*, 82; and W. J. Barlow, "Command, Control, and Communications Countermeasures (C^3CM) during Desert Shield/Desert Storm," June 1992, IDA paper P-2678, 137, HRA.

5. The Iraqis considered the Hawk far more effective than any of their Soviet SAMs during the Iraq-Iran War. See Anthony Cordesman and Abraham Wagner, *The Lessons of Modern War*, vol. 2, *The Iran-Iraq War* (Boulder: Westview Press, 1990), 461; Cordesman and Wagner, *The Gulf War*, 431; Mike Freeman, briefing, "Suppression of Enemy Air Defenses (SEAD)," December 1990, HRA; William Peters, "Background Paper on Captured Hawk Kuwaiti SAMs," 12 August 1990, HRA; Major Bell, information paper, "Captured Kuwaiti Hawk Air Defense Systems," 27 December 1990, HRA; and Robert Boyd, Memo for XOOSE, "Status of Iraqi I-Hawk," 27 December 1990, HRA.

6. *GWAPS*, vol. 4, *Weapons, Tactics, and Training*, 15.

7. Gen Charles Horner, testimony, Senate Committee on Armed Services, *Hearings before the Committee on Armed Services, United States*, 102d Cong., 1st sess., "Operation Desert Shield/Desert Storm," 12 May 1991, 235; and Cordesman and Wagner, *The Gulf War*, 407. However, the Airmen believed that the Iraqi air defense system was not as good as the Vietnamese one had been. See Gen Larry Henry at Horner briefing, "Extract of Major Comments of Questions: Notes from Horner Brief," 20 August 1990, HRA; and James Winnefeld, Preston Niblack, and Dana Johnson, *A League of Airmen: U.S. Air Power in the Gulf War* (Santa Monica, Calif.: RAND, 1994), 172. Also see Gordon and Trainor, *The Generals' War*, 108; and *GWAPS*, vol. 2, *Operations and Effects and Effectiveness*, 82.

8. The Iraqis unsuccessfully attempted to add an airborne early warning capability to this system. They installed French (Tiger) radars aboard Soviet Il-76 transports, but this makeshift effort had little capability. See Gordon and Trainor, *The Generals' War*, 105–8; Barlow, "Command, Control, and Communications," 140; and *GWAPS*, vol. 4, *Weapons, Tactics, and Training*, 6.

9. Gordon and Trainor, *The Generals' War*, 105; and *GWAPS*, vol. 2, *Operations and Effects and Effectiveness*, 83.

10. For a detailed discussion of the development of stealth and PGMs and their employment in the Gulf War, see Kenneth Werrell, *Chasing the*

Silver Bullet: US Air Force Weapons Development from Vietnam to Desert Storm (Washington, D.C.: Smithsonian Institution, April 2003).

11. Barlow, "Command, Control, and Communications," 136.

12. This was a change from the prior air campaigns that attacked air defenses first and then went on to hit other targets. This new kind of air warfare, parallel rather than serial, was credited to Col John A. Warden III, USAF. See his book, *The Air Campaign: Planning for Combat* (Washington, D.C.: National Defense University, 1988).

13. *GWAPS*, vol. 4, *Weapons, Tactics, and Training*, 171.

14. Cordesman and Wagner, *The Gulf War*, 495; and *GWAPS*, vol. 1, *Planning*, 5.

15. Cordesman and Wagner, *The Gulf War*, 397; and *GWAPS*, vol. 4, *Weapons, Tactics, and Training*, 172–74, 181.

16. Barlow, "Command, Control, and Communications," 148.

17. Bernard Trainor, "War by Miscalculation," 204, in Joseph Nye and Roger Smith, eds., *After the Storm: Lessons from the Gulf War* (Lanham, Md.: Madison, 1992).

18. Rick Atkinson, *Crusade: The Untold Story of the Persian Gulf War* (Boston: Houghton Mifflin, 1993), 40; Tom Clancy and Charles Horner, *Every Man a Tiger* (New York: Putnam, 1999), 339; James Coyne, *Air Power in the Gulf* (Arlington, Va.: Aerospace Educational Foundation, 1992), 104; "Desert Storm/Desert Shield: Preliminary Report on Air Force Lessons Learned," 25, n.d. (postwar) HRA; "Desert Storm: A Strategic and an Operational Air Campaign," briefing, n.d. (prior to the air war) HRA; Gordon and Trainor, *The Generals' War*, 90, 115, 132, 188; *GWAPS*, vol. 1, *Planning*, 151; R. A. Mason, *Air Power: A Centennial Appraisal* (London: Brassey's, 1994), 137–38; H. Norman Schwarzkopf, *It Doesn't Take a Hero* (New York: Bantam, 1997), 415; Bob Woodward, *The Commanders* (New York: Simon and Schuster, 1991), 340; David A. Deptula, "Lessons Learned: The Desert Storm Air Campaign," April 1991, 24, HRA; "Extract of Major Comments and Question: Notes from Horner Brief," interview with Brig Gen Buster C. Glosson, n.d. [6 March 1991], 4, HRA; and interview with General Glosson, n.d., 82–83, HRA. For another view of the estimated losses, see Cordesman and Wagner, *The Gulf War*, 399.

19. When launched from 40,000 feet and at minimum air speed, TALDs could reach 86 miles. Effective range under combat conditions would, of course, be somewhat less than that—30 to 40 miles as noted in the open sources. See Cordesman and Wagner, *The Gulf War*, 413; "Conduct of the Persian Gulf War: Final Report to Congress," appendix T, "Performance of Selected Weapon Systems," T-197; Barlow, "Command, Control, and Communications," 149; James Dunnigan and Austin Bay, *Shield to Sword: High-Tech Weapons, Military Strategy, and Coalition Warfare in the Persian Gulf* (New York: Morrow, 1992), 213–14; Gordon and Trainor, *The Generals' War*, 113, 217; *GWAPS*, vol. 2, *Operations and Effects and Effectiveness*, 133; and *GWAPS*, vol. 4, *Weapons, Tactics, and Training*, 186.

20. Gordon and Trainor, *The Generals' War,* 113–14; *GWAPS,* vol. 2, *Operations and Effects and Effectiveness,* 132; and *GWAPS,* vol. 4, *Weapons, Tactics, and Training,* 102–3. The decoys could fly as fast as 550 knots, as far as 450 nautical miles, and as high as 40,000 feet for about an hour but not at the same time. See Cordesman and Wagner, *The Gulf War,* 413.

21. Barlow, "Command, Control, and Communications," 149; Thomas Christie, John Donis, and Alfred Victor, "Desert Shield/Desert Storm Suppression of Enemy Air Defenses," Phase I report, IDA Document D-1076, January 1996, 4, HRA; and Glosson interview, 6 March 1991, 8, HRA.

22. Cordesman and Wagner, *The Gulf War,* 427; Marine lieutenant general Royal Moore cited in Winnefeld, Niblack, and Johnson, *A League of Airmen,* 179, note 46; and *Conduct of the Persian Gulf War, Final Report to Congress,* April 1992, 129, 218.

23. *GWAPS,* vol. 4, *Weapons, Tactics, and Training,* 92–93; and *GWAPS,* vol. 5, *A Statistical Compendium,* 339, 641.

24. Norman Friedman, *Desert Victory: The War for Kuwait* (Annapolis, Md.: Naval Institute, 1991), 166; and *GWAPS,* vol. 4, *Weapons, Tactics, and Training,* 94.

25. *GWAPS,* vol. 4, *Weapons, Tactics, and Training,* 94–96.

26. Ibid., 96–97.

27. Ibid., 104.

28. "AGM-88 HARM," *Air Force Magazine,* May 2000, 156.

29. Christie, Donis, Victor, *Desert Shield/Desert Storm,* II-4; Glosson interview, March 1991; Lt Gen Charles A. "Chuck" Horner interview, 4 March 1992, 55, HRA; Thomas Keaney and Eliot Cohen, *Revolution in Warfare?: Air Power in the Persian Gulf* (Annapolis, Md.: Naval Institute, 1995), 195; *GWAPS,* vol. 2, *Operations and Effects and Effectiveness,* 133; and *GWAPS,* vol. 5, *Statistical Compendium,* 550–53.

30. *GWAPS,* vol. 4, *Weapons, Tactics, and Training,* 114; and Stan Morse, ed., *Gulf Air War Debrief* (London: Aerospace, 1991), 154–57.

31. "Airborne Electronic Combat in the Gulf War," n.d., 2, HRA.

32. Later in the campaign, Horner lowered this altitude to 10,000 feet and then to 8,000 feet.

33. This accuracy is measured in circular error probable, with one-half of the bombs falling within that radius.

34. William Andrews, *Airpower against an Army: Challenge and Response in CENTAF's Duel with the Republican Guard,* CADRE Paper (Maxwell AFB, Ala.: Air University Press, 1998), 35; Atkinson, *Crusade,* 101–2; *GWAPS,* vol. 2, *Operations and Effects and Effectiveness,* 99; *GWAPS,* vol. 4, *Weapons, Tactics, and Training,* 51; Edward Marolda and Robert Schneller, *Shield and Sword: The United States Navy and the Persian Gulf War* (Washington, D.C.: Naval Historical Center, 1998), 183, 194; and Winnefeld, Niblack, and Johnson, *A League of Airmen,* 127.

35. Friedman, *Desert Victory,* 164.

36. In addition, US forces lost 13 aircraft, and the allies lost five aircraft to noncombat causes. See Keaney and Cohen, *Revolution in Warfare?,* 196;

GWAPS, vol. 2, *Operations and Effects and Effectiveness*, 142; and *GWAPS*, vol. 5, *Statistical Compendium*, 640–51.

37. "Fact Sheet," US Central Command Air Forces, 2, May 1998.

38. The United States also fired 325 TLAMs and 90 CALCMs. See Greg Seigle, "'Fox': The Results," *Jane's Defence Weekly*, 13 January 1999, 25.

39. Headquarters USAF, "The One Year Report of the Air War over Serbia: Aerospace Power in Operation Allied Force," October 2000, 34.

40. Allied Forces Southern Europe, Fact Sheet: Operation Deliberate Force; Federation of American Scientists, "Operation Deliberate Force"; Kevin Fedark and Mark Thompson, "All For One," *Time*, 19 June 1995; and Richard P. Hallion, "Control of the Air: The Enduring Requirement" (Washington, D.C.: Bolling AFB, 1999).

41. Apparently, Serb helicopters downed some UAVs. See Tim Ripley, "UAVs over Kosovo—Did the Earth Move?," *Defense System Daily*, 1 December 1999; Anthony Cordesman, "The Lessons and Non-Lessons of the Air and Missile Campaign in Kosovo," Center for Strategic and International Studies, September 1999, 24, 132, 209–10; David Fulghum, "Report Tallies Damage, Lists US Weaknesses," *Aviation Week and Space Technology*, 14 February 2000, 34; Joel Hayward, "NATO's War in the Balkans: A Preliminary Assessment," *New Zealand Army Journal*, July 1999; Headquarters USAF, "Air War over Serbia," 44; "Operation Allied Force: The First 30 Days," *World Air Power Journal* (Fall 1999): 18, 21; "NATO's Role in Kosovo," 30 October 2000, http://www.NATO.int/kosovo/ kosovo; USAF, "Air War Over Serbia (AWOS) Fact Sheet," 31 January 2000 [in USAF, One Year Report]; and Headquarters USAF, "The Air War over Serbia," 33, 44.

42. Headquarters USAF, "The Air War over Serbia," 19, 43.

43. David Donald, "Operation Enduring Freedom," *International Air Power Review* (Spring 2002): 16–29.

44. Michael T. Moseley, "Operation Iraqi Freedom: By the Numbers" (Shaw AFB, S.C.: USAF Assessment and Analysis Division, 30 April 2003); and Werrell, *Chasing the Silver Bullet*, 256, 258.

45. Moseley, "Operation Iraqi Freedom"; and David Willis, "Operation Iraqi Freedom," *International Air Power Review* (Summer 2003): 24.

46. Willis, "Operation Iraqi Freedom," 17.

47. Barry Posen, "Command of the Commons," *International Security* 28:1, 25.

48. Dexter Filkins, "At Least 17 Dead as 2 U.S. Copters Collide over Iraq," *New York Times*, 16 November 2003, 1.

Chapter 7

Ballistic Missile Defense in the 1990s

The breakup of the Soviet Union ended the Cold War and dramatically changed the balance of strategic power and the nature of the threat to the United States. On the positive side, the lessening of tensions between Russia and the United States greatly reduced the possibilities of an all-out nuclear exchange between the two. At same time, the fragmentation of the Soviet Union presented new challenges. There were fears for the security of Russian nuclear weapons, as underscored by the abortive August 1991 coup. The threat from Russia seemed to be less of a massive, planned strike and more of an accidental or unauthorized launch (action by a rogue commander or perhaps a rebel group).

Aside from Russia, another problem was the proliferation of weapons of mass destruction (nuclear, biological, and chemical [NBC]) and of ballistic missiles. If some could shrug off possession of such weapons in the hands of such responsible states as Britain, France, and Israel, the same was not the case with such terrorist-sponsoring states as Iran, Iraq, Libya, North Korea, and Syria. During a visit to Russia in 1991, a congressional delegation found that this was more than just a Western perception.[1]

In response to these changes, the United States refocused its BMD program. In his 1991 State of the Union address, Pres. George Bush announced that the American BMD would be redirected from defending against a massive Soviet ballistic missile strike to defending against a more limited missile attack of up to 200 warheads. His view was summed up in the system's new name, global protection against limited strikes (GPALS). It would shift the strategic defense initiative into a three-fold program consisting of theater warning to allies and forward-deployed US troops, defense of stateside Americans, and a space-based system to fend off an attack anywhere in the world.[2] GPALS was a two-layer system consisting of 1,000 space-based brilliant pebbles to intercept hostile missiles in their boost phase and 750 ground-based interceptors to defend against surviving missiles in midcourse. Cost estimates ranged from $100 to $150 billion. The shift from national to tactical ballistic missile defense is clear. By 1993, US spending on theater missile defense (TMD) greatly exceeded that spent on national (strategic) missile defense (NMD). The new administration continued this trend.[3]

In the 1992 election campaign, Bill Clinton promised a tighter defense budget than his Republican opponent and, upon taking office, cut defense spending. The new administration emphasized TMD at the expense of NMD in its funding for fiscal years 1995–99.[4] TMD received top priority based around three core programs: Patriot improvement, PAC-3; improvement of the Navy's Aegis program, the Navy Area program; and the Army's Theater High Altitude Area Defense (THAAD) program. Three other TMD systems would compete to join this select three: the Navy upper-tier system, a mobile Army system then known as Corps-SAM (surface-to-air missile), and a third system to provide boost-phase intercept capability. NMD dropped to second priority, focusing on technical problems.[5]

Congress also responded to the increased interest in ballistic missile defense. In 1991, Congress passed legislation that called for deployment of an advanced TMD system by the mid-1990s and for a cost-effective and operationally effective BMD system by 1996.[6] Although the Democratic administration saw international agreement as a better solution to the problem than a technical one, the Republican congressional victories in fall 1994 changed the Washington power equation. The Grand Old Party put forth a bold contract with America that included a commitment to deploy a limited NMD system. Congress persisted and in 1995 passed a measure that called for a limited NMD. Congress wanted to revise the ABM treaty, but failing Russian agreement, was willing to withdraw from the arrangement and build a multi-site BMD system with space sensors that could defend the 50 states. President Clinton vetoed the bill because it violated the existing treaty and responded with a program that called for a three-plus-three option. This plan consisted of three years of development that would be treaty compliant and then a decision that, if positive, would permit limited deployment in another three years. Thus, the United States might field BMD by the year 2002 or 2003.[7]

TMD Hardware: PAC-3, MEADS, Arrow, Naval Developments, and THAAD

The increased attention led to progress, the baseline of which is the Army's Patriot system. The Army planned a number of incremental improvements of missile, launcher, and radar to field the PAC-3 (Patriot Advanced Capability) version. This began with a quick-reaction program (improved radar sensing and remote launch capability) deployed in 1993. PAC-3 increased the area it could defend, previously about 10 by 20 kilometers (km), by a factor of five. At about the same time, the developers improved the missile with the guidance enhanced missile (GEM) that increased range by 30 to 40 percent. The Army began to deploy it and the next improvement, Configuration 1, that consisted of improved battle management, command, control, communications, and intelligence.[8]

The most noticeable change was to replace the missile. The existing Patriot missile with its blast-fragmentation warhead and improved multimode seeker was matched against an entirely different warhead concept, hit to kill. The Army had begun work on this idea, most notably in the Flexible Lightweight Agile Guided Experiment (FLAGE) in 1983. In May 1987, FLAGE successfully intercepted a Lance ballistic missile. The Army upgraded FLAGE to extend the missile's range and speed in a follow-on design called Extended Range Intercept Technology (ERINT). It used a hit-to-kill mechanism along with a lethality enhancer that dispensed small pellets. The Loral-Vought missile flew a number of successful intercept tests during 1992–94.

ERINT competed with the improved Patriot missile for use in the PAC-3 configuration. Patriot's multi-mode seeker enabled the missile to hit a target Patriot in July 1992, and it apparently performed better against cruise missiles, aircraft, and drones than did ERINT. Nevertheless, in early 1994 the Army picked ERINT as its PAC-3 missile. The Army stated that ERINT had greater range, accuracy, and lethality than its rival. One source claims it had about 10 times the footprint of the PAC-2 system.[9] As the new missile was considerably smaller than the previous Patriot missile, four could be fitted into each Patriot tube, allowing each launcher to carry 16 instead of four of the older missiles. ERINT also did considerably better than the multimode seeker in simulated tests against biological and chemical warheads. Its IOC was scheduled for late 1998 or 1999.[10]

The PAC-3 program encountered scheduling delays, cost overruns, and technical challenges in the 1990s. By mid-1999, it was two years behind schedule and 37 percent over budget. This forced the Army to cut the buy by more than 50 percent, resulting in cost escalation from $2 million to $4–$5 million per missile. The PAC-3 achieved mixed testing results, although most tests were successful. This encouraged the government to authorize limited low-rate production and schedule IOC for 2001. A decision on full-rate production was scheduled for late 2002. Full deployment is not expected before 2005. The Army intends to keep the weapon in inventory until 2025, with planned upgrades of ground equipment.[11]

Another system later upgraded to handle BMD is the Hawk. By the 1990s, it was no longer in the Army inventory but was in service with over 15 countries as well as with the Marine Corps. The Marines lacked the Patriot and required a stopgap TMD until they fielded the medium extended air defense system (MEADS) in the 21st century. As early as 1988, the Hawk demonstrated BMD capabilities against a simulated ballistic missile target. The Army started efforts to modify it for the TMD role and then passed it along to the Marines in 1992. There were two principal modifications. The first extended radar range to 400 nm and up to 500,000 feet, and the second increased warhead size and used a new fuze. Another development was to make the system interoperable with the upgraded Patriot system, allowing the Hawk to share data from the Patriot's more sophisticated and capable electronics. Cued by Patriot radar in May 1991, the system intercepted a ballistic missile. In September 1994, the modified system, called Improved Hawk II, downed two Lance ballistic missiles (fig. 95). The Marines modified Hawks to this new standard by 1999.[12]

Figure 95. Hawk intercepting Lance. The Hawk had the potential to intercept ballistic missiles, as it demonstrated in intercepting this Lance surface-to-surface missile. (Reprinted from Ballistic Missile Defense Organization.)

The Army wanted to replace Hawk with a SAM system possessing capabilities between that of the man-portable Stinger and the much larger, complex, and capable Patriot. It desired better range, mobility, and firepower than the Hawk and greater mobility and survivability than the Patriot. (Another goal of the program was to reduce the manpower required to man the SAM battalion from 500 to about 300.) The new system began life under the name Corps Surface-to-Air Missile, a joint Army-Marine project intended to replace the Hawk. It soon became an international project when the Germans, French, and Italians joined the effort, formalized in February 1995 when the system was renamed MEADS.[13]

Mounted on a wheeled or tracked vehicle, MEADS features both strategic and tactical mobility. Unlike the Patriot that required the C-5 for air transport, MEADS will be transportable on the ubiquitous C-130; in fact, this became the system's driving requirement.[14] The cost estimates fluctuate from the original $36 billion, and the IOC has been pushed back from 2007 to 2010.[15]

In May 1999, the three government consortium awarded Lockheed-Martin the MEADS contract. This surprised some observers in view of that company's difficulties with the THAAD program (see below). As the Americans desired, the missile will be based on the PAC-3 missile as a cost-saving measure that may cut the $5 billion missile development cost in half. MEADS will be a versatile weapon, able to intercept ballistic missiles, as well as defend against unmanned vehicles at lower altitudes.[16]

Another system under development to fulfill the TMD role is the Israeli Arrow (fig. 96). The Israelis began work on the project in 1986 and gained US support two years later. This evolved into an unusual weapon relationship that involved almost complete US funding of the missile's development, while the Israelis funded the early warning and fire control system.[17] The Arrow had considerable technical problems. In the period 1988 through 1991, its record was called disappointing, and the missile did not achieve its first interception until November 1999.[18] The Arrow was designed to have a footprint larger than the PAC-3 (one Arrow battery could cover as much area as four Patriot batteries according to one source) but smaller than the THAAD. Less mobile than the Patriot, it uses a blast-fragmentation warhead to destroy its target.[19] The Israelis declared the system operational in October 2000. They intend to field three batteries with an overall program cost of $2–$10 billion.[20]

In contrast to these lower-tier missile systems, the THAAD system is an upper-tier system. It is intended to engage targets at a minimum 200 km range and 150 km in altitude that will give it 10 times the footprint of the Patriot missile. This extended performance would permit a shoot-look-shoot capability— sequential shots at an incoming missile. It will be more portable than the Patriot, as it will be air-transportable aboard the C-130.[21] Like the more recent US BMDs, it has a hit-to-kill

Figure 96. Arrow launch. The Arrow is a joint US-Israeli development. The Israelis declared the theater ballistic missile defense weapon operational in 2000. (Reprinted from Ballistic Missile Defense Organization.)

warhead. THAAD uses radar early in the engagement and then an infrared sensor and computer aboard the missile for interception.[22] Estimated costs range from $10-$15 billion, with an IOC in 2007.[23]

THAAD began development in 1988 and accelerated with an award to Lockheed-Martin in September 1992 (fig. 97). The effort has been difficult with repeated test failures. Even the two (of 16 attempts) successes in 1984 and 1991 were disputed by critics who claimed they were rigged.[24] After six failed interceptions between 1995 and 1999, THAAD achieved its first interception in June 1999 when it hit a modified Minuteman missile 50 miles high and with a (combined) closing speed of 15,000 fps. On the next test in August 1999, THAAD scored another intercept.[25]

Less than three weeks after the second success, the Department of Defense (DOD) announced that the weapon would enter engineering and manufacturing development (EMD) without further testing. This changed the earlier requirement that a positive EMD decision would hinge on three successful intercepts. A few days later, the top DOD tester, Philip Coyle, the director of Operational Testing and Evaluation, stated that these successes were "not operationally realistic" and called for further testing. Coyle based his statement on the facts that the missile used was not the one that would be fielded, the targets were employed over a shorter range than the system might face, and test conditions were contrived. Coyle doubts the system can be deployed before 2010.[26]

Navy Systems

The push for a nautical BMD had two roots. First, the Navy required protection of its assets from ballistic missiles. Second, ship-based BMDs would permit shifting of scarce resources and eliminate the problem of host-country permission. Such mobility would represent a show of force and give the United States a political/diplomatic advantage.

The Navy developed two programs: the lower-tier Navy area-wide system and the upper-tier Navy theaterwide (NTW) system, both based on the standard missile. The short-range BMD

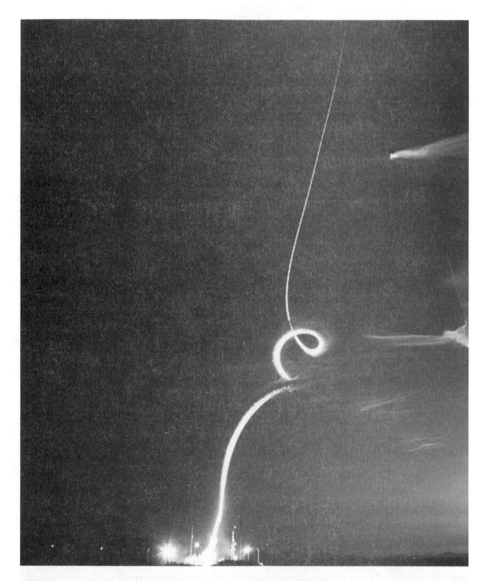

Figure 97. THAAD maneuver. THAAD maneuvering after launch. (Reprinted from http://army-technology.com/projects/thaad/images/Thaad3.jpl.)

called area, equivalent to the land-based PAC-3, was based on the Navy's SM-2 Block IV A missile. It has a blast-fragmentation warhead and the ability to hit targets up to an altitude of 35 km and out to a range of 125 km (another source states it can cover an area 50 km by 150 km). The Navy modified two *Aegis*-class cruisers with the system in September 1998 and successfully completed sea trials the next month (fig. 98). The Navy conducted the missile's first flight test in June 2000 and scheduled

Figure 98. Navy TMD launch. The Navy's Theater Ballistic Missile Defense system is being tested. (Reprinted from http://www.checkpoint-online.ch/ CheckPoint/Monde/Mon0010-Pro11.)

deployment of the first unit in 2003. This system was designed to protect against aircraft, cruise missiles, and short-range ballistic missiles. DOD cancelled the program in December 2001, as it was $2 billion over budget (60 percent cost growth) and two years behind schedule.[27]

DOD considered several missiles for the system. The trade press reported that the DOD was considering standardizing on one missile for both the Army and Navy programs. Because of the technical status of the two programs, this would probably mean using the THAAD. While that might make economic sense, and perhaps technical sense, it had political problems. That is, Republican legislators, holding the majority in Congress in the late 1990s, strongly supported separate Army and Navy programs.[28]

Another proposal was to mate the light exoatmospheric projectile (LEAP) to a Standard missile. LEAP began with a 220-pound device in August 1989, but within three years it appeared in five versions that weighed between 12 and 40 pounds. It was estimated to have a maximum speed twice that of THAAD and an altitude capability of 80 km. LEAP had its first successful test in September 1992.[29]

The NTW Ballistic Missile Defense program is also based on the standard missile aboard *Aegis* ships, but in contrast to the Area program, it is designed for longer range and higher altitude (outside the atmosphere) interception of ballistic missiles. It is comparable to THAAD. Designated SM-3, it is an SM-2 Block IV with a third-stage motor and a maneuvering hit-to-kill warhead that uses the LEAP IIR seeker. The missile had its first successful flight in September 1999, although this did not include the all-important third stage. But the system cannot handle ICBMs, which would require twice the interceptor missile speed and more powerful radars. Some believe that it might also require new ships. The original plan was to field an interim missile (Block I) by 2006, but by February 2001 the Navy rejected this concept to concentrate on the final version (Block II). The Navy now believes that 2010 is the earliest it can deploy this weapon, when it expects to get 80 SM-3 missiles aboard four *Aegis* cruisers.[30] A 1999 Heritage Foundation study asserted that NTW could be expanded into an NMD by putting 650 missiles

247

aboard 22 *Aegis* ships in less than five years, for an initial cost of $3 billion. However, a Navy estimate for a 12-ship system was $15 billion, while later estimates for such a system were between $16 billion and $19 billion. A sea-based NMD would violate the ABM treaty.[31]

The attractiveness of the Navy system was evident in 1999. In September, the Japanese agreed to conduct joint research with the United States for the NTW system. The two partners intend to jointly deploy a Block II Standard, with an undetermined IOC. The next month, naval representatives from the United States, Australia, Germany, Italy, and the Netherlands met to investigate a future cooperative naval effort. The Standard missile figured prominently in these talks.[32]

To jump a bit ahead of the chronology, the election of George W. Bush to the presidency in 2000 renewed interest in the Navy BMD programs. Bush, Senate Majority leader Trent Lott, Secretary of State Colin Powell, and former secretary of state Henry Kissinger all called for the deployment of a sea-based system.[33]

A New Threat

One reason for this increased activity was the recognition of an increased threat. Following the collapse of the Soviet Union and the overwhelming military victory in the Gulf War in the early 1990s, Americans relaxed, expected a peace dividend, and believed they were secure. They also began to cut the military. The politicians were also lulled by a 1995 national intelligence estimate (NIE) and the intelligence community's March 1998 annual report that held that it would take 15 years for a country without a ballistic missile infrastructure to deploy an ICBM. This would give the United States ample warning before such a deployment.[34] Critics noted that this estimate ignored the existing Russian and Chinese ICBMs, turned a blind eye to the vulnerability of Alaska and Hawaii, and disregarded missile and missile technology transfer.

This complacent view was jarred by events in the summer of 1998. First, a congressionally mandated committee chaired by former Secretary of Defense Donald Rumsfeld concluded that "the threat to the United States from emerging ballistic missile capabilities is broader, more mature, and is evolving more rapidly than contained in earlier estimates and reports by the US intelligence community."[35] It observed that part of the problem was that America's ability to get timely and accurate intelligence was declining, leaving the possibility "under some plausible scenarios" that "the US might well have little or no warning before operational ballistic missile deployment."[36] The committee specifically noted that "a fairly significant ballistic missile threat is emerging almost overnight in North Korea."[37] Further, the North Koreans, Chinese, and Russians were exporting ballistic missile technology to other nations. As some of these countries were making efforts to develop nuclear and biological weapons and all had chemical capabilities, the threat was obvious.[38]

The administration countered these dire warnings at the end of August 1998 with a letter from the top US military leader, chairman of the Joint Chiefs of Staff, Gen Hugh Shelton, to Senator James Inhofe. The four-star general wrote that the JCS "remain[s] confident that the Intelligence community can provide the necessary warning of the indigenous development and deployment by a rogue state of an ICBM threat to the United States."[39] He held that the current defense policy was prudent and that continued adherence to the 1972 ABM treaty was "consistent with our national interests."[40]

Events were not kind to either General Shelton or to the administration's course of action. A week after Shelton's letter, the North Koreans fired a three-stage missile (Taepo Dong 2) eastward, with the second stage landing east of Japan and the third stage near Alaska (fig. 99). Thus, North Korea, a failed state that was unable to feed its people, demonstrated alarming and advanced technological and military capabilities. The multistage missile showed a high level of competence, as did the fact that the third stage was powered by solid propellants. Particularly disturbing was that until this demonstration, North Korean expertise with solid fuels was unknown to US intelligence agencies. The Taepo Dong 1 missile with a 1,200-mile range could hit targets in South Korea and Japan. The Taepo Dong 2 had a nominal range of 3,700 miles that put Alaska and Hawaii within its reach. Lighter versions of that missile

Figure 99. Taepo Dong 1. The North Koreans developed a family of ballistic missiles capable of delivering nuclear weapons, based on this Taepo Dong 1 missile. (Reprinted from Ballistic Missile Defense Organization.)

could fly as far as 6,200 miles, threatening the western United States. A 1999 NIE concluded that the North Koreans could field an ICBM by 2005.[41]

These events galvanized the Japanese. Since 1945, they have been bound both psychologically and politically by a no-war constitution and attitude that led to miniscule rates of defense spending. Although the Japanese had been importing sophisticated US military technology such as the PAC-3, *Aegis* warships, and the airborne warning and control system, they showed considerable reluctance toward the BMD. While the Japanese military and elements of the government supported Japanese-US cooperation on BMD, Japanese industry and the powerful ministry of international trade and industry questioned such an action. However, events in both China and North Korea led to an increase in Japanese military spending and a rise in funding for ballistic missile defense by the end of 1999. In August 1999, the Japanese and Americans signed an agreement to conduct joint research on a BMD system.[42]

In contrast to the Japanese, who showed uncharacteristic concern over these developments in North Korea, South Korea was much less disturbed. This is remarkable in view of the closer South Korean geographic, emotional, and political proximity to the threat. The South Korean defense ministry stated that it would not join the joint American-Japanese BMD program, citing a lack of money and technology. For their part, the South Koreans wanted to modify their 20-year-old agreement with the United States that confined them to surface-to-surface missiles with ranges less than 180 km. They wished to extend the permitted ranges to 500 km, which would enable them to reach all of North Korea, while the United States appeared willing to extend the limit to 300 km. The South Koreans apparently put more value in deterrence and less in a direct BMD system than does the United States.[43]

Unlike the South Koreans, the government of Taiwan very much wanted BMD. In March 1999, it announced a $9 billion program over a 10-year period to develop a low-altitude air defense system. At the same time, there was intense speculation that the Taiwanese wanted to get under the US-Japanese BMD umbrella. This effort was aided by a US congressional request that the DOD study a defensive arrangement with Taiwan. In June 1999, Taiwan's president made it clear that his country wanted to join the theater ballistic missile defense program.[44]

American relations with Taiwan are sensitive. China opposes American BMD more than the Russians, but it is even more adamant about Taiwan. Therefore, American military aid to the island has been cautious. Nevertheless, in April 2001, the Bush administration announced the largest arms sale to Taiwan in decades. However, the United States deferred supplying BMD, although it reserved the right to transfer PAC-3 for deployment in 2010 under certain circumstances. Bush explicitly declared US intentions to defend Taiwan from a Chinese invasion.[45]

America's European allies criticized the American BMD effort. They saw it as another example of American arrogance and unilateralism, not as consultation and agreement among allies. They believed America was exaggerating the threat. More seriously, they feared that US BMD deployment would decouple the United States from Europe, as the partners would no longer share a nuclear risk. This, they postulated, would reinforce the ever-present American isolationist sentiment and the fortress America attitude and action.[46]

The chief European complaint centers on the impact of BMD development on the 1972 ABM treaty. These European critics believe that a modification of this agreement and development of the BMD would encourage the Russians to build up their offensive and defensive forces, nullify the deterrent forces of both Britain and France, and lead to an arms race with China and Russia.[47] French President Jacques Chirac noted that "the development of shields will always result in the proliferation of swords."[48] These advocates believed that the solution to the problem of nuclear weapons was not technology but diplomacy centered on the 1972 ABM treaty and the various agreements that limit both defensive and offensive systems. They insisted that the ABM treaty had to be maintained to achieve arms reduction.

At the same time, technical and political changes were buffeting the treaty.[49] In December 1993, the United States proposed modifications to the agreement to clarify testing of BMDs in what some perceived as being in the gray area. The treaty permitted BMD geared against tactical ballistic missiles but not against strategic missiles; however, these terms were not defined. Nevertheless, for years the United States had informally used the so-called Foster Box concept. It required approval by a treaty compliance panel for American BMD tests against targets exceeding 2 km per second and an intercept altitude of 40 km. Therefore, the United States proposed setting an upper limit on target speed and range against which the systems could be tested, specifically 5 km per second in speed and 3,500 km in range.[50] The Russians were willing to accept the target speed limit but also wanted to restrict the interceptor missile to a maximum speed of 3 km per second. In May 1995, the two nations agreed to this arrangement.[51]

At this point, these were the only concessions the Clinton administration made toward deploying or developing the BMD. In fact, earlier in a September 1993 five-year review of the treaty, the administration moved away from some of the changes proposed by the previous administration to relax treaty restrictions. In 1996, Clinton countered congressional pressure for BMD with a veto.[52]

Events, however, conspired against the treaty: the proliferation of missiles and NBC concerns with a number of countries; the Rumsfeld Report; North Korean missile developments; and domestic politics, especially Democratic fears that Republicans would use BMD as an issue in the 2000 elections. These events forced the administration to make key concessions, if not to capitulate, to BMD proponents. In January 1999, Secretary of Defense William Cohen announced a $6.6 billion, five-year program to develop a BMD system in addition to the almost $4 billion already budgeted. Cohen declared that the United States was seeking limited changes in the ABM treaty that would permit deployment of a restricted BMD and added that, failing such amendments, the United States might withdraw from the treaty. One journalist observed that Cohen's announcement "angered the Russians, dismayed arms control advocates and spurred new efforts by congressional hawks to abandon the 1972 Antiballistic Missile Treaty, which they believe inhibits US ability to protect itself against a growing missile threat."[53]

Meanwhile, the administration attempted to reassure the Russians and arms-control supporters. Within hours of Cohen's remarks, top administration officials, including Secretary of State Madeleine Albright and the president's national security advisor, Samuel Berger, clarified or, according to some, repudiated Cohen's words.[54] In an attempt to encourage the Russians to agree to treaty modifications, the administration went as far as to offer US financial support to help the Russians finish an important radar installation in Siberia and upgrade another in Azerbaijan. Although there were a few weak mixed signals from Moscow, the Russians held to the view that the ABM treaty had to remain intact.[55]

Nevertheless, Clinton bent to the political realities as the Congress passed, by a veto-proof margin, a National Missile Defense bill in March 1999. In July, Clinton signed the measure that called for a national BMD as soon as technically feasible. The president also pledged to make the hard and fast decision in June 2000, although it appeared to be a mere formality in view of the upcoming presidential election.[56] In early 2000, a number of influential individuals called for a delay in this decision. Some fervent BMD proponents feared that Clinton would opt for a minimal system and cut off the possibilities of a more robust one and thus preferred to wait for the hoped-for election of a Republican. Others wanted the decision taken out of the heated but not particularly enlightening glare of election-year politics. Meanwhile, the 2000 presidential nominees staked out positions on the subject. The Republican, George W. Bush, proposed support for not one but two missile defense systems (national and theater BMD) at the earliest possible date. His opponent, Al Gore, was more cautious. He supported the BMD concept but would not deploy the system without further testing, talks with the Russians, and international approval.[57]

Clinton made clear that he would approve BMD if it met four criteria. These included affordable cost, a real threat, workable technology, and tolerable diplomatic impact.[58] All four criteria were open to wide interpretations. For example, what cost is tolerable? How much is it worth to save one American city? What measure will define "workable technology"? That is, how well must the system work? Similarly, the appraisals of threat and diplomatic impact are subject to considerable subjective judgment.

Throughout the history of BMD, its opponents raised technical objections. These centered on the ease by which an attacker could deceive, or overwhelm, the system by using relatively simple decoys. A new issue was to point out that the booster for the missile would not be tested until after the system was deployed. The critics noted that it would produce 10 times the high-frequency vibrations as the test system, and, according to a Congressional Budget Office study, "distort or damage the kill vehicle's optics or electronics, rendering the interceptor impotent."[59] Three major science groups opposed the plan. Perhaps most impressive was a petition that about half of all living American science Nobel laureates sent the president urging him to reject NMD. They called the plan "premature, wasteful, and dangerous."[60] Opponents also raised the other perennial objection, cost. In early April 2000, the Ballistic Missile Defense Organization director announced that the first phase of the system would cost almost 60 percent more than prior estimates and $20.2 billion to develop, deploy, and support the 100-missile system in Alaska through 2025. The estimate increased from $26–$30 billion in July reports and to $40.3 billion in August. But, the number the press insisted on using was $60 billion, the same figure the Congressional Budget Office released in April for a much-expanded system.[61] Regardless of the specifics, clearly the costs were large and seemingly rising.

The Clinton administration proposed a plan for a midcourse BMD. America would build tracking radar on remote Shemya Island, a westerly island in the western Aleutians; upgrade five early-warning radars; and replace the current early-warning satellite system (Defense Support Program) with the space-based infrared satellite (SBIRS-High) system. Later, the United States would add ground-based radars and the space-based infrared satellite (SBIRS-Low) system. To protect western Alaska and Hawaii (along with the other 48 states)—politically important areas, although relatively few Americans live there—missiles initially would be sited in Alaska. Later, the United States would build a second interceptor missile site in the northern section of the United States to better protect the heavily populated eastern section of the country.[62] The plan's first phase called for new radar on Shemya by 2005, 20 missiles based in Alaska by 2005, and 100 missiles by 2007. The United States desired changes in the 1972 ABM treaty to permit upgrades of other radars in Alaska, Massachusetts, and California. The second phase would expand the radar system. In the third phase, the United States would add a second missile site in North Dakota with 150 missiles.[63]

Ballistic Missile Defense continued its oscillating course during the last half of 2000 and early 2001. The system suffered setbacks brought on by technical problems and diplomatic developments. The threat of a North Korean ICBM abated in 2000 as that country held encouraging talks with the South Koreans, including a meeting of the leaders of the two Koreas. In addition, and more to the point for the Americans, in late 1999, the North Koreans announced a moratorium on their missile tests. Then in late July 2000, Russian president Vladimir Putin announced that the North Koreans were willing to abandon their missile program in exchange for a booster to launch satellites into space. The much-emphasized North Korean threat seemed to be receding.[64]

The Russians waged a tough and effective diplomatic campaign to undermine the BMD program. President Putin's visits with American allies were troublesome to NMD proponents, but Russian and Chinese cooperation was worrisome to US decision makers. In a joint statement in July 2000, the two countries called the 1972 ABM treaty "the cornerstone of global strategic stability and international security" and warned of "the most grave adverse consequences" if the United States went ahead with the NMD.[65] In July 2001, Russia and China signed a friendship pact, with press commentators emphasizing that the NMD was a major factor in this development.[66] In another move, the Russians offered to share a theater missile defense with the West, specifically a boost-phase intercept (BPI) defense. Hitting hostile missiles as they were being launched had numerous advantages, as the missile would be a slower (and thus an easier) target during its first 120 to 210 seconds of flight. Destruction then would finesse the decoy problem and bring the missile debris down on the enemy's homeland. Such a system based in Russia would cover the United States from ICBM attacks from North Korea, and most from Iran and Iraq, although not from Libya nor launches from either China or Russia.[67] The BPI concept also had support from a number of long-time critics of BMD, including Theodore Postal, who opined that the concept "makes tremendously more sense. All the technology is in hand."[68] Others noted that BPI would be one-third cheaper than the Alaska plan and was less threatening to the Chinese and Russians. The only small Russian nudge toward the American position was an agreement by Putin in June that there was cause for concern over the issue of ballistic missile proliferation. Even here, however, the Russian generals insisted that the threat from rogue states was not as urgent as the United States maintained.[69]

More serious and certainly more dramatic were test failures. After achieving a success in its first intercept test in October 1999, the missile missed in January 2000. Because of the pending decision by President Clinton, the test scheduled in the summer of that year was critical.[70] Before the event, some claimed that the upcoming test was rigged. An article in *Time* stated that "little is being left to chance . . . . So little, in fact, that this may be a test in name only—an expensive piece of Potemkin performance art to win enormous military appropriations."[71] In any event, the program suffered a twin failure on 8 July 2000, when the kill vehicle failed to separate from the booster, and the balloon decoy did not deploy from the target missile. The *Los Angeles Times* called it a "spectacular test failure" and a "debacle of monumental proportions."[72] In addition, while a neutral observer might consider the incident a nontest, certainly it was bad public relations and politics.

With only one success on three attempts, diplomatic pressure from friends and nonfriends alike, domestic pressure magnified by the media, and escalating cost estimates, President Clinton was under great pressure to cancel the program. The close presidential election campaign did not help matters. On 1 September 2000, he announced that he was postponing a decision, leaving that responsibility to his successor.[73]

George W. Bush and BMD

That successor turned out to be the more enthusiastic BMD supporter of the two presidential candidates, Republican George W. Bush. With his election, the path of the BMD took another turn. In May 2000, well before the election heated up, candidate Bush proposed deep unilateral cuts of nuclear weapons along with a robust BMD that would be shared with allies and at a more distant date shared with both the Russians and Chinese.[74] Shortly after Bush's election, the Russians suggested an arrangement that would exchange cuts in offensive weapons for some level of cuts in defensive weapons. In mid-November, the commander of Russia's missile forces proposed a scheme that would limit each side to an agreed-upon number of offensive and defensive weapons but allow each to decide the exact mix. Bush repeated his call in January 2001 for building the BMD and nuclear arms reduction; he also seemed willing to consider the Russian proposal.[75]

By early 2001, the Russians were no longer pushing their joint BPI concept. They and the American allies had reluctantly accepted the idea that the new administration was going forward with BMD. In late February 2001, the *New York Times* reported that the Russians had begun serious talks about BMD. The Russian foreign minister, Igor Ivanov, stated that "we are ready and interested in starting a direct dialogue with the US administration."[76] For their part, the Europeans saw the way things were going and tried to make the best of the situation. There was press speculation that the Europeans would accept the American BMD plan in exchange for US acceptance of a proposed European Union deployment force that would be separate from NATO.[77]

President Bush continued to push NMD despite domestic and foreign criticism. The administration asked Congress to increase missile defense spending from $3 billion to $8.3 billion. At the same time, there were reports that the Pentagon planned to notify Congress that it would begin building a missile-defense test range in Alaska. Not only was this in violation of the 1972 ABM treaty that limited testing to White Sands, New Mexico, and Kwajalein Atoll in the Marshall Islands, but this facility could also be used for an emergency deployment. The Alaska site could field 10 interceptor missiles. This helps explains the high-level view that the testing could conflict with the treaty "within months, not years."[78]

The first two years of the Bush administration produced three sets of events critical to BMD development. The first event involved domestic politics: in June 2001, power in the US Senate shifted from Republican to Democratic hands. NMD was a signature issue for the Republicans, while the Democrats have been much more reluctant; the Republicans have tended to favor armaments, while the Democrats advocated treaties to deal with international threats. Or, in the incendiary words of the former speaker of the House of Representatives, Newt Gingrich, "It's the difference between those who would rely on lawyers to defend America and those who would rely on engineers and scientists."[79] Thus, NMD certainly will have a more difficult route than appeared to be the case after the November 1990

elections. The fate of the system may well depend on which political party controls the executive and legislative branches.

The second set of events was technological—successful missile
tests. As one reporter opened his piece on the July 2001 test,
saying, "The brilliant flash in the sky above the Pacific signified
not just a hit by the Pentagon's prototype missile interceptor
but an opening shot in President Bush's long political, diplomatic, and technical battle over a national missile defense system."[80] Avoiding a simple decoy, the interception demonstrated
that the system could work. For its part, the military was sub-
dued and modest in its reaction, noting that the full results of
the tests would not be known for two months and that this
was just the first step on a long journey. Critics noted that the
test vehicle would differ in both hardware and capability from
the deployed system and that even with the successful interception, a key component failed.[81] The next test (December
2001) was also successful against a warhead obscured by a
single balloon decoy and pieces of debris. A third consecutive
success in March 2002 was more impressive: the interceptor
missile picked the warhead instead of the three decoys.[82]

The third set of events was diplomatic. President Bush announced in December 2001 that the United States was with-
drawing from the ABM treaty. Despite the dire warnings of
BMD critics, relations with Russia did not spin out of control.
In fact, Bush was able to fulfill his campaign promise of reducing the numbers of nuclear warheads. When the Soviet Union
collapsed in 1991, each side had about 11,000 warheads. The
START II agreement (1993), signed but not ratified, called for
a reduction of 3,000 to 3,500. Nevertheless, by 2002, each
side had reduced its nuclear arsenal to approximately 6,000
warheads. With lessened tensions, further reductions were
possible and pursued. The United States was willing to accept
a figure of 2,000 to 2,500 warheads, while the Russians, severely
strapped for funds, sought even deeper cuts to 1,500 or less.
In May 2002, American and Russian leaders signed an agreement to reduce nuclear warheads to 1,700 to 2,200 by 2012.
The Russians accepted higher numbers than they desired but
did get a concession in a legally binding document. In addition, they got a role in NATO. The warming relations between

Russia and the United States, especially in the wake of the September 2001 terrorist attacks on the United States, held the promise of even wider collaboration in the future (fig. 100).[83]

Figure 100. Airborne laser. One futurist ABM weapon is the airborne laser. Seven of these aircraft are scheduled to enter service before the end of the decade. (Reprinted from http://www.sargentfletcher.com/bus_dew/yalla.jpg.)

Notes

1. David Dennon, *Ballistic Missile Defense in the Post-Cold War Era* (Boulder: Westview Press, 1995), 11.

2. Donald Baucom, *The Origins of SDI, 1944–1983* (Lawrence, Kans.: University Press of Kansas, 1992), 199; Ballistic Missile Defense Organization (BMDO), "Fact Sheet: Ballistic Missile Defense Organization Budgetary History," http://www.acq.osd.mil/bmdo/bndolink/htm/tmd.html; Dennon, *Ballistic Missile Defense*, 8–10; General Accounting Office, *Theater Missile Defense Program: Funding and Personnel Requirements Are Not Fully Defined*, December 1992, 1–2, AUL; James Lindsay and Michael O'Hanlon, *Defending America: The Case for Limited National Missile Defense* (Washington, D.C.: Brookings Institution, 2001), 114.

3. BMD funding shifted from $1,103 million on TMD in 1993 and $1,886 million on NMD to $1,646 million and $553 million in 1994. See BMDO, "Fact Sheet," 1.

4. *Theater Missile Defense: Systems and Issues, 1994* (Washington, D.C.: American Institute of Aeronautics and Astronautics, June 1994), 3, 8; and Dennon, *Ballistic Missile Defense*, 14, 54.

5. BMDO, "Fact Sheet," 2.

6. James Walker, Frances Martin, and Sharon Watkins, *Strategic Defense: Four Decades of Progress* (n.p.: Historical Office US Army Space and Strategic Defense Command, 1995), 107.

7. Ballistic Missile Defence Organization, "Fact Sheet, History of the Ballistic Missile Defense," http://www.acq.osd.mil/bmdo/bmdolink/html/tmd.html, 3; David Grogan, "Power Play: Theater Ballistic Missile Defense, National Ballistic Missile Defense and the ABM Treaty" (Master of Laws thesis, George Washington University Law School, May 1998), 57–64.

8. BMDO, "Fact Sheet: Patriot Advanced Capabability-3," 1–2, http://www.acq.osd.mil/bmdo/bmdolink/html/tmd/html; Tony Cullen and Christopher Foss, eds., *Jane's Land-Based Air Defense*, 9th ed., *1996–97* (London: Jane's, 1996), 286; Richard Falkenrath, "US and Ballistic Missile Defense," Center for Science and International Affairs (Harvard University), October 1994, 18; and Lisbeth Gronlund et al., "The Weakest Line of Defense: Intercepting Ballistic Missiles," in Joseph Cirincione and Frank von Hippel, eds., *The Last Fifteen Minutes: Ballistic Missile Defense in Perspective* (Washington, D.C.: Coalition to Reduce Nuclear Dangers, 1996), 57.

9. Gronlund et al., "The Weakest Line of Defense," 57.

10. Cullen and Foss, *Jane's Land-Based Air Defense*, 9th ed., 1996–97, 209, 284; Falkenrath, "US and Ballistic Missile Defense," 20–21; J. W. Schomisch, *1994/95 Guide to Theater Missile Defense* (Arlington, Va.: Pasha, 1994), 47, 49, 51; and Walker, Martin, and Watkins, *Strategic Defense*, 99, 102.

11. Philip Coyle, "Rhetoric or Reality? Missile Defense Under Bush," Center for Defense Information, Washington, D.C., May 2002; John Donnelly, "Patriot Interceptions Hit Targets in Tests," *Space and Missile Defense Report*, 24 March 2002, 2; John Donnelly, "Military May Cut in Half Buys of Anti-Scud Missiles," *Defense Week*, 17 July 2000; Bradley Graham, "Army Hit in New Mexico Test Said to Bode Well for Missile Defense," *Washington Post*, 16 March 1999, 7; "PAC-3 Missile Program Cost Overruns Soar to $278 Million," *Aerospace Daily*, 18 June 1999; James Hackett, "Missile Defense Skeptical Revival," *Washington Times*, 26 August 1999, 13; "Missile Defense Success Story," *Washington Times*, 20 October 2000; Gopal Ratnam, "U.S. Army Struggles to Lower PAC-3 Missile Costs," *Defense News*, 31 July 2000; Robert Wall, "Missile Defense Changes Emerge," *Aviation Week and Space Technology*, 30 August 1999, 30; "Lockheed's PAC-3 Knocks Down a Contract," *Baltimore Sun*, 17 September 1999; and Hunter Keeter, "PAC-3 Intercept Clears Way for LRIP Decision," *Defense Daily*, 17 September 1999, 1.

12. Centre for Defence and International Security Studies, "Current and Near-Term Missile Defences," 3, http://www.cdiss.org/near 1.htm; Cullen and Foss, *Jane's Land-Based Air Defense*, 289, 293–95; Falkenrath, "US and Ballistic Missile Defense," 19; and Federation of Atomic Scientists, "HAWK," 1–2, http://www.fas.org/spp/starwars/program/hawk.htm.

13. The French dropped out in May 1996. See BMDO, "Fact Sheet: Medium Extended Air Defense System," 1–2, http://www.acq.osd.mil/bmdo/bmdolink/htm/tmd/html; Center for Defense and International Security Studies, "US-Allied Cooperation," 3, http://www.cdiss.org/coopt.htm; and Vago Muradian, "Lockheed Martin Beats Raytheon to Win MEADS Effort," *Defense Daily*, 20 May 1999.

14. BMDO, "Fact Sheet," 1; Federation of Atomic Scientists, "Medium Extended Air Defense System (MEADS) Corps SAM," 1, http://www.fas.org/spp/starwars/program/MEADS.htm; Cullen and Foss, *Jane's Land-Based Air Defense*, 292; Ramon Lopez, Andy Nativi, and Andrew Doyle, "The Need for MEADS," *Flight International*, 17–23 March 1999, 34; and Schomisch, *1994/95 Guide*, 78.

15. BMDO, "Fact Sheet," 2; Cullen and Foss, *Jane's Land-Based Air Defense*, 292; Gronlund, "The Weakest Line of Defense," 47; Lopez, Nativi, and Doyle, "The Need for MEADS," 34; Greg Seigle, "US Spending Row Puts MEADS in Jeopardy," *Jane's Defence Weekly*, 25 August 1999; and Wall, "Missile Defense Changes Emerge," 30.

16. Muradian, "Lockheed Martin."

17. General Accounting Office, *US Israel Arrow/Aces Program: Cost, Technical, Proliferation and Management Concerns*, August 1993, 1–2; Arieh O'Sullivan, "Final Arrow Test to be Held Soon," *Jerusalem Post*, 22 October 1999; and Arieh O'Sullivan, "Air Force Welcomes Arrow 2," *Jerusalem Post*, 15 March 2000.

18. BMDO, "Fact Sheet," 1, http://www.acq.osd.mil/bmdo/bmdolink/html/tmd.html; Steven Hildreth, "Theater Ballistic Missile Defense Policy, Missions and Program: Current Status," Congressional Research Service, June 1993, 30; William Orme, "In Major Test, New Israeli Missile Destroys 'Incoming' Rocket," *New York Times*, 2 November 1999; Schomisch, *1994/95 Guide*, 125; and Greg Seigle, "Confidence Over US-Israeli Target Test of Arrow 2," *Jane's Defence Weekly*, 20 October 1999.

19. BMDO, "Fact Sheet," 2; Schomisch, *1994/95 Guide*, 124–25; and Seigle, "Confidence over US-Israeli Target Test."

20. Arieh O'Sullivan, "Arrow Anti-Missile Shield is Operational," *Jerusalem Post*, 17 October 2000; "The Arrow Shield," *Jerusalem Post*, 16 March 2000; Hildreth, "Theater Ballistic Missile Defense Policy," 30; William Orme, "Israel: Missile Defense Deploys," *New York Times*, 15 March 2000, A6; and Schomisch, *1994/95 Guide*, 125.

21. Cullen and Foss, *Jane's Land-Based Air Defense*, 9th ed., *1996–97*, 283; David Heebner, "An Overview of the U.S. DOD Theater Missile Defense Initiative," 53, in American Institute of Aeronautics and Astronautics, *Theater Missile Defense: Systems and Issues—1993* (Washington, D.C.: AIAA, 1993); and Earl Ficken, "Tactical Ballistic Missile Defense: Have We Learned Our Lesson?" Air War College, April 1995, 21.

22. Ballistic Missile Defense Organization, "Fact Sheet: Theater High Altitude Area Defense System," 2, http://www.acq.osd.mil/bmdo/bmdolink//

html/tmd.html; Ficken, "Tactical Ballistic Missile Defense," 21; and Cullen and Foss, *Jane's Land-Based Air Defense,* 284.

23. Confusion over cost may be due to the inclusion/exclusion of the ground-based TMD-GBR sensor that will provide search and tracking information to the TMD. See Cirincione and von Hippel, "Last 15 Minutes," 48; Cullen and Foss, *Jane's Land-Based Air Defense,* 283–84; General Accounting Office, *Theater Missile Defense Program: Funding and Personnel Requirements Are Not Fully Defined,* December 1992, 10–11, HRA; Bradley Graham, "Pentagon Gives THAAD a Boost," *Washington Post,* 20 August 1999, 2; Joseph Peterson, "Theater Missile Defense: Beyond Patriot?" Naval Postgraduate School, June 1994, 97; and Schomisch, *1994/95 Guide,* 250.

24. The Federal Bureau of Investigation cleared the contractor of these allegations. See Bradley Graham, *Hit to Kill: The New Battle over Shielding America from Missile Attack* (New York: Public Affairs, 2001), 228; Craig Eisendrath, Melvin Gorman, and Gerald March, *The Phantom Defense: America's Pursuit of the Star Wars Illusion* (Westport, Conn.: Praeger, 2001), 23; William Broad, "New Anti-Missile System to be Tested this Week," *New York Times,* 24 May 1999, 1; and Walker, Martin, and Watkins, *Strategic Defense,* 103.

25. BMDO, "Fact Sheet, THAAD," 1; Glenn Goodman, "Layered Protection," *Armed Forces Journal International,* November 2000; Bradley Graham, "Anti-Ballistic Missile Has 2d Hit," *Washington Post,* 3 August 1999, 6; James Hackett, "What the THAAD Hit Means," *Washington Times,* 15 June 1999, 18; Robert Holzer, "U.S. Navy Rips Missile Merger," *Defense News,* 8 February 1999, 3; and Philip Shelton, "After Six Failures, Test on Antimissile System Succeeds," *New York Times,* 11 June 1999.

26. John Donnelly, "THAAD Intercepts Were Unrealistic, Top Tester Says," *Defense Daily,* 23 August 1999, 1; Graham, "Pentagon Gives THAAD a Boost," 2; and "THAAD Test Flight Pushed Back as Accelerated Development is Mulled," *Inside Missile Defense,* 14 July 1999, 4; and Coyle, "Rhetoric or Reality?"

27. BMDO, "Fact Sheet: Navy Area Ballistic Missile Defense Program," November 2000, 1–2, http://www.acq.osd.mil/bmdo/bmdolink/html/tmd. html; "Navy Optimistic Following Recent Success of Navy Area Missile Defense System," *Defense Daily,* 28 August 2000; Peter Skibitski, "Navy Again Slides Date of First Area Anti-Ballistic Missile Shot," *Inside the Navy,* 13 March 2000; "White House Decision May Move Sea-Based NMD into Spotlight," *Inside Missile Defense,* 6 September 2000; Robert Wall and David Fulghum, "What's Next For Navy Missile Defense," *Aviation Week and Space Technology,* 24 December 2001, 44; and Ron Laurenzo, "Adridge Speaks on Osprey, Missile Defense, More," *Space and Missile Defense Report,* 3 January 2002, 1.

28. John Donnelly, "Pentagon Plans $5 Billion for 'Upper Tier' Missile Defense," *Defense Week,* 20 December 1999, 1.

29. Gronlund, "The Weakest Line of Defense," 48; Heebner, "An Overview," 56; Peterson, "Theater Missile Defense," 72; Schomisch, *1994/95 Guide,* 75,

77; and Simon Worden, "Technology and Theater Missile Defense," in American Institute of Aeronautics and Astronautics, *Theater Missile Defense: Systems and Issues—1993* (Washington, D.C.: AIAA, 1993), 94.

30. BMDO, "Fact Sheet: Navy Theater Wide Ballistic Missile Defense," 1–2; Wade Boese, "Navy Theater Missile Defense Test Successful," *Arms Control Today,* March 2002, 29; Goodman, "Layered Protection"; Anthony Sommer, "Defense Missile Test Will Be Held Off Kauai," *Honolulu Star-Bulletin,* 11 July 2000; and Robert Suro, "Missile Defense is Still Just A Pie in the Sky," *Washington Post,* 12 February 2001.

31. The *Aegis* ships already have cost the country $50 billion. See Coyle, "Rhetoric or Reality?"; Kim Holmes and Baker Spring, "Missile Defense Compass," *Washington Times,* 14 July 2000; Murray Hiebert, "Flying High on Blind Faith," *Far Eastern Economic Review,* 22 February 2001; and Lindsay and O'Hanlon, *Defending America,* 102–3.

32. Colin Clark and Robert Holzer, "U.S., Allies Move on Maritime TMD Partnership Plan," *Defense News,* 29 November 1999, 1; and Sandra Erwin, "U.S. Ponders Sea-Based Missile Defense," *National Defense,* October 1999, 25.

33. "Let President Defer Missile Deployment," *Minneapolis Star Tribune,* 11 July 2000; and Richard Newman, "Shooting from the Ship," *U.S. News and World Report,* 3 July 2000.

34. This reminds historically minded individuals of the interwar British 10-year rule that justified minimal defense budgets. This policy left the British unprepared for World War II, perhaps encouraging German aggression, and certainly leading to military setbacks early in the war.

35. Quoted in Clarence Robinson, "Missile Technology Access Emboldens Rogue Nations," *Signal,* April 1999; and James Hackett, "CIA Candor on Missile Threat," *Washington Times,* 20 September 1999, 19.

36. Lindsay and O'Hanlon, *Defending America,* 198, appendix C, "Excerpts from the 1998 Rumsfeld Commission Report."

37. Robinson, "Missile Technology."

38. Ibid. The report had considerable credibility due to its unanimous findings and its impressive authors. See Lindsay and O'Hanlon, *Defending America,* 197n.

39. Quoted in "Missile Controversies," *Air Force Magazine,* January 1999, 50.

40. "Missile Controversies," 50.

41. Specifically, the National Intelligence Estimate (NIE) stated, "We project that during the next 15 years the United States most likely will face ICBM threats from Russia, China, and North Korea, probably from Iran, and possibly from Iraq." See Lindsay and O'Hanlon, *Defending America,* 218, appendix D, "Excerpts from the 1999 National Intelligence Estimate"; John Donnelly, "Iran Has Makings of North Korea's Taepo Dong," *Defense Week,* 24 May 1999, 1; Jim Lea, "Report: N. Korea Using Japanese Technology for Developing Missiles," *Pacific Stars and Stripes,* 20 February 1999, 3; Jim Lea, "ROK Won't Join Missile Program," *Pacific Stars and Stripes,* 5 May 1999, 3; Robinson, "Missile Technology"; and Steven Myers and Eric Schmitt,

"Korea Accord Fails to Stall Missile Plan," *New York Times*, 18 June 2000.

42. "Budget Rise Sought to Cover Missile Shield," *South China Morning Post*, 21 December 1999; Steven Hildreth and Gary Pagliano, "Theater Missile Defense and Technology Cooperation: Implications for the U.S.-Japan Relationship," Congressional Research Service, August 1995; and Calvin Sims, "U.S. and Japan Agree to Joint Research on Missile Defense," *New York Times*, 17 August 1999.

43. Don Kirk, "U.S. to Back Seoul's Plan For Extended Missile Force," *International Herald Tribune*, 13 July 2000; Lea, "ROK Won't Join"; and Don Kirk, "U.S. and Japan to Join in Missile Defense to Meet Pyongyang Threat," *International Herald Tribune*, 29 July 1999.

44. Vanessa Guest, "Missile Defense is Wrong Call on Taiwan," *Los Angeles Times*, 3 May 1999, 17; "Missile Defense System Necessary," *South China Morning Post*, 25 June 1999; and "Taiwan Plans to Buy Missile Defense," *Washington Post*, 26 March 1999, 22.

45. William Tow and William Choung, "Asian Perceptions of BMD: Defense or Disequilibrium?" *Contemporary Southeast Asia*, December 2001; and Lindsay and O'Hanlon, *Defending America*, 124–25.

46. Joseph Fitchett, "Washington's Pursuit of Missile Defense Drives Wedge in NATO," *International Herald Tribune*, 15 February 2000.

47. Elizabeth Becker, "Allies Fear U.S. Project May Renew Arms Race," *New York Times*, 20 November 1999, 5; Clifford Beal, "Racing to Meet the Ballistic Missile Threat," *International Defense Review*, March 1993, 211; William Drozdiak, "Possible U.S. Missile Shield Alarms Europe," *Washington Post*, 6 November 1999, 1; "Experts: U.S., Europe Far Apart on Response to Ballistic Missile Threat," *Inside Missile Defense*, 14 July 1999, 1; and Schomisch, *1994/95 Guide*, 99.

48. Tow and Choung, "Asian Perceptions of BMD."

49. There were allegations of Soviet cheating on the treaty. While most of these cases fell into the gray category, matters that lawyers can argue endlessly over, the Soviet foreign minister Eduard Shevardnadze admitted in October 1989 that the radar installation at Krasnoyarsk was in violation of the treaty. See Ralph Bennett, "Needed: Missile Defense," *Reader's Digest*, July 1999.

50. ICBMs have a speed of 7 km per second and a 10,000 km range, while tactical ballistic missiles have speeds around 2 km per second. See Falkenrath, "US and Ballistic Missile Defense," 37, 39; and Gronlund, "The Weakest Line of Defense," 59.

51. Gronlund, "The Weakest Line of Defense," 59.

52. "Missile Defense," *Kansas City Star*, 24 January 1999, K2; and Schomisch, *1994/95 Guide*, 24.

53. Thomas Lippman, "New Missile Defense Plan Ignites Post–Cold War Arms Debate," *Washington Post*, 14 February 1999, 2; Steven Myers, "U.S. Asking Russia to Ease the Pact on Missile Defense," *New York Times*, 21 January 1999, 1.

54. The administration wanted to get further arms reductions, even though the START II agreement had not been ratified by the Russian parliament. There were hopes that START III would further reduce each power's strategic nuclear warheads from 6,000 to 1,500. See Sheila Foote, "White House Threatens Veto of Cochran's NMD Bill," *Defense Daily*, 5 February 1999, 1; Lippman, "New Missile Defense Plan"; Bill Gertz, "U.S. Missile Plan Hits Roadblock," *Washington Times*, 22 October 1999, 1; Frank Gaffney, "What ABM Treaty?" *Washington Times*, 4 March 1999, 17; Bradley Graham, "U.S. to Go Slowly on Treaty," *Washington Post*, 8 September 1999, 12; and Jonathan Weisman, "U.S., Russia to Develop a Joint Missile Defense," *Baltimore Sun*, 1 August 1999.

55. Michael Gordon, "U.S. Seeking to Renegotiate a Landmark Missile Treaty," *New York Times*, 17 October 1999, 1; Graham, "U.S. To Go Slowly on Treaty," 13; Jane Perlez, "Russian Aide Opens Door a Bit to U.S. Bid for Missile Defense," *New York Times*, 19 February 2000; "Russia: Talks with U.S.," *New York Times*, 23 December 1999, A8; "Russia Rejects Changes in ABM Treaty," *Washington Post*, 4 March 2000, 14; and Weisman, "U.S., Russia to Develop."

56. Bennett, "Needed"; and David Sands, "U.S. Considers Placing Missiles at Alaska Sites," *Washington Times*, 9 September 1999, 17.

57. Elizabeth Becker and Eric Schmitt, "Delay Sought in Decision on Missile Defense," *New York Times*, 20 January 2000; Justin Brown, "Two Views of Security, as Seen in 'Star Wars,'" *Christian Science Monitor*, 13 March 2000; Bradley Graham, "Missile Shield Still Drawing Friends, Fire," *Washington Post*, 17 January 2000; James Hackett, "Sorties Against Missile Defenses," *Washington Times*, 27 December 1999; and Jane Perlez, "Biden Joins G.O.P. in Call for a Delay In Missile-Defense Plan," *New York Times*, 9 March 2000.

58. In February 1985, long-time government policy maker Paul Nitze proposed that SDI should be judged by its military effectiveness, survivability, and cost effectiveness at the margin; that is, it should be cheaper for the defense than the offense to add additional systems. See Eisendrath, Goodman, and Marsh, *The Phantom Defense*, 16; and Mary McGrory, "Going Ballistic," *Washington Post*, 30 March 2000.

59. "A Misdirected Missile Defense Plan," *Los Angeles Times*, 30 April 2000, M4.

60. Davis Abel, "Missile System's Best Defense is Public Opinion," *Boston Globe*, 28 January 2001; William Broad, "Nobel Winners Urge Halt to Missile Plan," *New York Times*, 6 July 2000; and Elaine Sciolino, "Critics Asking Clinton to Stop Advancing Missile Plan," *New York Times*, 7 July 2000.

61. Jim Abrams, "Report Puts $60 Billion Tag on Shield," *USA Today*, 27 April 2000; Tony Capaccio, "National Missile Defense Cost Estimate Rises nearly 20 Percent," *Defense Week*, 11 September 2000; Helen Dewar, "Clinton is Urged to Defer to Successor on Missile Shield," *Washington Post*, 14 July 2000; and John Donnelly, "Missile Defense Costs 60 Percent More than Advertised Price," *Defense Week*, 3 April 2000.

62. Dean Wilkening, "Keeping National Missile Defense in Perspective," *Issues in Science and Technology* (Winter 2001); and Lindsay and O'Hanlon, *Defending America*, 89.

63. "Pentagon Delays Test of Defense Using Missiles," *New York Times*, 22 March 2000; Steven Myers and Jane Perlez, "Documents Detail U.S. Plan to Alter '72 Missile Treaty," *New York Times*, 28 April 2000; "Misdirected Missile Defense Plan," *Los Angeles Times*, 30 April 2000; and Robert Suro and Steven Mufson, "GAO Report Finds Fault with Missile Shield Plan," *Washington Post*, 17 June 2000.

64. Center for Defense Information, *National Missile Defense: What Does It All Mean?* (Washington, D.C.: Center for Defense Information, 2000), 4; Michael Gordon, "North Korea Reported Open to Halting Missile Program," *New York Times*, 20 July 2000; and Steven Myers, "Russian Resistance Key in Decision to Delay Missile Shield," *New York Times*, 3 September 2000.

65. Ted Plafker, "China, Russia Unify Against U.S. Missile Shield," *Washington Post*, 19 July 2000.

66. American economic and military dominance was, of course, the major factor in driving these two countries together.

67. Christopher Castelli, "Russian BPI Could Help Negate Missile from North Korea, Iran, Iraq," *Inside the Navy*, 19 February 2001; Michael Gordon, "Joint Exercise on Missiles Seen for U.S. and Russia," *New York Times*, 29 June 2000; and James Hackett, "Putin's Missile Defense Policy," *Washington Times*, 21 July 2000.

68. Tom Bowman, "Consensus Grows for 'Boost-Phase' Missile Defense," *Baltimore Sun*, 18 July 2000.

69. Ibid.; David Hoffman, "Russian Generals Diverge from Putin-Clinton Stance on Missile Threat," *Washington Post*, 30 June 2000; and Eisendrath, Goodman, and March, *The Phantom Defense*, 107.

70. Coyle, "Rhetoric or Reality?"; and Graham, *Hit to Kill*, 188.

71. Mark Thompson, "Missile Impossible?" *Time*, 10 July 2000.

72. Tom Plate, "The Costs of a Ridiculous 'Defense,' " *Los Angeles Times*, 12 July 2000; and Tom Bowman, "Missile Defense Supporters Still Hopeful After Failed Test," *Baltimore Sun*, 9 July 2000.

73. Charles Babington, "Clinton's Decision Presents Challenges to Gore, Bush," *Washington Post*, 2 September 2000.

74. Eric Schmitt, "In Search of a Missing Link in the Logic of Arms Control," *New York Times*, 16 July 2000.

75. John Barry, "Looking Forward to NMD," *Newsweek*, 29 January 2001; Steven Myers, "Bush Repeats Call for Arms Reduction and Missile Shield," *New York Times*, 27 January 2001; and Miles Pomper, "Political Turmoil May Up Odds for Missile Defense Accord," *Congressional Quarterly Weekly*, 18 November 2000.

76. Michael Gordon, "Moscow Signaling a Change in Tone on Missile Defense," *New York Times*, 22 February 2001.

77. Joseph Fitchett, "Bush Can't Afford to Ignore Missile Defense, Envoys Tell Europeans," *International Herald Tribune*, 6 February 2001; and David

Sands, "Shadow Official Backs Missile Shield Guarding NATO," *Washington Times*, 15 February 2001.

78. The Alaska site could be ready between 2003 and 2005 with an emergency capability before two other systems deemed to have emergency capabilities—the airborne laser and Navy systems. See Carla Robbins and Greg Jaffe, "Bush's Planned Missile-Shield Program May Violate ABM Treaty 'Within Months,' " *Wall Street Journal*, 12 July 2001; James Dao, "Pentagon Sets Fourth Test of Missile For July 14," *New York Times*, 7 July 2001; and Wayne Specht, "Pacific 'Test Bed' for Missile Defense Raises Questions about ABM Treaty," *Pacific Stars and Stripes*, 16 July 2001.

79. "Conservatives Determined to Carry Torch for US Missile Defence," *London Financial Times*, 12 July 2001.

80. John Diamond, "Missile Test Inspires Praise and Caution," *Chicago Tribune*, 16 July 2001.

81. Ibid.; Vernon Loeb, "Interceptor Scores a Direct Hit on Missile," *Washington Post*, 15 July 2001. Radar that was supposed to report the successful interception failed. This is important, as without indication of a successful interception, the system will launch backup interceptors against the destroyed target, wasting limited defense missiles. See Peter Pae, "Crucial Radar Failed Missile Defense Test," *Los Angeles Times*, 18 July 2001.

82. Coyle, "Rhetoric or Reality?"; and Robert Wall, "Missile Defenses New Look to Emerge This Summer," *Aviation Week and Space Technology*, 25 March 2002, 28.

83. Coyle, "Rhetoric or Reality?"; Graham, *Hit to Kill*, 245; David Sanger, "NATO Formally Embraces Russia as a Junior Partner," *New York Times*, 29 May 2002; and Michael Wine, "U.S. and Russia Sign Nuclear Weapons Reduction Treaty," *New York Times*, 24 May 2002.

Chapter 8

Summary, Trends, and Conclusions

Ground-based air defenses have been a problem for Airmen almost from the onset of manned flight. Although seldom able to stop air power, air defenses have made air operations more dangerous and costly. Just as aircraft have become more capable, so too have air defenses. This extended offensive versus defensive battle shows no sign of abating. In fact, every sign points to it becoming more complex and costly as it continues.

Summary

Airmen have had to contend with ground-based air defense since it downed the first aircraft in 1912. In every war except World War I, more American aircraft have been lost to ground-based air defenses than to fighters; nevertheless, air-to-air combat has dominated both the public's and the Airmen's mind. While this mistaken and romantic attitude is probably understandable and excusable for the public, it is not for Airmen, who must be held to a higher standard. They should, and must, know better.

Probably this attitude of denigrating AAA and the defense (the idea that the bomber would always get through) peaked in the 1930s and 1940s. In the late 1920s and the early 1930s, aviation made great strides, and the gap between offense and defense widened. During the early years of World War II, the offense held the advantage, as flak was relatively ineffective. However, between 1935 and 1944, almost to the end of the war, aviation advanced modestly. (For example, the B-17 that first flew in 1935 was still frontline equipment in 1945, as were such fighters as the Me 109 and Spitfire, which first flew in 1935 and 1936.) These aircraft and others like them are more representative of air combat in World War II than the better performing and better remembered B-29s and Me 262s that both went into combat in June 1944.

In contrast, defense technology made great strides during the war. Flak grew from an ineffective nuisance weapon into a potent force by 1944. Although AAA could not stop determined Airmen, it could inflict heavy losses on the flyers, disrupt accuracy, and, in general, make air operations much more expensive. The notable antiaircraft successes, such as Allied guns in the V-1 campaign, German flak defense of the oil targets, and American defense of the Remagen Bridge, all strongly support this point. Relative to defensive aircraft, flak proved inexpensive and very cost effective.

The two major technical advances responsible for the improvement and success of ground-based air defenses during World War II were radar and proximity fuzes. Radar stripped the cloak of surprise and invisibility from aircraft. It provided detection and warning of attacking aircraft, allowed control of defensive fighters, and permitted more accurate all-weather, day/night firing of AAA. Other devices increased the lethality of flak, none more so than proximity fuzes. Fortunately for the Allies, only they fielded this device.

As a result, Airmen learned that AAA constituted a dangerous and powerful force. The World War II experience also proved that low-level operations in the face of flak were costly because guns were increasingly effective at lower altitudes. The increasing lethality of the guns exposed an enduring problem, the gunner's difficulty in correctly identifying friend or foe—not engaging the former and always engaging the latter. Experience showed numerous instances, however, of friends downed by friendly fire and gunners letting foes slip by.

To counter ground fire, Airmen adopted tactics that would be used repeatedly in subsequent air wars. Besides avoiding flak areas, the flyers took advantage of surprise, the sun, the terrain, and one-pass attacks. They also employed electronic countermeasures, specifically, chaff and jammers. Finally, however Airmen attacked their tormentors, although direct action seldom proved effective, it usually was expensive. The trade-off of cheap guns for valuable aircraft made direct attack a high-risk proposition with low return.

Therefore, during the course of World War II, the balance between air offense and air defense tilted toward the defense. Yet, events in the last stages of the war obscured these facts. The introduction of jets markedly improved aircraft performance, just as the atomic bomb enormously expanded firepower. Therefore, both the public and military saw the offensive as supreme.

However, the combatants used only the jet, not the atomic bomb, in America's next war. Korea was different from World War II and the wars that the prophets and theorists had forecast. The peasant hordes on the periphery of Asia stalemated the strongest nation in the world. This war was limited by both sides (at least by the major players, the United States, China, and the Soviet Union; the Koreans understandably had a different view) in terms of means and objectives. With the exception of the MiG-15, the Communists used only obsolete equipment to thwart and impose considerable losses on United Nations' airmen. Air power was not decisive in the war. At the same time, the war reemphasized many of the basic AAA lessons from World War II—the lethality of flak, the danger of low-altitude operations, and the usefulness of antiflak countermeasures.

In many respects, the Vietnam War repeated the same pattern. Again, American Airmen were unprepared for the reality of combat and especially AAA, their chief opponent. Once more, the lessons of World War II and Korea had to be relearned. Yet again, the air power of the strongest nation in the world proved indecisive against Asian masses armed with simple weapons.

The one new air defense weapon introduced into combat in Vietnam was the SAM. Although these missiles claimed relatively few aircraft, they made air operations more difficult and expensive. American tactics and equipment were able to overcome the SAMs, but the missiles forced the Airmen to increase the number of support aircraft and to operate at lower altitudes where AAA proved even more deadly. American Airmen learned to cope with the ground-based defenses. They used modified tactics, ECM, and new technology, such as antiradiation missiles (ARM) and standoff weapons. Linebacker II (December 1972) clearly demonstrated that modest numbers (compared to World War II) of second-rate air defense equipment could not stop large-scale air efforts by a major power but could inflict both a burden and a loss on the attacker.

271

Shortly after American involvement in the Vietnam War ended, air operations in the Middle East seemed to indicate the predominance of the defense. Unlike the 1967 Arab-Israeli War in which the Israeli Air Force was overwhelmingly triumphant, the 1973 war indicated the renewed power of the defense. The Arabs violated two concepts of conventional war: attacking a country with superior military forces and attacking without air superiority. They advanced under a dense umbrella of SAMs and guns that downed many Israeli aircraft. Although the Israelis won the war, they suffered heavy aircraft losses, and their air force was unable to influence operations as it had in 1967. Ground-based air defenses appeared to have regained the edge. Operations in 1982 between the Arabs and Israelis cast doubt on these findings. In a short and sharp action, the Israeli air force won an air battle against Syrian MiGs and SAMs, a battle that was even more lopsided than their 1967 victory.

A few months earlier, on the other side of the world, the lessons of another conflict were less clear. In the Falklands, a small force from a Western power with superior technology defeated a larger force from a less-developed country. However, the Argentine air force battered the Royal Navy despite the restrictions of range, old aircraft, old bombs, and lack of ECM. Although the British air defense imposed heavy losses on the attackers, the Argentines did get through to severely punish the defenders.

The war in Afghanistan seemed to indicate the superiority of the defense. This action pitted a modern air force against a lightly armed guerrilla force in rugged terrain, similar to the Vietnam War. The Soviet air force did reasonably well until the guerrillas employed advanced, man-portable SAMs. These inflicted substantial losses on the airmen, forced them to modify their tactics to reduce their vulnerability, and by so doing reduced their effectiveness. As a result, the military advantage shifted to the insurgents, who eventually drove the Soviets from the country and the war.

In contrast, the offense scored a quick and decisive victory over the defense in the 1990–91 war in the Persian Gulf. It matched a large, well-equipped military—certainly by third world standards—against an even larger, better equipped and trained international coalition. The coalition used mass and superior technology to neuter the defenses; especially effective and noteworthy in the war were precision-guided munitions (PGM) and stealth aircraft. The result was an overwhelming military triumph obtained with unexpectedly low friendly casualties. Modern technology had won over mass; the offense again dominated the defense. The Gulf War spurred hopes that a new kind of war had arrived and stimulated thoughts of a revolution in military affairs.

Air action in the Balkans and Iraq in the 1990s and in Afghanistan in the early 2000s showed that the offensive had retained its supremacy. In these ground-based air defenses there were few casualties inflicted on the attackers. Nevertheless, the defenses were important, as they increased the cost of operations and represented an ever-present threat, similar to the fleet-in-being concept of a potential force. These observations need to be tempered, however, for in all of these recent cases there has been an extreme mismatch of forces.

In contrast to the overall picture of the advantage shifting back and forth between offense and defense, the ballistic missile defense (BMD) story is consistent. It is overwhelmingly one more of promise and disappointment than of battlefield success. There has been a long quest for BMD since the first ballistic missile combat during World War II. Most American interest has centered on BMD as a strategic defense against nuclear-armed ICBM. Yet, despite great effort over the past half century, developers have encountered substantial technical difficulties, great costs, and complicated politics. Throughout, proponents have been imaginative and optimistic, while the critics have been insistent and politically sophisticated. BMD achieved political success in the Gulf War, although its tactical and technical performance was controversial. Despite almost 60 years of development, BMD is better known for its cost and controversy than its proven performance. It remains to be seen if it will be the Edsel or Frankenstein of the 21st century or the key to a more secure future.

Trends (Speculations)

What does all this mean? What are the lessons of the past? And what do they tell us about the future? Just as in weather

273

forecasting, it is probably a safe bet to generally expect more of the same, along with some unpleasant surprises. We can expect to see more capable air defense systems fielded in the future. The capabilities of SAMs on the drawing boards indicate that they will become harder to jam, more difficult to evade, and more effective against many more attackers. The key to advancements in air defense appears to be in the area of electronics. Certainly, stealth technology has broken the impact of radar on air defense, at least for the moment. Clearly, the defenders will seek means to counter this new development. Surely, the devices will become more complex as they become more capable. Sensors will improve, and the almost total reliance on radar will end. Different types of sensors will be tied together and give more data more quickly to the air defenders. All of this will be much more expensive in terms of dollars and trained manpower.

A second expectation is that effective air defense weapons will spread in numbers and geography. We can expect most countries to equip their forces with more and better missiles, and sometimes we will even see our own weapons used against us. In addition, man-portable SAMs will give antiaircraft protection to guerrilla groups and become a potent weapon for terrorists.

Future military conflicts may be decided not so much on the combat performance of weapons—that is, their probability of kill, time of flight, lethal radius, launch envelope, ECM, and electronic counter-countermeasures (ECCM)—but on other factors. These will include nontechnical factors such as numbers of weapons in the field and in the supply depots; maintainability and reliability; cost; and human factors, including training, adaptability, and motivation. Most of all, the result will depend on how well the military puts together this complicated array.

What are the big payoff areas in the future? Improved ECM will be useful but increasingly difficult because of effective ECCM and the introduction of multisensors on a large scale. Most of all, the Airmen need capable and versatile standoff weapons: the attacker must get away from the defenders. These weapons offer the promise of increased accuracy (thereby requiring fewer sorties) and increased reach (permitting less risk to the Airmen). The air defenders also need more ECM and

ECCM. The big area of opportunity is in the field of multiple sensors. Both friendly air defenders and their airmen partners would benefit greatly from the introduction of effective identification equipment. Until the problem of rapidly and accurately sorting out friends from foes is solved, the effectiveness of both the offense and defense will be greatly reduced. In short, the area that needs to be exploited is electronics. Advances in civilian technology indicate that much can be expected from electronics—less expensive, smaller, and more capable equipment. Therefore, the future seems to belong to those who can best use—not just field—modern, high-cost high technology in combat. This will decide the outcome of wars and the balance between the offense and defense.

Conclusions

Historically, US Air Force assumptions about future conflicts have proven to be in error. Since 1945, the Air Force has geared itself for air-to-air combat and a nuclear exchange with a major power. Although this certainly was America's most serious challenge during the past 60 years, the reality of war since 1945 has proven to be far different. Since World War II, the US Air Force has fought in three wars against minor powers, used conventional weapons, and found its chief opposition to be ground-based air defense weapons.

These conflicts proved different from their anticipation, but again they indicated the power of the defense. The first two, Korea and Vietnam, demonstrated the problems of fighting an extended campaign against a primitive, determined, and resourceful enemy. Vietnam also saw the introduction of the SAM, which tilted the balance away from the offense toward the defense. Americans countered these threats using ECM, direct action, and tactics; however, they never found an acceptable solution at a reasonable price. The US military was forced to relearn old lessons at considerable cost.

It is important to note that since 1945 the United States has not faced a peer competitor in direct air-to-air combat as it did over Europe in World War II. With the exception of Korea, where the United States faced a larger force of equivalent quality air-

275

to-air fighters, the US Air Force has had the advantages of numbers, technology, training, command and control, and spirit. That American effort paid off in the air-to-air battle, but victory tended to obscure another threat to air operations. For at the same time, the Airmen paid far less attention to the peril of ground-based defenses in peacetime and, as a result, paid a high price in wartime.

The Gulf War was primarily a tale of offensive superiority, although it again demonstrated the continuing importance and cost to Airmen of ground-based defenses. The overwhelming triumph in the Gulf War was due to many factors; however, two of the most important technologies clearly were stealth and the improvement of standoff PGMs. In the long and continuing contest between offense and defense, the Gulf War indicated that currently the offense is ascendant. This impact is magnified by the emergence of the United States as the sole superpower with overwhelming dominance in the areas of economics, technology, and military. Nevertheless, actions over the Balkans and Iraq reinforce the view that although the offensive is dominant, ground-based air defenses are still a force to be reckoned with and can still impose costs on the Airmen.

The situation is far from static. American Airmen should realize that increased capabilities of ground-based air defenses challenge them in two important ways. The first and most obvious is to make their job more difficult and dangerous, whether it be in a major conflict with a major foe or in a minor conflict with a minor foe. The other aspect is the impact of this air offense/defense balance on friendly powers, who will undoubtedly request US assistance for their air force problems.

This study indicates the potential pitfalls of air defense systems and possible solutions to counter these systems based on past and recent experience. Clearly, ground-based air defense weapons are a vital issue to American Airmen of today and tomorrow. If our Airmen are to be successful, they must pay more attention to ground-based air defenses than they have in the past and meet and master the challenge of these systems. The world is not static; the duel between offense and defense will continue.

Index

GPO ☆ U.S. GOVERNMENT PRINTING OFFICE : 2005—736-181